THE
GIRLS' HANDBOOK

THE
GIRLS' HANDBOOK

First published in 1981 by
Octopus Books Limited
59 Grosvenor Street, London W1

Copyright © 1981 Octopus Books Limited
Reprinted 1981, 1982, 1983
ISBN 0 7064 1546 9

Printed in Czechoslovakia
50425/3

CONTENTS

LOOKING AFTER YOURSELF

Beauty and Health

Although your body has an amazing built-in ability to repair and renew itself, it can do this successfully only if you give it the proper basic care and attention. Proper care leads to good health, good health makes you feel and look your best, giving you the kind of vitality and confidence which enables you to tackle and enjoy all the experiences that come to you.

Eat your way to beauty and health

Mention diet and most people think of slimming. However, the word 'diet' really means 'a way of eating' and a normal diet means a way of eating which gives your body all the ingredients it needs to keep it in tip-top condition.

Meat, fish, cheese, eggs, nuts and pulses (various peas and beans) are full of protein. Protein is the material the body needs for growth, and for replacing parts like hair and nails. It also gives you energy.

Fruit and green vegetables provide you with roughage – the material that makes your digestion work efficiently. They are also full of mineral salts and vitamins. Vitamin C, found in citrus fruits and green vegetables is essential if you want glowing, healthy skin. As this vitamin cannot be stored in the body, you need a good supply every day.

Milk, cream and cheese supply you with calcium for your teeth, bones and nails. Milk and yoghurt also supply you with vitamins A and D – the vitamin which you also get from sunshine. These are also good for your skin and for your hair.

Wholemeal bread also provides roughage and is a valuable source of vitamin B.

The foods to avoid, if you want to stay slim and healthy, are the ones that are fattening without being very nutritious. These are white bread, cakes, sweets, biscuits, jams, fizzy drinks – everything, in fact, which contains lots of starch and sugar. Sugary foods are also very bad for the teeth (they are the main cause of decay) and for the skin (they cause spots).

If you are overweight, you are eating more food than you need. Eating less doesn't mean skipping meals and starving yourself; what it does mean is eating less of the wrong foods and more of the right ones. So concentrate on the proteins, vegetables and fruits, and cut out the sugars and starches.

In order to lose weight, an average girl needs to limit herself to an intake of 1,200–1,300 calories a day. Use the following calorie chart to help you regulate your daily intake. But before you do, be sure to get the permission of your doctor as diets can be dangerous as well as unnecessary.

The calorie value of most of the items is based on a sample weight of 28g (1oz). For special cases the amount is listed next to the item. Anything cooked in oil has a higher calorific value than it has when raw.

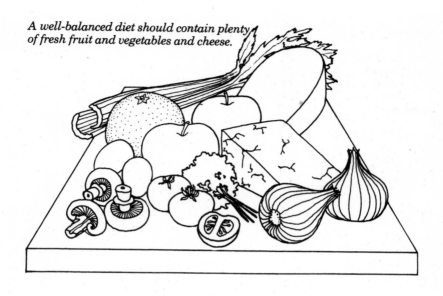

A well-balanced diet should contain plenty of fresh fruit and vegetables and cheese.

Food	Calories
All-Bran	69
Almonds	170
Anchovy fillets	40
Angel Delight	43
Apples, dried	50
fresh	10
Apricots, canned	30
dried	50
fresh	5
Artichokes, Globe	5
Jerusalem	5
Asparagus	5
Aubergines	5
Avocado pear	25
Bacon, fat	130
lean	115
Bagel, one	125
Baked beans and Frankfurters	37
Bananas	15
Bass, steamed	20
Bean sprouts, fresh	8
Beans, Baked	25
Broad (lima)	10
French	5

Food	Calories
Haricot (navy)	75
Runner	5
Beef, fat	75
lean	50
Beefburger, one	155
Beetroot (beet), fresh	10
Bilberries, fresh	10
Biscuit, plain	110
sweet	140
Blackberries	10
Blackcurrants	10
Blueberries, *see* Bilberries	
Bread, white or brown large loaf, average	70
slice	80
small loaf, average slice	50
ginger	108
Broccoli	5
Brussels sprouts	10
Butter	225
Buttermilk, 600ml/1pt	235
Cabbage, red or white	5
Cake, plain	75
rich	105

Carrots	5	Gooseberries, fresh	10
Cauliflower	5	Grapefruit	8
Celery	3	Grapes	15
Cheese, Cheddar	120	Haddock, raw	20
Cottage	30	smoked	20
Edam	90	Hake fillets, raw	25
Processed	120	Halibut, raw	30
Cherries, fresh	10	Ham, lean	65
glace	60	fat	95
Chicken, flesh only,		Hamburger, *see*	
raw	35	Beefburger	
Chicory	3	Herrings, raw	65
Chives	10	Honey	80
Chocolate, milk	165	Ice Cream	55
plain	155	Jam and jellies	75
Chutney, average	50	Kidneys raw	35
Cocoa (half milk),		Kippers, raw	30
300ml/½pt	110	Lamb, lean	75
Cod, raw	20	Lard	260
Consommé, canned,		Leeks, fresh	10
300ml/½pt	40–65	Lemon, fresh	5
Corn, *see* Sweetcorn		Lentils, fresh	85
Cornflakes, and most		Lettuce, fresh	3
cereals	105	Liver, raw	45
Cornflour (Cornstarch)	100	Loganberries	5
Courgettes	2	Macaroni, boiled	30
Cranberry, fresh	4	Mackerel	30
sauce	35	Margarine	225
Cream, double	130	Marmalade	75
single	60	Marrow, boiled	2
soured (sour)	55	Melon	5
Cucumber	3	Milk, whole, 600ml/1pt	380
Currants	70	skimmed,	
Custard powder, made		600ml/1pt	190
up	30	Mushrooms, fresh	2
Damsons	10	Nuts, Almond	170
Dates, dried	85	Brazil	180
Doughnuts, jam filled	100	Chestnuts	50
Duck, meat only, raw	70	Peanuts, salted	180
Eggplant, *see*		Walnuts	155
Aubergines		Oil, Corn, 30ml/1fl oz	250
Eggs, whole, 1 small	70	Olive, 30ml/1fl oz	265
1 large	90	Olives	25
white	10	Onions, fresh	5
yolk	100	Orange, fresh	10
Fish finger, one	54	Parsnips, raw	5
Flour	100	Pasta, cooked	29
Fudge	100	Peaches, raw	10
Gelatine (Gelatin)		Pears, raw	10
powder	100	Peas, canned	20
Goose, meat only, raw	63	canned, processed	25

dried	30	Squash, *see* Marrow		
fresh, boiled	15	Stock cube, each		15
frozen	20	Strawberries, fresh		5
Peppers, red or green	10	Suet		260
Pineapple, canned	20	Sugar, white or brown		110
fresh	15	Sweetcorn, canned or		
Plaice, raw	15	frozen		25
Plums, fresh	10	on the cob		35
Pork, fat	110	Syrup		85
lean	55	Tangerines		5
Potatoes, boiled, two		Tomatoes, ketchup		
medium	95	(catsup) 30ml/1fl oz		28
fried, two medium	270	puree		40
Rabbit, meat only, raw	50	raw		5
Radishes, fresh	5	Tongue		85
Raspberries, fresh	5	Trout, raw		25
Redcurrants, fresh	5	Tuna, canned in oil		75
Rhubarb, fresh	2	Turbot, steamed		30
Rice, boiled	35	Turkey, meat only,		
Salmon, canned	40	raw		35
raw	55	Turnips, raw		5
smoked	45	Veal fillet, raw		30
Sardines, canned	85	Vinegar, 30ml/1fl oz		1
Sausages, average,		Waffles, one		216
raw	100	Water chestnuts		23
Sole, raw	15	Watercress		5
Soup, consommé,		Watermelon		5
300ml/½pt	40–65	Whiting, raw		15
thin, e.g. chicken		Yogurt, natural low		
noodle, 300ml/½pt	65–100	fat, 30ml/1fl oz		15
thick, 300ml/½pt	90–200	fruit flavoured,		
Spaghetti, boiled	35	30ml/1fl oz		25
Spinach	5	Zucchini, *see*		
Spring greens	3	Courgettes		
Spring onions	10			

SOFT DRINKS	Portion	Calories
Apple juice, unsweetened	small glass	50
Blackcurrant concentrate	1 × 15ml spoon	35
Grapefruit juice, unsweetened	small glass	55
Lemonade	600ml/1pt	120
Orange juice, unsweetened	small glass	60
Tomato juice	small glass	25
Low-calorie Minerals		0
Low-calorie Orange Squash	30ml/1fl oz	5
Low-calorie Lemon Squash	30ml/1fl oz	2

EXERCISE

Many people think of exercising only when they are overweight. This is a great pity. Regular exercise keeps your body supple and strong so that it can do everything you ask of it with ease and grace, after practice, of course.

Try to take part in some active sport at least once a week: tennis, squash, or hockey if you enjoy playing with a team or a partner; skating, riding, running or jogging if you are a loner. Swimming is especially good because it exercises just about every muscle in your body. If you do not care for any of these activities, have you considered dancing or walking?

If lack of exercise has made you feel a bit stiff and awkward or if you have a few extra inches you would like to lose, try these exercises and see how beautifully you begin to move, and how unwanted bumps and bulges begin to melt away as you strengthen and firm the flabby muscles that cause them.

Fast roll

1 Sit cross-legged on the floor.

2 Take hold of your left foot with your right hand and your right foot with your left hand.

3 Bend slightly forward and tuck your head in towards your knees.

4 Pull on your feet and let yourself roll backwards on to your shoulders, allowing your momentum to bring you back up again.

You can do this up to ten times. It will massage your spine and all your back muscles, and it is marvellous for improving your posture. Be sure to do this exercise on a rug or a folded blanket, never on a hard floor.

The butterfly

This one is good for firming flabby thighs and removing surplus fat from the hips and bottom.

1 Sit on the floor (against a wall if you want to make sure your back is straight).

The fast roll

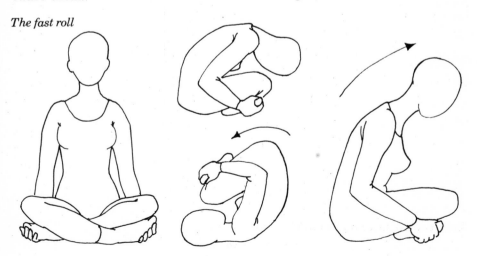

15

2 Bend both knees and bring the soles of the feet together.

3 Clasp the feet firmly with both hands.

4 Breathing in, raise the knees up and hold them there for a second or two.

5 Breathing out, lower the knees as far as they will go without strain. Repeat two or three times.

6 Now, with your legs in the open position, gently move them up and down, making very tiny movements, like trembling butterfly wings.

7 Finally, keeping your knees in the open position, rock your bottom from side to side.

The scissors

This is an excellent exercise for flattening your tummy and strengthening your legs and lower back muscles.

1 Lie flat on your back, arms at your sides.

2 Raise one leg until it is as near 90° from the floor as it will comfortably go. Lower it. Repeat with the other leg.
If you do this very fast, it is quite easy. What you have to work towards is raising your leg as slowly as possible.

3 Repeat the exercise, this time pausing for a count of five when your leg reaches an angle of 45°.

4 Now repeat the whole exercise, raising both legs together.
When your stomach muscles have become strong enough to do this without strain (and not until then) add this next stage to the exercise.

5 Raise both legs until they are 45° from the floor.

6 Now sweep them apart and together again, letting one leg cross over the other; sweep them apart and together, letting the other leg cross over. Make the movement as flowing and rhythmical as you can.
Do this exercise just once or twice at first, increasing the number of times gradually as your muscles get stronger.

The scissors

16

Neck roll

Neck, shoulder and back muscles tense up when they get tired; especially when you have been hunched over a table or desk for some time. These and the following exercises will help to rest and to relax them.

1 Sit comfortably on a chair, or kneel on the floor and sit back on your heels. Let your head drop forward, very gently, as far as can.

2 Slowly roll your head round to the right shoulder and hold it there for three seconds.

3 Continue rolling the head slowly back through another 90° and hold it there for three seconds.

4 Roll the head slowly to the left shoulder and hold it for three seconds.

5 Roll the head forward again and hold for three seconds.

6 Now repeat the exercise, rolling the head in the other direction. This exercise should never be done quickly. The object is very gently to stretch and then relax all the neck muscles, and to do it with smoothness and grace.

Shoulder loosener

1 Sit erect, arms hanging loosely by your sides.

2 Close your eyes.

3 Very slowly, circle the right shoulder backwards three or four times and then forwards three or four times. Make the circle as big as you can, without straining.

4 Repeat the exercise with the left shoulder.

5 Now circle both together.

Waist trimmer

1 Stand with your legs comfortably apart.

2 Breathing in, raise your arms to shoulder level, palms facing downward.

3 Holding your breath in and keeping your arms on a line with your shoulders, bend as far as you can to the left.

4 Breathing out, return to the upright position and lower your arms.

5 Repeat the exercise, bending to the right.

6 When you become supple enough to grasp your ankle, raise your other arm over your head until it is parallel with the floor.

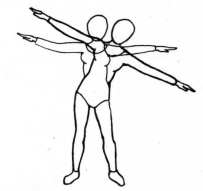

The waist trimmer

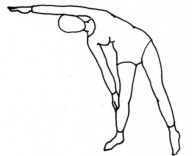

Chest expander

This is a two-in-one exercise. It helps you towards a pretty bustline and keeps your back supple.

1 Stand with your heels together, arms at your sides.

2 Breathing in, bring your hands up in front of you until your fingertips are together and your thumbs are touching your chest.

3 Stretch your arms straight out in front of you, the backs of your hands facing each other.

4 Now take them behind you, keeping them as high as you can, until you can interlace your fingers.

5 Holding your breath in, bend very slightly backwards.

6 Now begin to breathe out, bending slowly and gracefully forward as you do.

7 Hold this position for a few seconds, breathing normally and keeping your neck and head completely relaxed.

8 Straighten up slowly and let your arms fall back to your sides.

The tree

Finally, an exercise which will improve your balance and help you to stand and move gracefully.

1 Stand up straight. Bend your right leg and place the sole of your foot, flat against the inner thigh of your left leg.

2 Breathing in, slowly raise both arms to shoulder level.

3 Breathing out, raise your arms over your head and bring the palms together.

4 Breathing normally, stretch

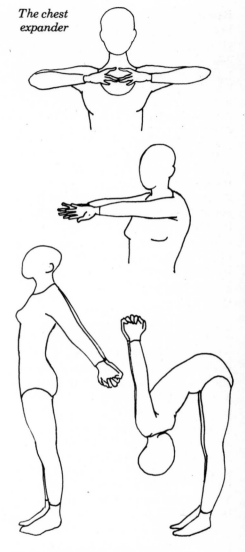

The chest expander

gently upward once or twice.

5 Breathing in, lower the arms to shoulder level.

6 Breathing out, lower your arms to your sides and your right leg to the floor.

7 Repeat with the other leg.

Breathing

Because our breathing goes on automatically, we very seldom pay any attention to it. The body needs a continual supply of oxygen with which to repair and re-energize itself, so giving it an extra supply now and then, by taking a few good deep breaths, has a marvellous effect.

Try this. Stand, feet slightly apart, near an open window. Breathe only through your nose. First, breathe out until there is no air at all left in your lungs. This expels all the stale air and allows your lungs to take in as much fresh air as they will hold. Now breathe in to the count of seven and out to the count of seven, three or four times.

Breathing deeply and slowly doesn't only give you more energy. It also has a calming, relaxing effect – so it's worth trying if you're in a situation that makes you feel nervous.

Relaxing

Knowing how to relax is just as important as knowing how to exercise. Try it for ten minutes after you've been doing something strenuous or for ten minutes before you go out on an important date. You'll be surprised how good it will make you feel.

Lie flat on the floor, preferably on a rug or folded blanket. Cover yourself with a blanket, too, if the room is at all chilly. Have your arms stretched out a little way away from your sides, and your legs slightly apart. Close your eyes.

Turn your attention to your feet, and for a moment tense all the muscles in your feet as tight as you can – then let them go, and be aware of your feet feeling relaxed and heavy. Gradually work up your body, doing the same thing with your legs, your bottom, your stomach, your chest, your back and shoulders, your hands and arms, your neck, your head and your face. Imagine yourself feeling heavy, like a sack of potatoes, and be conscious of the floor pushing up underneath you. When you feel completely heavy all over, turn your mind to something pleasant – a beautiful place you enjoy being in, for example.

When you feel you've relaxed for long enough, turn your attention back to your feet and give them a little wriggle. Then work up your body, wriggling each bit in turn, until you've got every bit of it moving again. Then sit up, take a deep breath, and you'll be ready for anything.

*The perfect position
for relaxation*

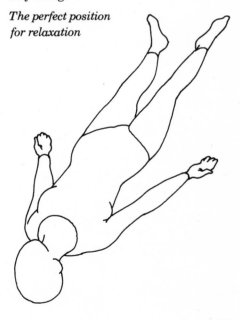

GOOD GROOMING

Good grooming begins with scrupulous cleanliness. Take a daily bath or shower to remove dirt, dust and dead skin cells – all of which can build up to clog the pores and cause unsightly spots and blemishes. If you can't have an all-over wash every day, then at least wash your face and hands, and the areas which perspire most.

Perspiration is important – it helps keep the body at the right temperature. Perspiration begins to smell when the bacteria on the surface of the skin start attacking it, and the smell becomes strongest in areas which are closed off – under the arms and between the legs. The staler the perspiration the more it will smell, so thorough and regular washing is essential for these areas.

Under the arms, where perspiration becomes stale very quickly, you can use an anti-perspirant or deodorant immediately after washing. An anti-perspirant actually stops you perspiring, while a deodorant just stops the odour.

Whenever you have the time, turn your bath into a beauty treatment. Make the water soft and fragrant by adding some nicely perfumed bath salts or bath oil. You don't have to buy expensive products – a tablespoon of olive or almond oil and a few drops of triple strength rosewater does just as good a job. If these aren't available, try a tablespoon of borax. If you like the smell of herbs, gather a handful from the garden (lavender, rosemary, lemon balm or thyme are particularly

good) and allow them to soak for 20 minutes in half a pint of boiling water. Then strain the liquid into your bath.

What sort of temperature should your bath or shower be? Avoid extremes of hot and cold. These can be bad for your skin. If you are just going to bed or want to relax, a warm bath is best. A cool bath or shower will wake you up and make you feel fresh and vigorous.

A mild, creamy soap is kindest to your skin. A good baby soap is ideal (and usually fairly inexpensive). If your skin is very sensitive avoid soaps that are highly perfumed; in fact, you might do best with a soap that contains no perfume at all.

If your skin is very dingy or spotty, a brisk rub with a loofah or bath brush will improve your circulation and help get rid of blemishes.

If you have very rough skin – on your feet or elbows, for example – pour a little olive oil and coarse salt into the palm of your hand and massage the rough area with it before you get into the bath. You'll see a great improvement after only one or two treatments.

After an invigorating bath, give yourself a brisk rub-down with a fairly rough towel and follow with a relaxing one by wrapping yourself in a big soft towel and patting yourself dry.

After your bath try a splash of light cologne to make you smell sweet and a light dusting of talc to make you feel silky.

Hair care

Your hair, like every other part of

you, reflects your general health. When you are feeling well it will look silky and bouncy. When you feel tired it becomes dull and limp.

There are three main types of hair – greasy, dry, and balanced. Balanced hair is the easiest to care for. If you have greasy or dry hair, however, you will have to take extra care to control the condition and to avoid damaging the hair.

Greasy hair

Don't be tempted to wash it too often. The oil glands will work overtime to replace the oil that has been washed out. Leave at least four days between washes and use a shampoo formulated specially for your type of hair.

Brushing also stimulates the oil glands, so moderate this, too, but don't give it up altogether. Try putting a very thin, worn piece of towel over your hairbrush before you use it. This will help to pick up quite a lot of excess grease and dirt.

Dry hair

Always use a cream shampoo. Occasionally give yourself an oil treatment which will improve the texture of your hair and stop the ends splitting.

Put some olive oil or almond oil in a basin and stand it in a bowl of hot water to warm. Working from one side of your head to the other, make partings every half inch and rub the oil into them. (Or you might find it easier to apply it with an eye-dropper.) Then wrap your head in a warm towel and relax for 15 or 20 minutes, while the oil soaks in. Finally, shampoo in the normal manner.

Hair washing

When you wash your hair, massage your scalp at the same time. This stimulates the circulation and brings a beneficial supply of fresh blood to the roots.

Thoroughly wet your hair, then work in your shampoo, using as little as possible – just enough to produce a good lather.

Make sure that the shampoo you use is right for your hair. Your hairdresser or chemist will put you right.

When you have worked the shampoo well in, place your fingers directly onto your scalp and, pressing down firmly, move them and the scalp in tiny circles. When you have massaged the whole of your scalp in this way, rinse thoroughly and then shampoo again. Rinse with at least three lots of clean water, to get rid of all traces of lather. (Careless rinsing will leave you with dull, sticky hair and an irritable, flaky scalp.) For a final rinse, use the juice of a lemon in half a pint of cool water. This will leave your hair nice and shiny.

Cutting

Whether you wear your hair long or short, always have as good a cut as you can afford. Once it has been properly shaped your hair will fall beautifully into place and need the minimum of attention between washes.

Drying

If you are lucky enough to have naturally wavy hair, towel off the excess water, comb your hair into shape and leave it to dry by itself.

If you set it on rollers, this is best done while the hair is damp, not soaking wet. Divide your hair carefully into sections, hold each one up at right angles to your scalp and wind the roller downwards. Don't try to cram too much hair on to one roller and be careful not to stretch the hair or roll it too tightly as this can cause it to split and break. If you want your set to last longer, comb setting lotion or gel on to each section before you roll it.

Too much heat can frizzle your hair and make it dry and brittle. So if you use a hair dryer, don't let it get too hot.

Heated rollers work best on hair which is practically dry. They are quick and convenient but, once again, beware of 'overcooking' your hair and spoiling its texture.

Swimming

Chlorine and salt water both make the hair dry and brittle, so after swimming it is important to rinse thoroughly with lots of clean water. If you swim a lot, treat your hair to a conditioner fairly regularly.

Perms

Home perms are very effective and much cheaper than a professional one. They are, however, difficult to manage by oneself, so enlist the help of a relative or friend. Be sure to carry out the instructions properly. Try a very soft, short-term perm to begin with. If you don't like it, you won't have to live with it for long.

Bleaching and dying

Both can do your hair and skin a great deal of damage – sometimes irreparable – so they are best left to the experts. If you're longing to experiment, try one of the temporary colour rinses that are on the market. If it looks awful, you can just wash it out again.

Face

Fashions in make-up are always changing but there are some basic beauty rules that are always the same. A spotlessly clean skin is an essential foundation as badly cleaned skin will soon develop spots and blemishes.

Washing with mild, creamy soap and warm water is sufficient for most young skins, followed by a warm rinse and perhaps a splash with cool water to close the pores. If your skin is very greasy or has very open pores, after washing you can wipe it gently with a piece of cotton wool moistened with an astringent (rose water, witchhazel or a mixture of the two).

Changes in body chemistry often cause outbreaks of spots in teenagers. These are usually temporary and clear up of their own accord. Bad and persistent cases of spots can be caused by poor eating habits (check with the diet section) and made worse by using grubby face flannels and powder puffs (use a fresh piece of cotton wool every time you cleanse or make-up your face). If spots irritate badly or become infected, consult your doctor straight away. Resist the temptation to squeeze and pick spots as this can easily make them worse and might even leave you with permanent scars.

Make-up

Young skins do not need heavy make-up. They are attractive enough in their natural state and need only the slightest addition of cream and powder to enhance their natural beauty.

If you have fine, dry skin which feels tight after it has been washed and which easily becomes rough and flaky, it will benefit from a light skinfood or moisturiser during the day and a slightly richer one at night. Baby cream is ideal for this kind of skin.

If your skin is oily, with a tendency to open pores and spots, always use an astringent before making-up and paying particular attention to the area around the nose and chin. For this type of skin a vanishing cream is best.

Most people's skin is a combination of these two types – dry and flaky around the cheeks with a greasier line running up the centre of the face. Use a mild astringent on the greasy areas and feed the dry areas with skinfood. (Never use astringent on fine dry skin, this will cause it to dry up even more.)

Always apply creams and lotions sparingly. Remember to massage creams into the skin very lightly, using an upward movement. Be specially gentle with the skin around the eyes, as it is easily dragged downward and damaged. By the way, do not forget to treat your neck in the same way as you treat your face.

Applying powder, lipstick and eyeshadow in a way that suits your individual face is a great art. A good idea is to ask for a visit to a beauty salon as a birthday or Christmas present. There you can learn from an expert the very best way to make your particular face look its most attractive.

Eyes

Eyes are very good indicators of your general state of health, so if they're dull and lifeless or puffy underneath, check your diet and make sure that you're getting enough sleep.

If your eyes get sore and tired after being in a hot, smoky atmosphere or in a windy, gritty one, use an eye lotion and eye bath. Remember that eye lotions are best kept for emergencies and should not be used as a regular habit.

Or you can try palming. Sit down and rest your elbows on a table. Cover your eyes with the palms of your hands. Your fingers should meet and cross above your eyebrows; your palms should cover, but not touch, the eyelids. Sit quite still and think of something pleasant for five minutes (so that you relax). Tension in the neck and shoulders can also affect your vision – so relax them with your neck and shoulder exercises.

Blinking rests and lubricates the eyes naturally. If you're doing lots of close work, break off every so often and spend a few seconds blinking rapidly.

If you want to make your eyes sparkle before a special occasion, soak two cotton-wool pads in witchhazel and put them on your closed eyes while you lie and relax for five or ten minutes. Alternatively, you can place a slice of cucumber on each eye.

Unruly eyebrows can be coaxed into shape with a brush or comb if you put a tiny trace of oil on them first. Plucking eyebrows can make them grow thicker and coarse, so confine yourself to removing the odd straggly hair.

Mouth

The skin of the lips is very sensitive. Keep it soft and supple by giving it a little light skin food each night. If your lips crack easily, a colourless, scentless lipsalve applied at night and before you go out into the sun or wind will help. Cracked lips are very painful and can take a long time to heal, so prevention is very much easier than cure in this case.

A pretty smile depends on well-cared-for teeth. Clean them after breakfast and last thing at night without fail. Ideally you should clean them after every meal but if you can't manage this, finish your meal with a crisp apple or raw carrot and then rinse your mouth with ordinary water. Sugar is the great tooth destroyer, so aim never to leave sugary solutions lingering in your mouth.

When cleaning your teeth, don't do it haphazardly, you should follow a regular routine. First brush the backs of the teeth and then the fronts. Always brush down from the gum towards the crown. If you brush towards the gums you can gradually push them back, exposing the very sensitive area which bacteria can attack more easily. Finish by brushing the biting surfaces in all directions. Remove any food particles still lodged between the teeth with dental floss or a toothpick. Once a week put a little toothpaste on your finger and massage your gums. And remember that toothpaste containing flouride does combat tooth decay.

Until you are twenty-one, visit your dentist every three or four months for a check-up. You may need minor fillings but you will greatly reduce the risk of losing your teeth.

Bust

There are so many pretty bras to choose from that if you're buying one for the first time it's difficult to know exactly what to look for.

Try to find a teenage bra, this is one which has been specially designed for a developing figure, and will support the breasts gently without constricting the new and delicate tissue.

For a bra to fit well, you need to know two measurements: your general size and your cup size. The general size is found by measuring round your back and over the fullest part of your bust. To find your cup size, measure again, this time directly under the bust, and subtract this measurement from the general size: under two inches difference is an AA cup; up to three inches an A cup; three to four inches, a B cup; over four inches, a C or D cup.

Try on your bra before you buy it. It should fit snugly under the arm without gaping. The cup itself must support the bust from underneath and you should not have to rely on tightening the straps (this just gives you nasty

sore, red marks on your shoulders!).
It should fit closely but without
feeling tight or restricting.

A very small bust may not need a
bra but a heavy bust will feel more
comfortable with one and it will
run less risk of drooping and
becoming shapeless.

Good posture is essential if you
want a pretty bust line. Have a
look at the exercise section.

Girdles

There is no better corset than your
own stomach and buttock muscles.
It is a sad mistake to wear heavy
foundation garments which just
allow your own muscles to grow
lazier and lazier. Unwanted inches
don't really vanish when you put
on a girdle. Look carefully and
you'll find them bulging out round
your thighs and waist. In the long
run, you'll find it more worthwhile
to lose the unwanted fat by paying
careful attention to what you eat
and to firm up the muscles by
regular exercise.

To smooth away the odd bulge
under a closely fitting skirt, a very
light pantie girdle should be quite
adequate.

Hands and feet

These do a lot of work for you and
are grateful for a little loving care
and attention. Both can get very
dry, so keep them well nourished
by rubbing in a little oil or cream
every time you wash them. And if
you have your hands in water a
lot, invest in a pair of rubber
gloves.

Nails should not be scrubbed if it
can be avoided as this tends to
split them. Instead, use an orange
stick with a little damp cotton
wool wound round the tip to
remove stubborn dirt.

To keep them looking their best,
give toe and finger nails a weekly
manicure. For this you'll need: a
bowl of warm, soapy water; cuticle
cream; skinfood or baby cream; an
orange stick; an emery board;
cotton wool.

Wash your hands (or feet)
thoroughly, rub cuticle cream
gently into the cuticles and then
put them back into the water for a
few moments. Then dry them
thoroughly.

Wrap a wisp of cotton wool
round the tip of the orange stick
and with this clean the nails.
Remove the cotton wool and use
the stick to push back the cuticles.
Don't do this too vigorously or
you'll make them sore. Never cut
your cuticles, it will make them
ragged and unsightly.

Now use the emery board to
shape your nails, remembering
always to work from the side of the
nail up towards the centre. Rubbing
the board backwards and forwards
tends to split the nail as does the
use of a metal file. Shape your
fingernails to suit the shape of
your fingers but file your toenails
square. Filing toenails down at the
sides causes ingrowing toenails.

Finally buff your nails with a
pad of cotton wool or a small piece
of chamois leather to give them a
natural sheen. Finish off with a
generous application of skin food
or baby cream.

For special occasions, you may
want to try nail varnish. Choose a
colour which looks pretty against
your skin and which complements

the outfit you are wearing.

Have handy some nail varnish remover and an orange stick with a little cotton wool wrapped round the top. Place your hand on a firm surface, fingers well spread out. Apply the colour, using just three strokes for each nail – one up the centre then one up each side. Finish off by using the orange stick dipped in remover to tidy any places where the varnish has gone astray. (Don't have the cotton wool too wet or you'll remove the varnish from the nail, too.)

When the varnish is completely dry, you can apply a second coat. This will make the colour more intense. If you want a paler effect, try a second coat of colourless varnish or of a special transparent sealer, which helps to prevent the varnish chipping. Chipped varnish does look very ugly, so if yours gets damaged, remove it straight away.

Hand care is very important

Nail biters may find that carefully manicured and varnished nails help them not to chew. If, at the moment, your nails are bitten too far down to be manicured properly, try this tip. Allow yourself to bite just one or two nails while you grow the rest. When you can get these looking good, you will have more incentive to stop biting the others. It may help to obtain a preparation of bitter aloes from the chemist. Nails painted with this taste horrid.

Ragged, splitting nails are a temptation to biters, so stop your nails splitting by wearing gloves for rough jobs. Always carry a new emery board in your purse so that you can smooth down those tempting rough edges as soon as they appear.

If your nails have white flecks in them or are in very poor condition, it could indicate a lack of calcium in your diet. Take a course of calcium tablets as an emergency measure, and make sure you include plenty of protein and calcium-rich foods (meat, fish, eggs, cheese and milk) in your diet to prevent it happening again.

Reward your feet for all the work they do by giving them well-fitting shoes. Corns, bunions, dropped arches and numerous other unpleasant conditions result from wearing shoes that do not fit properly or which distort the feet into unnatural shapes and positions. Make sure that your foot lies stretched to its full extent in the shoe and that your toes have room to move. The shoe should grip the heel snugly and not slide up and down. Medium heels are kindest to your feet particularly if you do a lot of standing or walking. High heels should be kept for rare occasions. They throw your whole body out of balance and ruin your posture if they are worn too often.

If your feet get very hot and tired, try this. Bathe them first in hot, then in cold water. Give them a quick massage with a little cream or cologne and a light dusting with talcum powder. Then put on a fresh pair of socks or stockings and shoes.

First Aid and Home Remedies

It is important to stress that the following instructions provide only a brief introduction to the important subject of first aid. Readers are urged to contact their local first aid training centre if they wish to study first aid thoroughly.

There are other vital points to be kept in mind whenever presented with a serious accident or case. The first essential is to contact medical aid – a doctor, nurse or ambulance – and then to attend to the casualty. Remember that an injured person should not be moved. You should, however, take steps to guard the casualty from traffic or any other danger. If it is possible try to divert the traffic rather than move the patient.

Keep the person's head low and the body warm with any suitable covering. Do not give the casualty anything to drink while waiting for help to arrive. If there is severe bleeding or the person has stopped breathing, however, treatment should be given immediately (*see* appropriate entries).

Bleeding
When bleeding is severe, the following five steps should be taken at once:
1 Ensure that whatever caused the cut or cuts cannot inflict any further damage. Try not to move the casualty but clear the area instead;
2 Using a clean cloth, towel or your fingers, if nothing else is available, press the wound's edges together. Continue doing this until the bleeding ceases. This can be anything up to 15 minutes;
3 As soon as possible, get the patient to lie down, raising the feet higher than the head;
4 When you are sure that the bleeding has stopped use any handy material, such as a sock or stocking, to bind round the wound;
5 Telephone for an ambulance, or doctor, if you think the patient's condition is serious enough.

In less serious cases, such as when the bleeding is slight, you should expose the wound and remove any foreign matter from it. Be very careful not to disturb any blood-clots. Gently wash away any dirt by pouring water freely over the wound. Apply an antiseptic and cover the wound with a dry dressing and then cotton-wool or lint, finally followed by a bandage. Support the injured part and make sure it is not moved. Treat for shock if there are any signs of it.

A nose-bleed should be treated in the following way. Sit the patient in an air-current from an open window. The head should be thrown slightly back. Loosen any tight clothing around the neck and chest. The patient must keep the mouth open to breathe through, and should on no account blow the nose. Applying something cold to the nose and the spine at collar level generally helps to stop the bleeding.

Shock
Accidents can cause a wide range

of injuries. They may be external or internal, such as broken bones or damaged organs. In all such cases, first aid must include treatment for shock.

Shock always occurs when there is a severe injury, blood loss or pain. It is caused by an insufficient supply of blood to the brain, which results in oxygen deficiency. The patient may feel faint, or cold and clammy, and possibly sick. Treatment should be carried out as follows:
1 Ensure that the casualty is not in danger of further injury. Never move the person unless it is *absolutely essential.* Just provide as much comfort as you can by using cushions for example;
2 Raise the patient's legs higher than the head if this can be done without affecting the injured part of the body. If you are unsure of the extent of the injuries move the patient as little as possible;
3 Make sure that warmth is maintained by covering the casualty with a light blanket. Never use hot water bottles or fires to provide artificial heat.

If the injured person shows any sign of the shock becoming worse, an ambulance should be called at once. This should be done anyway whenever a patient has been seriously injured. In the case of a heart attack, the casualty should be propped up, in order to aid breathing, before you call for an ambulance.

Burns, scalds and bruises
Dry heat, such as a fire or hot metal, causes burns; and moist heat, boiling water or steam, causes scalds. Treatment is the same in both cases, except for the first step:
1 *Burns*: If the person's clothing is on fire, approach the casualty, holding a rug, blanket, coat or table-cover in front of you. Wrap it round the patient to smother the flames and lay the person on the floor as fast as possible.
Scalds: Remove soaked clothing and anything tight, such as bracelets, belts or boots;
2 Cool the burnt or scalded parts with cold water for at least ten minutes;
3 Do not move the patient if the burn or scald is serious, but do all you can to make the person comfortable;
4 Cover the burn or scald lightly with a pillowcase or sheet to prevent infection. Never touch the affected areas with your hands or prick any blisters;
5 For serious cases, call an ambulance.
N.B. The treatment for sunburn is the same as that for other burns.

Bruising can be eased by rubbing the affected area gently with olive oil or by applying something cold to it, such as ice or a cold compress.

Choking
When somebody has something stuck in the throat, bend the person's head and shoulders forward and thump the back hard between the shoulder-blades. If this is not successful, try to make the person vomit. Pass two fingers right to the back of the throat. Should the choking continue – perhaps because a fishbone is lodged in the throat – call a doctor.

Foreign matter in the eye
Usually, grit or an eyelash can be removed simply by rolling the eyelid back from the eye and carefully applying a soft cloth or handkerchief. If, however, a quantity of sand, grit, or some chemical such as ammonia, is in the patient's eye, persuade the person to put her head into a basin of cool water and blink several times. Repeat the process after you have changed the water. Generally you will find the eye is clear of the foreign matter.

Poisoning
In cases of poisoning it is vital to telephone for an ambulance immediately. Only a hospital can cope properly with poisoning. Keep a sample of the poison, if possible, to show to the doctor so that the correct treatment can be given. While waiting for the ambulance to come, keep the patient as quiet as possible. Do not give her anything to drink or eat. In cases when the patient complains of a burning mouth or throat she has most certainly swallowed an acid. Give her plenty of water to drink in order to dilute the acid. Continue until the burning stops. Avoid making the patient sick as vomit may be inhaled and cause choking.

Squeezed fingers, splinters and stings
After squeezing the top of a finger, hold it in warm water for a few minutes. This causes the nail to expand and soften. The blood beneath it now has more room to flow, thus lessening the pain.

Splinters can be removed by nearly filling a wide-mouthed bottle with hot water, and then holding the injured part over this and pressing it down tightly. The suction acts as a poultice and draws the flesh down. The splinter will normally come out quite easily after this.

When a sting is still present it should be extracted, if possible, with the point of a sterilized needle. For bee stings, apply spirit, toilet water, sal volatile, a solution of baking soda or washing soda to relieve the pain. For wasp or hornet stings, use a weak acid such as vinegar or lemon juice. Then, put on a dry dressing and treat for shock.

Sprains
Place the affected limb in a comfortable position and prevent movement. Next, expose the sprained joint and apply a firm bandage. The bandage should be wetted with cold water and kept wet. Repeat this process, whenever necessary to provide relief. When in doubt, treat the injury as a break (fracture).

Sunstroke
In cases of sunstroke, get the patient to a cool and shady place. Strip the person to the waist and lay her down with the head and shoulders well raised. Fan the patient rigorously and also sponge the body with cold water all the time. Apply ice-bags or cold water to the head, neck and spine.

When the person is conscious, give her drinks of cold water. Do all you can to help the patient to become conscious and do not try to give her a drink until then.

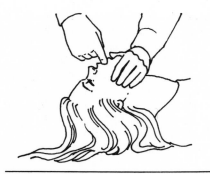

The first step is to clear the person's airway because, once it is cleared, the casualty may start breathing again without further ado. Anything that you find in the mouth (blood, vomit, false teeth, etc.) must be instantly cleared out. It is also vital to tilt the casualty's head well back, as an unconscious person's tongue falls back and obstructs the airway.

Tilting the head extends the neck and moves the tongue clear of the airway.

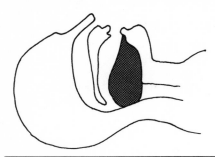

If you then breathe into the casualty's mouth and the person's chest rises and falls, you will know that the airway is clear; otherwise, you must immediately repeat the first step. Again clear the mouth of any obstruction and make sure that the head is tilted back far enough.

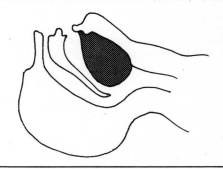

When applying mouth-to-mouth breathing remember to pinch the casualty's nostrils to close them. This will stop any of the air you are breathing in from escaping by way of the person's nose.

You are now ready to start mouth-to-mouth breathing. Begin with four quick breaths *in order to replenish the casualty's blood with a good supply of oxygen. There is a sufficient amount of oxygen in your breath when exhaled.*

Now settle down to a steady breathing at the normal rate of 10–15 breaths per minute. Remember to keep the casualty's nostrils pinched all the time. This must be kept up until medical help arrives, somebody takes over from you or, of course, the person starts breathing properly again without your help.

When a casualty does start breathing, place the person carefully in the recovery position shown in the illustration. This makes it possible for the casualty to breathe easily without the tongue falling back across the airway or any further vomit being inhaled.

Should you have to deal with a heavy person, use the following method to turn her into the recovery position: kneel alongside the casualty; place the arms at the sides of the body; cross the far leg over the near one and then pull the person over by the clothes at the hip. After that, put the casualty's arms and legs into the proper recovery positions, as illustrated.

Finally, there are a few additional points to keep in mind for special cases. Gentle breathing is essential for young children and babies, and you may have to seal your lips over both the child's nose and mouth. When injury to the casualty's mouth makes it impossible to give breathing aid by the usual method, you must as an alternative apply mouth-to-nose breathing.

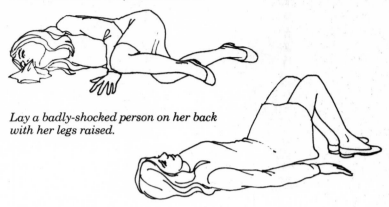

The correct treatment for convulsions

Lay a badly-shocked person on her back with her legs raised.

Convulsions

If a person is having convulsions (a fit) remove any objects nearby which can cause injuries. Protect the patient but do not restrain her in any way. If choking occurs, put a piece of cloth or anything soft into the mouth but *never* use force. Stay by the person after the convulsions have stopped as she may suffer from a temporary loss of memory and a headache.

Electric shock

Before any assistance can be given to the victim of an electric shock, the electric contact must be broken. Do this by switching off the appliance, turning off the current at the mains or pushing the person away with a piece of dry wood. Next see if the casualty is breathing. If she is not, give her mouth-to-mouth breathing (*see* below).

A badly shocked but conscious person should be laid on her back with the legs raised. If she is unconscious, she should be laid in the recovery position (*see* diagram on page 30).

MOUTH-TO-MOUTH BREATHING

It is very important that as many people as possible know how to apply 'mouth-to-mouth breathing' as it is the surest method of saving the life of a person who has ceased to breathe due to an accident, heart attack, drowning, electric shock or other reason.

Practice, after studying this form of first aid in the following description, is a very good idea. *Never* practise on another person but try to attend a proper class at which mouth-to-mouth breathing can be practised on dummies.

As soon as you are certain that the casualty is not breathing at all, start giving her mouth-to-mouth breathing. Delay can cause damage to the brain in three minutes!

HOBBIES
AND PASTIMES

Outdoor Activities

Exercise in the fresh air, especially on a fine day, can be a very rewarding way to spend one's leisure time. Although some outdoor pursuits require special equipment, you need spend little or nothing to go for a walk in the country when the weather is good. If you live in a city you may have to find the bus or train fare to get to the country, but that is all.

For more strenuous hiking and hill walking, special boots and protective clothing are advisable. Walking boots are not only tough and flexible with a good, thick sole, but they also give support to your ankles when you walk on rocky, uneven surfaces.

In cold conditions it is better to wear several layers of thin woollen clothing than just one thick sweater. If you become too warm you can always take off one or two garments. Woollen trousers are warmer than denim jeans. When wet, wool dries more quickly than cotton. For added protection, take along some waterproof nylon overtrousers.

On mountains and the tops of high hills you will find that even on a beautiful summer's day temperatures can be icy, so be prepared. If you are too lightly dressed as well as wet, prolonged exposure to the cold can cause you to suffer from hypothermia. This is an inability to maintain adequate body temperature. The symptoms are uncontrollable shivering and slurred speech, leading to extreme sleepiness and, eventually, death.

A waterproof cagoule will help keep out the wind and rain, although one small snag is that it will tend to trap condensation inside, making you hot and sticky. A hooded anorak is another wind-proof garment. It should be large enough to cover your sweaters amply and long enough to reach well below your hips. The hood and hem should be fitted with draw strings and the sleeves should be elasticated so that in bad weather all the openings can be sealed up as much as possible.

On short hikes a small frameless rucksack is useful for carrying spare clothing and your maps, compass, first aid kit and a packed lunch. The rucksack will leave both your arms free and you will scarcely notice its weight when it is properly adjusted. For walking tours covering several days, when you might be camping at night or staying at youth hostels, you will want a larger rucksack for all your equipment. It is very important to choose one that is comfortable during long walks. Basically there are two types for this purpose. First there is the sort that is mounted on a metal frame which fits on your back with a curved waist support. The wide leather or webbing straps are adjustable and take the load. If you are thinking of getting a second-hand one beware of buying a badly designed, old-fashioned rucksack that tends to hang too low. This causes the wearer to lean forward. The better types are fairly narrow at the

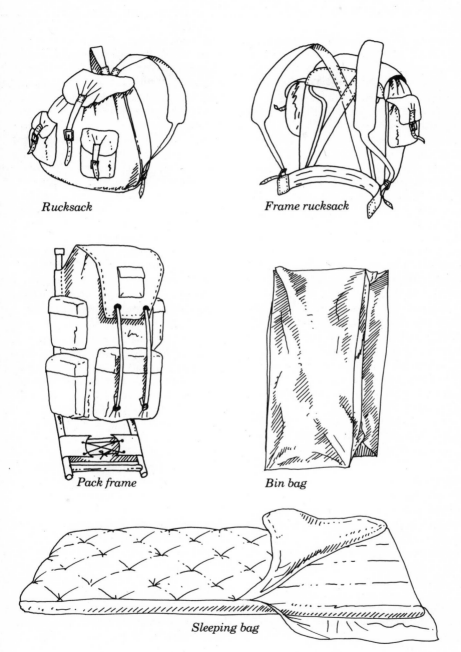

Rucksack

Frame rucksack

Pack frame

Bin bag

Sleeping bag

bottom and widen out at the top, fitting the contours of the back and shoulders.

Second, there is the pack frame and sack which is a most effective means of carrying a large load. The pack frame is made of a light alloy to which is attached two well-padded adjustable shoulder straps as well as the sack which is usually of nylon and has large external pockets.

Whatever type of carrier you use, the principles of packing are the same.

1 The heaviest items are packed at the top. It is easier to carry them high on the back.
2 Items that you may want to get at quickly should be readily available.
3 Light items and those which will be wanted last, such as a sleeping bag, should be packed first or wrapped in a polythene bag and strapped to the bottom of the frame below the sack.
4 Make sure that no hard object will dig into your back.
5 Never pack too heavy a load, it will spoil your trip. Take only the essentials.

Backpacking
If you like the idea of exploring remote areas on foot where there are no shops to obtain supplies, no hotels, not even youth hostels, then backpacking is the way to do it. Everything you need to survive for several days in the wild will have to be carried with you. This should include a tent, a sleeping bag, clothing, food and drink, and cooking utensils.

There are special lightweight tents for backpackers, some weighing 1.4 kg (3 lb) or less. They are made of nylon and have very little room inside, making them unsuitable for ordinary, leisurely camping. They are designed to give just sufficient protection for sleeping and often fit only one person.

An alternative to a tent is what is known as a bivibag. One type, made of polythene, gives cover for two people and is very cheap but it cannot be expected to last very long. Or you could rely on a waterproof sleeping bag with an improvised head cover made from a sheet of polythene tied to sturdy sticks. Various kinds of bivouac can be devised, but these are only a good idea if you can be certain that the weather will remain warm and dry.

Take care when choosing a sleeping bag for backpacking. The cheaper ones are rather heavy to carry and none too warm. The most expensive and the lightest in weight, are made of down. They can be rolled up into a very small bundle. There are now some polyester sleeping bags which are also very light and almost as warm as the down-filled sleeping bags, and much less expensive. These have the advantage that they do not attract the damp and if they happen to get wet they can be dried out easily.

Another way of exploring the country is by cycling. Long distances can be covered easily with a fair load carried in panniers and saddle-bag. There are many ways in which the load can be

distributed. It is important,
however, to spread it evenly and to
keep it low, otherwise the bike will
be difficult to handle and you could
have an accident.

Types of lightweight camping tent

The most commonly used type of
tent is the ridge tent. It has two
poles, normally consisting of three
sections of aluminium or wood. In
some designs there is a third pole
which lies horizontally, holding the
two vertical poles apart. Guylines
attached to the roof or walls of the
tent run to pegs (usually made of
metal) which are driven into the
ground at an angle. These hold the
tent down in windy conditions and,
if properly fixed, ensure that it
stands symmetrically. A sewn-in
ground-sheet is an advantage as it
reduces draughts and helps prevent
rainwater getting into the tent. A
flysheet gives added insulation by
trapping air between it and the
tent walls, especially if it is the
type that stretches down to the
ground. Furthermore it helps to
keep the tent waterproof by taking
the initial impact of rain drops
which then run off the sloping
edge.

You can choose a cotton canvas
tent, or one made of nylon or
terylene. Both have their
advantages and disadvantages. The
cotton fabric, which should be
treated against rain and rot, will
allow air to filter through the fine
weave. As a result moisture will
not tend to form inside. Nylon and
terylene are lighter fabrics and do
not shrink but condensation will
form on the inner walls if there is

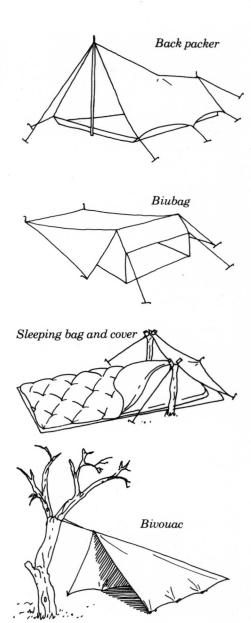

Back packer

Biubag

Sleeping bag and cover

Bivouac

Ridge tent

Mountain tent

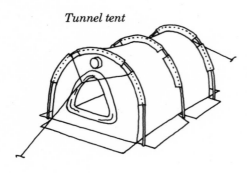

Tunnel tent

insufficient ventilation. An excellent compromise is to select a tent with cotton inner walls and a nylon flysheet.

There are various other kinds of tent on the market, some for special purposes such as the mountain tent which has a sleeve-like opening. Some tents are supported by A-frames (because they look like the letter A). Tents with an exterior frame have hangers to which the fabric is attached.

Selecting a camp spot

Finding a suitable spot at an organized camp site should present few problems. But suppose you wish to camp at a natural site where there are no laid-on facilities, with just a stream, perhaps, for water? First, obtain the permission of the landowner before you start pitching your tent. Make sure that the spot you choose is level, and free from lumps, rocks, tussocks, and thistles – and from too many flies. Be sure that any over-night rain will not cause you to be flooded out.

Don't pitch your tent under trees. In bad weather branches may break off and fall on you. Leaves tend to drip heavily long after a rain shower. Furthermore, it is dangerous to be at the foot of a tall, isolated tree during a thunderstorm. Long grass is also best avoided because it holds dew and will remain damp for a long time.

A site near a clear stream is a good one as you can use the water for personal washing and for washing up. You can use the water for drinking provided it is sterilized. Boil it for at least five minutes before drinking it. You can buy, at a chemist, water purifying tablets which you simply dissolve.

Camp cooking

There are several points to be borne in mind when planning meals for a lightweight camping expedition. The food you take should be light in weight and not so bulky that it takes up too much room in your rucksack. It should keep well. Fresh meat or fish won't last long in hot weather. Of course, you will need to produce balanced, nutritious meals, including carbohydrates, proteins and fats, and they should be as appetizing as possible. Fortunately fresh air and exercise tend to produce a terrific appetite and simple food cooked in a primitive manner will taste more delicious than it would if dished up on the dining room table. You also feel exhilarated with a sense of achievement when you have produced a meal from very basic resources.

There are various kinds of dried vegetables that you can buy beforehand that are very light to carry as well as reasonable in price and so ideal for campers. Types available include mashed potato, onions, peas, beans and mixed vegetables. Dried fruits such as apricots, apple-rings and prunes can be very handy, and don't forget packet soups. Remember, too, that some dehydrated fruits and vegetables need to be soaked for several hours before use, which is a drawback if food is wanted quickly.

You will not be able to carry a large amount of fuel, so food that needs a great deal of cooking should be left out. Aim for a hot breakfast and evening meal. During the day, cheese, nuts, raisins and chocolates can be eaten. They are quite sustaining and may be all you need until later in the evening. Instant coffee and tea-bags weigh next to nothing and a good brew-up revives the spirit and the body.

Porridge or muesli will make a nourishing breakfast. If you hanker after fried eggs and bacon, however, carry your eggs already cracked in a lidded container. Vacuum packed bacon will keep for several days in the cool.

Fresh vegetables, eggs and milk may be obtainable from a nearby farm. Fresh greens will certainly make a welcome change from the packaged or canned variety. Boil the water first before adding the vegetables to conserve the vitamins as much as possible.

Macaroni and spaghetti will provide a useful foundation for many dishes. Put it in salted water and boil until tender. Then mix with grated cheese, tinned meat or vegetables. For variety, a simple curry sauce may be made by frying a little onion, stirring in a few teaspoonfuls of curry powder and then adding water or gravy. A small quantity of lemon juice and sugar will improve the taste.

Bread is a bulky item which could be left out altogether. Crispbread could be taken instead. If you want jam on it, try mashing up soft wild fruit such as bilberries with sugar. You may even prefer it to cooked jam you use at home.

It is fun to make your own camp bread using self raising flour. Make a biscuit dough by mixing four parts of flour to a little over one part of water and a good pinch of salt. Having mixed the dough there are several ways you could cook it.

Dampers Pull off small balls of dough about the size of eggs and flatten them in your hands to make discs. Put them on a hot pan or in front of a reflector fire (*see* below). If you put them in a pan, shake them in the early stages to prevent them sticking. As soon as one side is brown, turn them over. The dampers should rise a little like a small cake. Cut the dampers in half and butter them.

Ember bread This is made on an open fire. Take a dollop of dough and slightly flatten it. Rake over your fire to expose the hot earth. Place the dough on the ground and rake the embers over it. Cook for about 15 minutes. The outside may be burnt but all you have to do is to scrape off the outside to get at the nicely cooked bread within.

Bread twist Cut a green stick about 2.5 cm (1 in.) thick, peel it and heat it until the sap bubbles out at the end. Now make the dough into a long sausage and twist it around the heated stick leaving a gap between the coils. Hold the stick over the embers, turning it frequently until the dough is golden brown. Be sure the stick is really hot before you put the dough on it otherwise the outside will be cooked and the inside uncooked. When baked it should easily slide off the stick and can be filled with cheese or jam.

When using sticks for cooking you need a fire of coals, not flames. Avoid resinous woods and willow because they have an unpleasant taste which can flavour the food. Any kind of food suitable for grilling can be cooked with the aid of sharpened sticks over a fire.

Cooking stoves

Several types of lightweight cooking stove are available from camping suppliers. They burn either solid fuel, methylated spirits, petrol, paraffin or camping gas.

One of the cheapest is a little picnic stove which houses the fuel container within the combined pot stand and windshield. Meths is poured into the centre of the hollow, cup-shaped container to a set level. A lighted match is then applied to the surface which produces a ring of fire. Although this stove is comparatively safe care must be taken not to pour in more meths when a flame is still left. The meths will flare up and could cause a serious accident. It is well to remember that meths burns with an almost invisible flame. One of the disadvantages of this stove is that it uses a fair amount of fuel.

The solid fuel stove is the lightest of all. It consists of a small steel box which when folded up is not much larger than a pack of playing cards. It opens out to form a pot stand and burner plate with supporting legs. The best results are obtained when lightweight cooking utensils are used. A disadvantage of the solid fuel stove is that it does not cook quickly.

The primus stove uses paraffin. It is a powerful cooker, burning for a

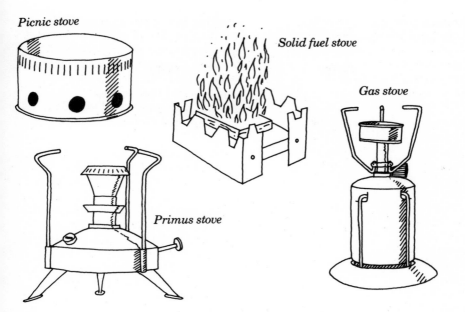

Picnic stove

Solid fuel stove

Gas stove

Primus stove

considerable time on one filling. However, it is a little more difficult to manage, needing some practice beforehand. It also needs priming to get going and for this you will need a second fuel such as methylated spirits or a solid fuel.

A petrol stove is also powerful, but it is a little risky to run and uses an expensive fuel.

There are several makes of lightweight stoves using camping gas. They are all easy to operate. You light them by simply turning on a valve and applying a match to the gas ring. When it is cold, below 1° C, butane gas liquifies and cannot be lit. There is no such problem, however, with propane.

Whatever type of cooking stove you use, do not run it inside your tent or too close to the canvas. Do not refuel it inside the tent either. Spare fuels should be kept outside,

away from the tent and away from the stove. A windshield will be necessary when using your stove unless it is one of those with the windshield built into it.

Cooking utensils
The absolute minimum you will need for lightweight camping is a frying pan and a pot. But there are some extremely practical and inexpensive camping canteens on the market which are well worth considering. Normally they consist of a number of aluminium cooking and eating utensils that nest compactly one inside another when packed. One of these canteens is illustrated. The handle of the frying pan is hinged and it is so constructed that it can be folded over the nest of pans to snap them tightly together. To lift the pot you will need a bulldog grip.

Pot

Frying pan

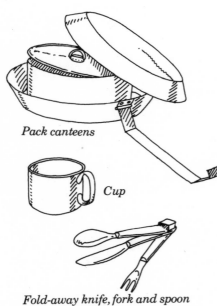

Pack canteens

Cup

Fold-away knife, fork and spoon

Plate

A plastic mug is a must, and it is useful to have an extra plate, either plastic or aluminium. Make sure it is a fairly deep one that can hold soup or stew. Aluminium cutlery sets consisting of knife, fork and desert spoon that clip together neatly for packing purposes can be found in camping shops. Don't forget a can-opener and a box of matches.

Camp fires

Camp stoves are so efficient and reliable that it is not really necessary to light a fire. On the other hand a camp fire can be a great comfort in cold weather and will help to conserve the limited amount of stove fuel that you carry. You must remember that fire can spread and cause damage, so always be very careful and never leave the fire unguarded.

To make a fire you will need to collect some tinder – material that will ignite easily and burn long enough to enable the fire to catch the kindling wood. Suitable materials for tinder are dry fir cones, dry grass and weeds knotted into bundles and fallen tree bark.

Collect larger pieces of fuel for kindling and still larger pieces for the basis of the fire. The logs may be arranged in several different ways and there are many ways of supporting the pots and pans. It all depends on how quickly you wish to cook the food.

A criss-cross fire is a very good cooking fire because it supplies an even bed of coals and all the sticks burn uniformly. Make it by laying a row of sticks alongside each other on the ground. A second row

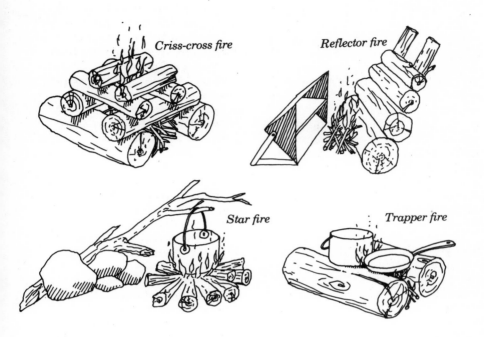

Criss-cross fire

Reflector fire

Star fire

Trapper fire

is placed crosswise on top of them, another row crosswise on top again until the pile is the desired height. When the sticks have burnt down there is a glowing bed of hot coals.

A *reflector fire* is often used to reflect heat into a bivouac or shelter. It is an ideal arrangement for baking. Drive two poles into the ground so that they slope backwards slightly. Stack several logs against them to form a wall. The fire is then built against this wall. The reflector oven is placed in front of it. As the bottom logs burn away the others drop down and the fire keeps burning. This is a good all-night fire. A reflector oven can be improvised by propping up a frying pan in front of the fire.

The star fire is a slow-burning fire which is very economical on fuel and which requires little attention. Make it by building up a small fire until you have a good blaze. Then place the ends of several long timbers into the blaze, igniting the ends one at a time. By the time you have finished the timbers radiate like the spokes of a wheel which burn only where the ends meet. As the ends burn away you push the logs inwards to keep the fire going steadily.

The trapper fire is another effective cooking fire. Place two green logs, or two long stones, just far apart enough to support your cooking pot. They should be laid so that one end catches the breeze and so fans the flames.

Crafts

Most handicrafts are based on very simple techniques and most of them date back to prehistoric times. When our ancestors first began to twist fibres together, to make ropes and nets, to spin hair and wool, and to combine these with knots or weaves to make fabric, they had very little to work with. You will find, often, that the most interesting things are produced with a few pieces of basic equipment and some scraps of material or yarn.

The next few pages will show how you can start to use some of the different techniques to make things yourself. You may know some of these techniques already, but there are always new ideas to try out and new ways of making a particular thing. Have you tried knitting a cushion cover? Or making an owl out of knots?

Equipment

The following items will be of use to you and some of them will be necessary for several techniques, so you should try to obtain or borrow:

a pair of scissors for material and a
    pair of scissors for paper and card
tape measure
pins, both large and small
tacks
cardboard
fine sewing needles
embroidery needles
a bodkin or large blunt needle,
    with a large hole
a piece of insulating board or
    fibreboard, about 18 inches square

beads, sequins and buttons of
    different sizes and colours
empty cotton reels
sticks – plant supporting cane, for
    example
as many scraps of different yarns
    (e.g. wool, cotton and silk)
scraps of different materials (used
    or unused)
sewing threads
embroidery threads
adhesive transparent plastic
paintbrush
blotting paper
pencil and paper
pair of compasses
ruler
crochet hook
pair of knitting needles
rubber solution glue
optional – rigid heddle and box
loom
embroidery ring

ROPES AND CORDS

To make a length of twisted cord, take a strand of yarn (wool, cotton, string, etc.) and fasten one end to something secure, such as a drawer handle. Pull tautly on the yarn and begin to twist it in the direction of the twist already on it. When it begins to look very twisted, still holding it tautly, take hold of the middle of the yarn and bring the end you are holding to meet the other fastened end. Carefully allow the end you are holding to unravel into itself, undo the fastened end and tie the two ends together with an OVERHAND KNOT (*see* diagram).

You can vary the type of cord in

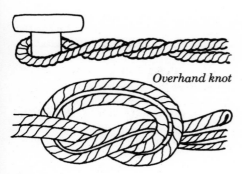

Overhand knot

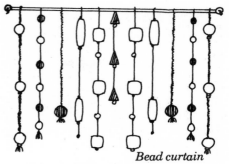

Bead curtain

these ways:
– use two or three yarns together, twisting them as if they were one;
– take two strands of yarn and twist each separately;
– put more or less twist in the yarn. Always remember to secure the ends with a knot. When measuring your strands make allowance for the twists, you will find that you need more than twice the cord's finished length in yarn.

PROJECT IDEA
bead curtain
You will need
lengths of coloured and/or natural yarn
beads with large holes
strong holding cord or string for the top of the curtain
With cords alone, you can make something extremely attractive and eye-catching to hang in front of a window or on a wall!

When you have decided on the size of the curtain and the colours you want to use (a mixture could be very effective), you will be ready to start. The strong holding cord or curtain cord, which is to be the top of the curtain, should be secured to a convenient working place such as between two drawer handles on a chest of drawers. Take the colour

you want to begin with and measure at least three times the length of the finished cord in your chosen yarn. Double it and place it around the holding cord. Now start twisting both strands of the yarn and let it unravel into itself. Thread some beads onto your new cord and secure each bead somewhere on the cord by tying a knot underneath it so that it won't slip down. Then tie a knot at the bottom of the cord, where the two ends are. Repeat until you have as many cords hanging from the holding cord as you wish. Vary the points at which you secure the beads on the cord. You can also thread beads on before you start twisting or tie beads into the knot, as well as leave the bead above the knot. Let some cords hang without beads or knots and some cords hang with a knot or two only. Finally, tidy the ends of the cords and the curtain is ready to hang up.

Macramé
The word macramé comes from the Arab word *mukharram* meaning trellis and the technique is based on a few knots which are repeated in various ways. All that is needed is the yarn to work with, a board to pin the work on (for example, an

The Larkshead

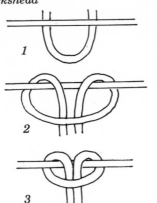

1

2

3

The Half-knot

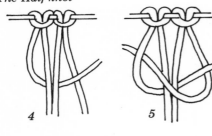

4

5

The Square-knot

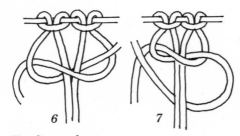

6

7

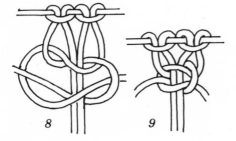

8

9

insulating board covered with cotton), large-headed pins or tacks, and scissors. The kinds of yarn to try are dishcloth cotton, crochet cotton, parcel string, rope, leather strips, nylon cord, piping cord, wool etc. but the easiest sort of yarn to work with is a medium-thick, smooth yarn with a good twist in it.

The square knot and the half knot

To start the work, tie a short length (20–30 cm/8–12 in) of any strong string or cord to two large pins, spaced 15 cm (6 in) or so apart on your working board. Cut four lengths of yarn, each about 1 m (40 in) long, and mount them onto the holding cord in the following way: fold each length in half and pass the loop formed behind the holding cord, pushing both long ends through the loop. This is known as the LARKSHEAD. (*See* diagrams 1, 2 and 3.) In the end, you should have eight strands hanging off the holding cord, on the board. Take the first four strands and pass the left-hand one of these behind the next two and over the fourth (diagram 4). Pass the right-hand strand over the centre two and through the loop formed by the left-hand strand (diagram 5). Pull the two outer strands up firmly. This is the HALF-KNOT (diag. 6).

Now continue with this knot to make the SQUARE KNOT. Take the right-hand strand (this was on the left-hand side originally) and pass it under the centre two and over the strand lying on the left-hand side (diagram 7). Next, take the left-hand strand and pass it over the centre two and through the loop on the right-hand side (diagram 8). Pull the two ends tightly. This is the completed square knot (diagram 9).

Work five square knots on both sets of four strands. Then take the centre four strands (so that there are two strands left over on either side) and make ten half knots. You will find that it tends to want to curl round in a spiral and this is part of its pattern. Now take the side pairs and make overhand knots (*see* previous section on ropes and cords) with them. On one side, use the same strand each time to tie the knot (diagram 1a or 1b) and on the other, alternate the strands (diagram 2). The second method gives a pretty bobbled effect and looks especially good in a fringe.

You have worked the square knot or flat knot (which is, in fact, similar to the reef knot), half knot, and overhand knot.
Practise these knots on the strands you have and try combining them in different ways. For example, use different groups of four for the knots, as well as repeating a knot on the same strands. Try to build up little patterns using these knots. One pattern you can try makes a kind of net effect (diagram 3) using the square knot. Another variation of it is shown in diagram 4.

Finally, you can use the square knot to make a PICOT edging. If you make one knot below another, using the same strands but leaving a space between them, and then push up the lower knot, you will find a little loop has formed

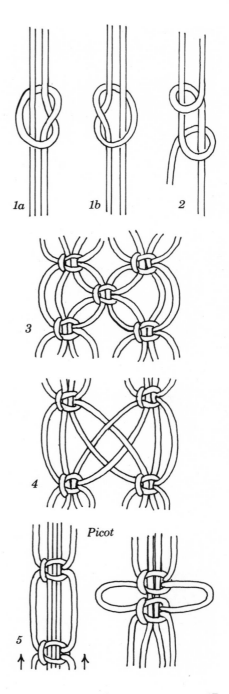

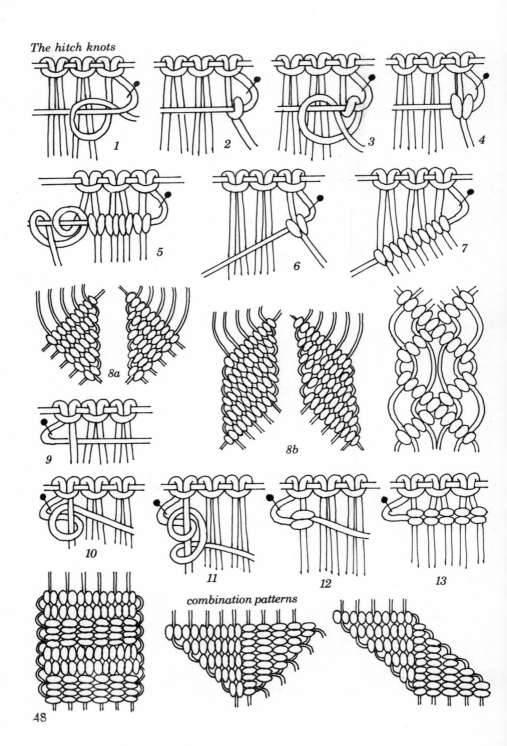

The hitch knots

1

2

3

4

5

6

7

8a

8b

9

10

11

12

13

combination patterns

between the knots. This is a picot (diagram 5). Try some picots in different sizes.

Take this sample off the holding cord by sliding it off and keep it for reference.

The half hitch, the double half hitch or clove hitch

Cut four more lengths of yarn, a little longer this time. Mount them on the holding cord using the lark's heads as before. You are now going to try the other basic macramé knots – the HALF HITCH and the DOUBLE HALF HITCH. These knots can be worked upwards and downwards (vertically), or sideways (horizontally) or on a slant (diagonally).

Start at the very right-hand side and take the first strand as your 'knot-bearer'. Place the strand at a right-angle to the other strands as in diagram 1 and pick up the second strand from the right. Wind it clockwise round the horizontal strand and pull (diagram 2). This is one half hitch. Repeat this and you will have the double half hitch. (diagrams 3 and 4). Complete the row in this manner (diagram 5). Try several rows, starting at the right each time. You will find that the rows start coming in on a slant. If you then do a few rows working from left to right, you will find, the slant travels in the opposite direction.

Now try working the double half hitch on the diagonal as in diagrams 6 and 7. This is a little more tricky but, if you do a few rows, you will see that it is not as hard as it first seemed. The most important thing is to take care that you pull the strands evenly. Now try a few of the patterns using the double half hitch diagonally (diagrams 8a and 8b).

Finally, try the double half hitch vertically. For this, each of the hanging strands becomes a 'knot-bearer', and the strand on the left or right of the work is the actual knotter. Start with your first strand underneath the next one as in diagram 9. Then make the clockwise knots as in diagrams 10 and 11 and continue along the row, remembering to place the knotting strand under the next strand each time (diagrams 12 and 13). And lastly, try a few of the patterns using combinations of horizontal and vertical double half hitches.

PROJECT IDEAS

If you liked trying out these knots and think that you would like to do something with them, why not try and make a little knotted picture? All you need is a stick or rod to hang your strand on, the yarn and extra beads or buttons as desired. You can use the diagonal double half hitch to make curved shapes for flowery and leaf patterns, adding beads onto the strands for extra interest. Another shape from nature that would suit macramé technique is an owl. Remember you don't have to use each single strand for a knot; you can take

groups of the strands and use them as one. This way you can bring two sides of a piece in towards the middle. You can leave the ends of strands hanging to make a fringe.

When you have a design in mind that you would like to try, draw it roughly on some paper. Think what texture you want – should it be rough, shiny, smooth etc.? And decide what colours you are using – are they natural, contrasting, toning? Finally, cut enough yarn for the work: square knots use up over half the length and double half hitches take up at least four to eight times as much! So allow for the types of knots you make.

A simpler project might be to make a small bag. You will need two wooden rings for the handles. Start by mounting at least 24 doubled strands of yarn onto each handle. Fasten the handle onto your working board or a door handle and work a few rows on each handle separately as in the pattern on page 48, diagram 3. This way you will have two slits at the top of the bag. Then take a piece of cardboard, roughly the size of your bag, or a cushion, or a block of foam, and work the knots all round until you have reached the length you want for your bag. A pair of strands from each side (two pairs) are then knotted together at the bottom of the bag with an overhand knot.

WRAPPING, TASSLES AND POM-POMS

There are several ways of making attractive finishes and extra decorations to add to what you are making. Tassles and pom-poms can also be used by themselves to make little dolls, furry animals, balls, bells etc.

WRAPPING is an excellent way of making ends look very neat (for example with a knotted curtain or bag). To wrap a group of ends, first smooth them out. Then, holding them firmly together, take a length of the yarn you are using for wrapping, make a loop as shown in diagram 1 and hold it against the group of ends. Start winding the yarn firmly over the loop and the group of ends (diagram 2). Work upwards, covering the loop, but leave a small part of the loop showing, and thread your wrapping yarn through this loop (diagram 3). Now pull the lower end of your wrapping yarn showing and you will see the top end of your wrapping yarn tuck under the wrapped section as the loop disappears. You can then cut the top end off and neaten the lower pulling end (diagram 4).

You can use wrapping to make TASSLES. Start by cutting off a group of threads the same length. A simple method for doing this is shown in diagram 5; just make sure that the width of the card you wind the yarn around is the length of the tassle you want. Cut another length longer than the tassle threads and tie it round the middle of the group with an overhand knot (diagram 6). Alternatively you could use a lark's head (see the

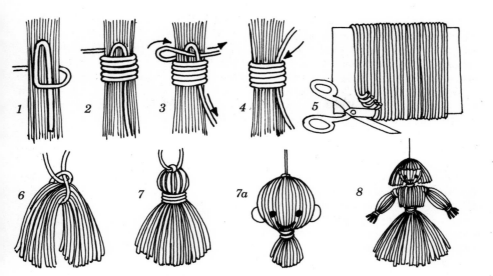

section on macramé). If you wrap
the threads firmly a little way
down, you will make a neck as in
diagram 7.

Now, if you try putting a bean,
or a bead into the top part of the
tassle, before you wrap it, you can
make its head even rounder. The
bigger the object you use for
stuffing it, the more threads you
will need for the tassle. Try using
an empty cotton reel which you
have covered with the same yarn
as you have used for your tassle.

These little shapes can be used
as Christmas tree figures or even
presents. You can sew on sequins
for eyes, use felt for ears or wings,
extra wool for hair (7a), and you can
combine more than one tassle to
make a tassle doll (diagram 8).

To make POM-POMS, you will
need some strongish cardboard and
a pair of good cutting scissors, as
well as the yarn you are using for
your pom-pom. Draw out two discs
on your card, each with a large

hole in the middle (for example, use
a saucer for the outer circle and a
glass for the hole in the middle).
The size of the pom-pom depends
on the size of the disc. You then
begin winding your yarn round the
two discs together, as in diagram 1.
You might need to use a thick-eyed
blunt needle towards the end, but
you can equally well do this with
your fingers.

Pompom

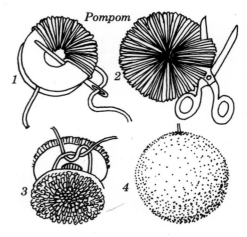

51

Continue winding until the centre hole is completely filled and no more yarn can be pushed through, as in diagram 2. The yarn is then cut with sharp-pointed scissors, which you guide carefully between the outer edges of the two cardboard discs (diagram 2).

When the discs are free and all the yarn is cut, you push them apart slightly and tie a length of yarn round the cut threads between the discs, as in diagram 3. Fasten this thread securely. The ends of this length of yarn are left long so that the pom-pom can be attached to whatever you are making. The cardboard discs are then gently pulled off (diagram 4).

PROJECT IDEA
Try making a mobile out of different kinds of tassles and sizes of pom-poms.
You will need
either some light but firm wire
or some gardening sticks
different coloured yarns
sequins, buttons, felt, and sewing things

It is better not to try and make a mobile that is too big and it is much easier if you start from the lower part, balancing each new section against the rest as you create your colourful mobile.

CROCHET
You may have done some crochet already and, if you have, you will know that all you need is a crochet hook and some wool. There are just a few basic stitches and, with these, you can make many things, for which there are plenty of

An attractive mobile

patterns available. In a short time, with a bit of practice, you can also start to make things for yourself or others.

The first stitch
Make the first loop or slip knot as follows. Hold the end of your wool between the thumb and the second finger of your left hand while you pass the strand around your first finger, from the side nearest to you. Bring the wool round to the left of the circle this makes and hold the loop in place with your thumb. Pick up the crochet hook, as if you were going to write with it, slip it under the loop where it crosses the top of your first finger and draw the strand of wool through. Drop the loop off the finger and draw the wool up to the hook. (*See* diagrams 1 and 2.)

Keep the wool away from the work by looping the long thread round the little finger of your left hand, across the palm and behind the first finger (diagram 2). You have now made one CHAIN-STITCH. Hold the end of this stitch between your thumb and first finger (diagram 3) close to the hook and pass the crochet hook under the wool behind the chain. Catch it from left to right (diagram 4) and draw it through the first stitch. Repeat this until you have a short length of chain (diagram 5). Try not to pull the stitches too tightly and keep them as even as possible. You have now made a foundation row.

Slip-stitch or single crochet

To make the second row, you can now do the basic crochet stitch – SLIP-STITCH. Pass the hook into the stitch below to the left of the hook, you now have two loops on your hook. Catch the wool again from left to right and draw it through both loops. When you turn to come back, make one chain and this counts as the first slip-stitch in the next row. The stitch makes a flat chain, which is useful for edges or for joining two edges together (diagrams 6 and 7).

Double crochet

Instead of making one chain extra at the end of your last row, make two. Put your hook into the next stitch, under both of its top loops, then under the wool from left to right and draw it through, which gives two loops on the hook (diagrams 1 and 2, p. 54). Pass the hook under the wool again and draw it through both loops (diagram 3). This leaves one loop on the hook. Continue along the row and start

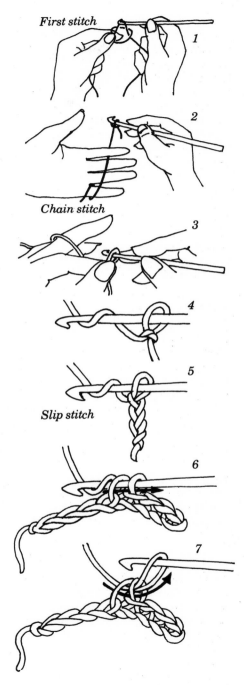

First stitch

Chain stitch

Slip stitch

1

2

3

4

5

6

7

Double Crochet

1

3

2

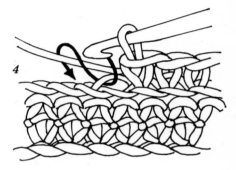

4

the second row of DOUBLE
CROCHET by making two chains
again. If you wish to have a ribbed
effect with this stitch, instead of
passing the hook under both loops
of the stitch below, just pass the
hook under one of these loops
(diagram 4). The other loop then
forms a little ridge and creates the
rib effect. This applies also for
single crochet.

Half treble
Begin the row with three extra
chains. Pass the hook under the wool
and then straight into the first stitch
below. This makes three loops on
the hook. Catch the wool once
more from left to right and draw it
through all loops on the hook,
leaving one loop (diagrams 5 and 6).

Treble crochet
Start by making three extra chains
at the end of the last row and pass
your hook under the wool from left
to right and then under the stitch
below, making three loops on the
hook. Pass the hook under the
wool again and draw it through
two of the loops (diagram 7), pass
the hook again under the wool and
draw it through the two remaining
loops (diagram 8). Remember to
make the extra chains at the ends.

Double treble
For this stitch, you make four
extra chains at the end of each
row. Pass the hook twice under the
wool, and then under the next
stitch. Pull the wool through to
make four loops on the hook. Pass

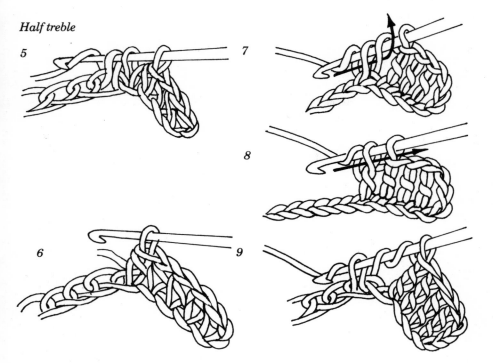

Half treble

the hook under the wool and draw it through two of these loops. Put it under the wool again and draw through two more loops, again, and then through the remaining loops (diag. 9).

To complete crochet
Cut off the wool, leaving about 15 cm (6 in). Draw the wool through the last loop on the hook until it has all come through and tighten. Sew in the rest of the wool with a thick-eyed needle.
Note: For those who are left-handed, the instructions are reversed and the diagrams will be correct if seen in a mirror.

PROJECT IDEA
Once you feel more comfortable about the crochet stitches you have learnt, you can begin to make articles by following patterns or experimenting yourself. Here is a simple pattern for a crochet square that you can try. It is known as 'Old America'. It could be used for a baby blanket or a shawl, or even a rug, depending on the thickness of the wool you choose. Remember, you will need a larger crochet hook for thicker wool. When joining up the squares for the article you are making, oversew the edge loops of the sides of each square and be careful not to draw the stitches too tight. Use wool or silk to match your work and try not to stretch one edge more than another. Press the seams lightly with an iron on a damp cloth.

The pattern

This square is very effective if done in two contrasting colours but you could make it multi-coloured, or just plain, and vary the squares. Make 6 chains in a light colour and join into a ring with a slip-stitch.

Round 1: With the light colour, make two chains, two trebles and three chains, * three trebles, three chains into a ring and repeat from * twice, then slip-stitch to first two chains.

Round 2: With the dark colour, slip-stitch to first space, (two chains, two trebles, three chains, three trebles) into first three chain space, * (1 chain, 3 trebles, 3 chains, 3 trebles) into next 3 chain space, repeat from * twice, join with a slip-stitch.

Round 3: With the light colour, slip-stitch to first space (2 chains, 2 trebles, 3 chains, 3 trebles) into first 3 chain space, * 1 chain, 3 trebles into 1 chain space (1 chain, 3 trebles, 3 chains, 3 trebles) into each corner, repeat from * ending 1 chain, slip-stitch to join.

Round 4: With the dark colour, slip-stitch to first space (2 chains, 2 trebles, 3 chains, 3 trebles) into first 3 chain space * 1 chain, 3 trebles into each 1 chain space (1 chain, 3 trebles, 3 chains, 3 trebles) into each corner, repeat from * ending 1 chain, slip-stitch to join. Fasten off, leaving a thread long enough to join the squares later.

When making up the final article, you could add a little flower at each corner join. These are very simple to make and can of course be used in many other ways. For the flower you simply need some of the wool you are using and a pencil. Cut a length about the size of the pencil and another length two or three times longer. Hold the shorter length against the pencil and wind the other length of wool around the pencil and wool.

Tuck the beginning end under the next loop. When you have wound the wool around, hold the pencil firmly in one hand, taking care the wool does not unravel, and pull the two ends of the short length of wool up. Tie them together and when you have slipped the whole row of loops of the pencil, fasten the knot tightly. The loops will bunch out into a flower. Use the ends of the holding strand of wool for sewing the flower on.

If you wish, you can add an extra row of slip-stitch all the way around the finished article to make it even more attractive.

KNITTING

We shall only be dealing with knitting with two needles here. You can also do circular knitting, in tubes. If you have knitted before, you will have seen that, even more than with crochet, the size of the needles and the type of yarn affect the finished product. For the best results, use rigid knitting needles with good (not sharp) points made in a light metal alloy.

Wool is definitely the most common material used in knitting. It has great elasticity, unless this is spoilt by careless washing, and it is of course warm and, up to a point, weatherproof. Cotton does not stretch so much and may not

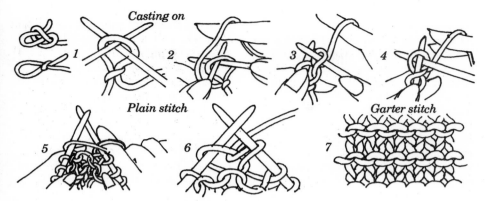

Casting on

Plain stitch

Garter stitch

keep its shape so well when knitted.

Try out different yarns to see how they look when knitted. What does parcel string do? However, when making something special, you should follow the pattern or try out the yarn on different needles until you get the required effect and the right amount of stitches per centimetre.

Holding the needles

In your left hand, the needle should be between your fingers and thumb and against the palm. In the right hand, the needle should rest on top of the hand between the thumb and the first finger. The wool lies across the top of the first finger of the right hand and is looped under the second finger to hold it firm.

Casting on

With your wool, make a loop 10 cm (4 in) from the end. (*See* section on crochet.) Hang it onto the left-hand needle and push the right-hand needle into the stitch (diagram 1). Pass the wool around the point of the right-hand needle in a clockwise direction (diagram 2).

Pull the wool through the stitch on the left-hand needle, using the point of the right-hand needle (diagram 3). Slip the new stitch from the right-hand to the left-hand needle (diagram 4). Repeat until you have the number of stitches you need on the left-hand needle.

Plain stitch

Push the point of the right-hand needle into the first stitch on the left-hand needle from left to right and pass the wool, from behind, clockwise around the right-hand needle (diagram 5). Pull the loop through the stitch on the left-hand needle (diagram 6) and slip the stitch off the left-hand needle, keeping the new stitch on the right-hand needle. The wool stays behind the needles when doing this stitch.

Garter stitch

This is a strip of knitting where every row is plain stitch. It is very stretchy and thick (diagram 7).

Note: At the end of a row, turn the right-hand needle round so that it becomes the left-hand needle.

Purl stitch

The wool is kept in front of the needle for this stitch. Push the point of the right-hand needle through the front of the first stitch on the left-hand needle from right to left (the opposite to plain stitch). Pass the wool around the right-hand needle from the front in an anti-clockwise direction (diagram 1). Keeping this loop on the right-hand needle, draw it through the stitch on the left-hand needle (diagram 2) and slip the stitch off the left-hand needle.

Stocking stitch

This is knitting where one row is purl and the next row is plain, and continuing in this way. It is often used in patterns (diagram 3).

Ribbing

This is made by knitting one purl stitch and one plain stitch repeatedly along the row and is worked with an even number of stitches, to give a rib effect (diagram 4). A variation is to knit two purl and two plain to give a wider rib (diagram 5).

Increasing

Knit the stitch as usual, but do not slip it off the left-hand needle. Instead, push the point of the right-hand needle through the back of the same stitch on the left-hand needle and knit it again. Slip the stitch off the left-hand needle, keeping the two new stitches made from it on the right-hand needle (diagram 6).

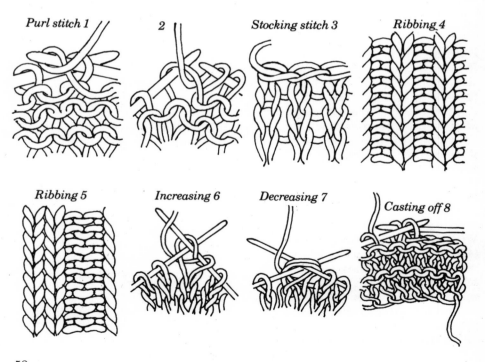

Purl stitch 1 2 *Stocking stitch 3* *Ribbing 4*

Ribbing 5 *Increasing 6* *Decreasing 7* *Casting off 8*

Decreasing
Simply knit two stitches together (diagram 7).

Casting off
Knit two stitches and with the point of the left-hand needle, slip the first stitch on the right-hand needle over the second. Knit another stitch onto the right-hand needle and again slip the first over the second (diagram 8). Repeat until the row is finished, and one stitch remains. Break the wool and draw it through the last stitch, pulling firmly. The end is now ready to be sewn.

PROJECT IDEA
There are so many patterns available for different kinds of knitted garments and objects that it would be worth trying out some ideas here which you might not find in a bought pattern. There is nothing to stop you knitting with strips of paper if you want and you can certainly include beads and sequins on to your yarn before you start knitting. You can also change your yarns in the middle of the knitting. Either knit the two yarns together for a section and then drop the old one behind, cutting it to leave about 10 cm (4 in), or leave 10 cm (4 in) straight away and sew the ends in later.

Try making four equal-sized patches or squares from as many different textures as you like, using both different stitches and different yarn for effect. You could try to make one diagonally, i.e. start from one or two stitches and increase at either end until you come to the centre diagonal and then start

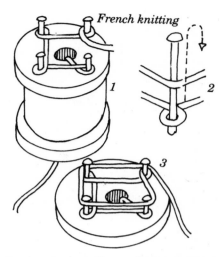

French knitting

decreasing until you have a square.

Remember that a ribbed pattern will pull the knitting much more than a garter stitch or stocking stitch. You can join your squares with a crochet or embroidery stitch and use this as the front of a cushion.

French knitting
This is a basic form of circular knitting which is done on an empty cotton reel that has four small nails or tacks pushed into one end, equally spaced apart. The only other item you need apart from the yarn is a blunt needle. To begin, pull the yarn through the hole in the middle of the reel and loop it round the nails, going from right to left (diagram 1).

When all the loops have been made, pass the yarn right round the four nails (diagram 2) and hold in place. Take the needle and slip the first loop around the first nail and over the yarn held around the nail. You now have a new loop (diagram 3). This is the basic stitch

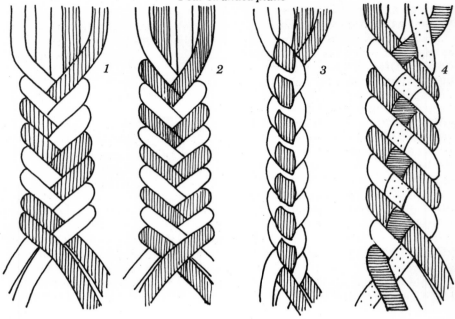

and it is repeated continuously.

Soon the knitted tube will appear at the lower end of the reel and will grow longer as you go on knitting. When the tube is long enough, break the working yarn, leaving enough to put into a needle and thread through the loops on the reel. Slip all the loops off and pull the yarn tight.

PROJECT IDEAS

The lengths of tube can be used to line clothes, oven cloths, added on to toys and used as cords for bags. You can also coil them around so that they look like a snail's shell and stitch them in this shape to make little mats. If you have used different colours in your knitting, the little mat will look bright and interestingly patterned.

FOUR-STRANDED PLAITS

These can also be used in many ways. Like the tube of French knitting, plaits can be used for edging on bags, jackets, tablecloths, and also coiled and stitched together to make mats and even baskets. Again, the colour of the yarns provides new patterns. The plaits shown here can be made with only your fingers and the yarn. If you have a board handy, one end can be pinned onto it, but you can also tie the end of your plait to a handle, or even your big toe, as the women in some tribes do.

To practise these plaits, start by using two contrasting colours only. Cut two lengths of the yarn, fold them in half and secure them. Arrange them first, as in diagram 1, in the order Light 1, Dark 1, Light 2, Dark 2. After you have tried this plait and worked a small length of it, arrange the strands as in diagram 2, in order Light 1, Light 2, Dark 1, Dark 2. The plaiting sequence is the same for both:

Left strand over middle two strands, right over left strand
New left strand over middle two strands, right over left strand
Repeat.

This plait is flat. You can also make a round plait from four strands. Take them in the order Light 1, Light 2, Dark 1, Dark 2, as in diagram 3. The plaiting sequence now is:

L1 behind L2 and D1, over D1,
    the order now is L2, L1, D1, D2
D2 behind D1 and L1, over L1,
    the order now is L2, L1, D2, D1
L2 behind L1 and D2, over D2,
    the order now is L1, L2, D2, D1
D1 behind D2 and L2, over L2,
    the order now is L1, L2, D1, D2
Repeat.

Once you see how the pattern is made you will find the plaiting becomes quite easy. Lastly, you can try a plait with a diagonal pattern running over it. Arrange your four strands in this order, as in diagram 4; Dark 1, Light 1, Light 2, Dark 2. The plait is made as follows:

Take the left strand over the one next to it
Take the right strand under the one next to it, and over the next strand
Repeat.

Now you have tried the plaits in light and dark contrasting colours, you can try to vary the colours, the thicknesses and the texture of the yarns, and see what effects you get.

FINGER WEAVING

If you tried making the plaits, you will have made narrow strips of cord or band, depending on whether it was a rounded or a flat plait. Plaits can be made wider, by adding more strands and continuing to cross the strands over and under each other. Wider plaits are, however, not always as firm and strong as braids and belts made by FINGER WEAVING. It is easier to pull the yarn tighter with the latter method. Mostly, you will find finger weaving used for straps, trimmings and belts, for daintier objects such as chokers or bracelets, and for softer bands such as neck-ties. Your hands can only

Finger weaving

1

control a certain number of strands at once! Plaiting and finger-weaving may look alike, but the difference between making plaits and finger weaving is that plaits are made with the threads being worked over and under each other diagonally, whereas in finger weaving you use the strands as warp threads and weft threads, as you do in all types of weaving. WARP threads are a set of vertical yarns (each length of yarn making the warp is called a WARP END). WEFT is the thread or threads that pass through the warp ends horizontally. In finger weaving, the warp and weft threads are actually the same threads, depending on how you are using them. This is not the case with most kinds of weaving.

You will need
a pencil
coloured yarns of about the same
    thickness
scissors

Cut 10 equal lengths of yarn. The finished article will be about $\frac{1}{3}$ the length of your cut yarn, if you want a fringe as well, and about $\frac{1}{2}$ if you do not want a fringe. Gather the ends of your yarn together and tie an overhand knot. Fasten this knot somewhere securely. Then, take a pencil and wind each strand of yarn around it, about 5 cm (2 in) below the knot. It is neater if you wind all the strands the same way. Now, working from left to right, take the first strand, weave it under the second strand, over the third, under the fourth and so on until you have come to the end of

the row. Pull the strand parallel to the pencil (this strand has now been used as a weft). Keep this strand pulled up towards the pencil until the next row is completed, when it will become another new warp end hanging downwards. Repeat from left to right, You can see how this works out in diagram 1, and note that you are using the same strands both downwards (as warp ends) and across (as wefts). It is not always easy at the beginning to keep your strands untangled and to keep the work firm. But after a few rows you will begin to see your band growing.

To finish, you can either leave the strands at an angle, or continue to weave each new row, leaving one strand spare at the end each time, until you have an edge at 90° from the sides. Then you can either tie overhand knots close to the last strand passed across to make a loose fringe, twist the strands together to make a corded fringe or plait a few of the strands at a time to make a plaited fringe. Finish cords and plaits off with another overhand knot. You can add beads onto the fringe or even onto the band itself but, for the latter, you must start by threading the beads on your strands.

For a hem, tie the strands in pairs with a square knot, trim the ends close to the knot and turn the ends over to the wrong side. Fold again 2·5 cm (1 in) from the edge. Using the same yarn as in the weaving, stitch right through the work to prevent the ends unfolding.

Patterns
Diagonal stripes Set the strands in colour groupings, e.g. 6 of green,

Chevron

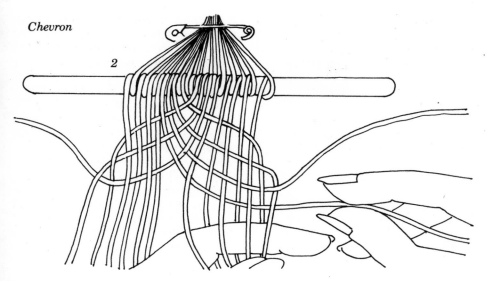

2

6 of cream, and 6 of rose.

Wavy lines Again use stripes of coloured strands, as with the diagonal stripes, but when you have used each strand once for the weft, working from left to right, begin taking your weft from right to left. Continue working from this direction, and when you want to change the angle of the stripes again, start working from the opposite side. You can make your own wavy pattern – large, small, or mixed.

Chevron Take an even number of colours and strands and divide into two groups, each with the same sequence of colours, Mount them on the pencil as shown in diagram 2. The colour sequence on one side reflects but does not repeat the colour sequence on the other side. Take the first warp end at the right of the left group and weave this end over to the very right. Pull it parallel to the pencil. Now take the first warp end on the left of your

right hand group and weave it over to the left hand side, again pulling it parallel to the pencil. Repeat. You will notice that you now have two different weft strands making new warp ends at either side. Using this pattern, the band does not slope out at an angle as it did with all of the previous examples in this section.

Diamond in chevron Mount the strands on the pencil in the same sequence as for the chevron pattern above, but start half way down. Tie one lot of warp ends in a loose knot to keep them out of the way. With the free strands, work the chevron pattern to the length you want. Then untie the loose knot, take the pencil out, turn the work round so the other half of the warp ends are hanging ready for you to work them, and continue the chevron pattern. You are now working in the opposite direction and forming a diamond in the centre of your band.

PROJECT

Make a colourful belt or headband for yourself, using any one of the patterns above. Remember to allow 2 to 3 times more yarn than the length of the finished article. Also try using different textures of yarn – fluffy, smooth, tightly twisted, bobbly – in a combination that you like.

NEEDLE WEAVING

You will need

a sheet of strong card the size of the article you are making (e.g. if it's a little bag, you will need a card twice the length of the bag and a little wider)

card-cutting scissors

a blunt needle with an eye thick enough for your chosen yarn

yarn (wool is easier to start with).

To prepare the card Make a set of holes at either end of the card, 1 cm (0·5 in) apart, with the point of the scissors. The holes should be parallel to one another (diag I).

To make the warp Thread your needle with a good length of yarn. Tie a double overhead knot at the end and thread it through the first hole on one side, down through the parallel hole on the other side, up through the next hole on the first side and so on until you have reached the last hole. Keep the yarn pulled firmly, but not too tight, and check that all the strands are at about the same tension. Make another double overhand knot on the wrong side (the right side is where the strands pass straight down the card). You are now ready to start weaving.

To weave Thread another length

Needle weaving

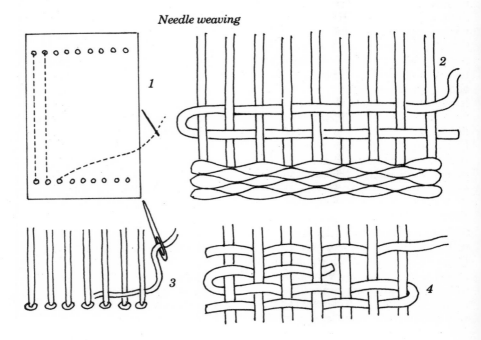

of yarn through your needle and pass your needle over and under a few warp ends near the edge as in diagram 2. This will keep the end in neatly. Then pass the needle alternately over and under each warp end until you come to the end of the row. If you are over this last warp end, you now go under it to start your next row, and vice versa. Push each row down with your fingers, so that it looks like the weaving in diagram 3. This is called PLAIN WEAVE.

To make a stripe Make at least two rows in another contrasting colour. Try and see what happens if you do just one row in a contrasting colour, the next row in your main colour, then another row in a contrasting colour and so on. Do you get some other stripes?
What happens when you use weft yarns of different thicknesses?
And what happens when you weave with strips of rag cloth?
With a thicker weft, do you see more of the warp ends or less?
Can you make new patterns using thick and thin wefts?
Remember not to pull tight on your weft or you will find your weaving becoming narrower and narrower. If your warp ends need to be a little tauter, slide a ruler or a pencil underneath to give some extra tension. Begin a new weft by doubling over a few centimetres of the old weft, as in diagram 4.

To finish off When you have woven as much as you can up the front of the card, tuck your weft over and under a few warp ends as you did at the beginning. Turn the card over and cut the strands in the middle. The ends can now be finished as suggested in the section on finger weaving.

PROJECT IDEA
You will see that it is possible to make a scarf or a little runner using card and needle. But you can also use needle weaving with finer threads and a smaller card, with the holes spaced closer together, to make tapestry pictures. These can be very delicate and can be left on the card to be framed as it is.

You have learnt to make stripes and different patterns through texture. You can also build up areas of colour without weaving right across all the warp ends.

In diagram 1 (p. 66) a method for making a triangle shape is shown and diagram 2 shows a method for a zig-zag join between two different wefts. You can also build up square shapes, so that there is a little slit between them, and then bring the slit together by weaving right across, as shown in diagram 3. And you can weave curves, as shown in diagram 4. Try and weave a circle.

It would be better to practise some of these shapes first on a sample warp and then design or paint a little picture you would like to weave. You could of course, just try to build up a pattern as you go, but it might look more effective if you chose a theme, e.g. bricks using square shaped areas over each other.

In tapestry, there are many more wefts than in ordinary weaving. If you are patient, you can weave all the ends in, but this is not necessary, as the picture will be seen only from one side. Therefore you can just leave a few

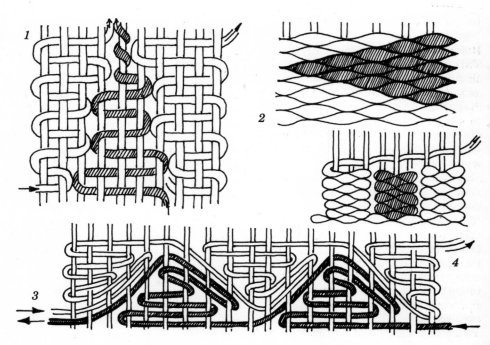

centimetres of weft tucked in at the back.

EMBROIDERY

You will need
needles of varying sizes to take
   thick and thin threads
embroidering threads and yarns

Embroidery can be used on any fabric, including knitting and crochet. Generally it is best done with a type of yarn similar or complementary to that of the fabric. If the fabric is fine, it is better to do the work using embroidery rings, which are two wooden rings, one completely enclosed, and the other open with a screw for adjusting the tension over the opening. The fabric is placed over the closed ring, the

other ring is placed on top, the fabric is pulled gently to stretch it while the outer screw is tightened to keep the fabric taut.
Method: The embroidery thread can be fastened with a small overhand knot at the end, which stays on the wrong side of the fabric. However, knots can make bumps, so it is better to avoid them. Here are a few other ways to begin your work. Take a few running stitches toward the starting point and cover with the stitch you are using (diagram 1). Use half the length of thread at the beginning of a row and use the rest for your next row (diagram 2). Diagram 3 shows how to end by passing the thread under about three stitches before cutting it, and diagram 4 shows how to start a new thread by passing it under a

few stitches to secure it.

Running stitch or darning stitch
This stitch should be regular in
size, about twice the length above
as it is below the fabric, as in
diagram 5. It can also be whipped
in a contrasting colour, as in
diagram 6, or it can be threaded
with one or two colours giving a
wavy or circular pattern, as in
diagram 7. Running stitch can be
made in two rows and threaded to
make a loopy pattern (diagram 8),
or it can be made in two rows at
right angles to each other
(diagram 9).

Back stitch This stitch makes a
continuous line. Working from left
to right, take the thread up from
the back and then make a
backwards stitch. Bring the needle
up a little way in front of the first

stitch and make another backwards
stitch, taking the needle through
the point where it first came up
(diagram 1, p. 68).

Pekinese stitch This is made on
back stitch with a contrasting
colour by looping the thread back
into the previous stitch and taking
it up and then under the next
stitch along (diagram 2, p. 68).

Stem stitch This is used mainly
for outlines, usually curvy, and
stems. It is worked from left to
right in diagram 3, p. 68. Make
slightly slanting stitches along the
line you are to stitch. The thread
always comes up a little behind
and to the left of the stitch you
have made. This stitch can be
whipped in a contrast colour, as in
diagram 4, p. 68.

Satin stitch This stitch is used for
filling in small areas. Take the

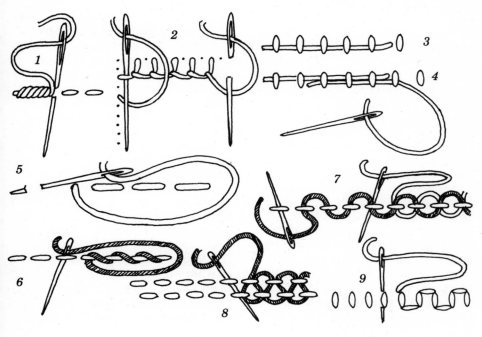

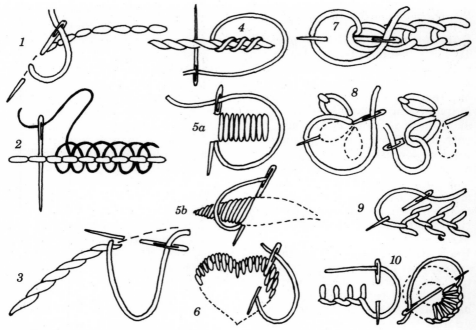

needle up at one edge of the design and draw it through to the back at an opposite point. Take the needle up again on the starting edge, very close to the first stitch (diagrams 5a and 5b).

Long and short stitch This is a type of satin stitch using long and short stitches that begin also inside the design area. Different colours can be used for shading or effect (diagram 6).

Chain stitch Bring the needle to the right side of the fabric and hold the thread down with your left thumb. Push the needle back through the point from where it has just come out and bring it up again a short distance away. Pull gently to make a loop and repeat (diagram 7).

Lazy daisy stitch The chain stitch is used to make little petals

and leaves. Instead of continuing a second chain, the thread is passed back under, catching the loop down, and the needle is brought up at the starting point of the next leaf or petal (diagram 8).

Feather stitch The needle is taken up at the top of the line of stitches. Hold the thread down with the left thumb, push the needle through a little to the right on the same level and bring the needle up a little way down between these points. Keep the thread below the needle. Pull up the thread and you will have made an 'open chain'. Hold the thread with your thumb and push the needle through a point a little to the left of where it has just come up. Bring it up a little below, between these two new points. Pull the thread up, making a second 'open' chain.

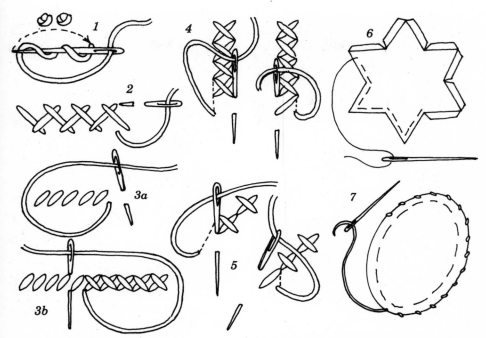

Repeat (*see* diagram 9.)

Blanket or buttonhole stitch For buttonholes, this stitch is worked closer together. Working from left to right, bring needle up on a lower level. Hold the thread down with the left thumb and push needle through a little to the right of the starting point, on the upper level. Bring up again directly below and pull through catching the loop of thread (diagram 10).

French knots Bring thread up at the place for the knot, hold the thread down with your left thumb and wind the thread twice (or more, as desired) round the needle. Holding the needle firmly, pull it through the twists and push them down to make a little 'knot' next to the fabric. Then push the needle back through at the point it came out (diagram 1).

Herringbone stitch Working from left to right, bring the needle up, make a diagonal stitch and take a very short stitch backwards behind the fabric. Bring needle up and over to form another diagonal stitch over the first one and continue, alternating from side to side, as in diagram 2.

Cross stitch The simplest method is for the horizontal row, as in diagram 3. Working from left to right, make half the cross with a diagonal stitch to the upper right corner, push through and bring up directly below. Keep the line even, and work the second half from right to left (diagrams 3a and 3b). A method for working a few vertical cross stitches at a time is shown in diagram 4, and for working diagonal cross stitches is clearly illustrated in diagram 5.

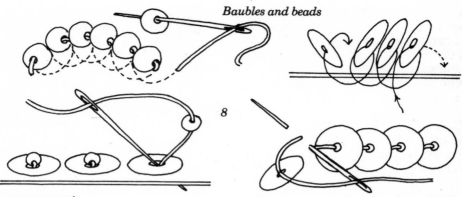

Baubles and beads

8

APPLIQUÉ

Embroidery is particularly useful for APPLIQUÉ work. Appliqué is simply the French for 'applied'. A smaller shape is applied to another larger area. It could be a patch on some old jeans or it could be a piece of felt cut into a motif and embroidered onto a cushion cover.

You will need

scraps of material and felt – avoid slippery and stretchy fabrics, and fabric that frays easily. Cotton is the most suitable.

background fabric for the motifs
needle, sewing cotton and embroidery threads
scissors – small and sharp are better
pins
pencil, tracing paper and rubber for designs

Draw your design onto a piece of tracing paper and pin it onto the scrap of material you are using for the appliqué. Cut out the shape, leaving 6 mm (0·2 in) for turning at the edge. With felt, no extra width is required and the motif can be stitched on as it is. If you want to

embroider extra details, do so now. Turn the edges under and baste the motif into place – using a long running stitch which can be pulled out easily later (diagram 6, p. 69). Stitch into place using a very fine slip-stitch (diagram 7, p. 69) or buttonhole stitch. If you want to raise the design, you can stuff it with a bit of wadding before finishing the stitching.

Motifs can also be stitched on top of other motifs, and so building up more interesting patterns. The work can be decorated with sequins and beads, some ways of applying these are shown in diagram 8.

PATCHWORK

This handicraft has been popular for centuries, particularly in Ireland and America. It has been used for home furnishing as well as for garments. Many types of fabric have been used for patches, but as with appliqué, cotton is the most suitable. It is generally better to start by taking the same type of fabric for all the patches in one piece of work, because otherwise the work will not lie flat. Small prints together can make lovely designs, whereas patches from bold stripes and checks can be very eye-catching. If you use a one-colour fabric, then you must be extra neat and careful when cutting the shape and stitching it, as these become more obvious.

You will need
card
scissors
pair of compasses
brown parcel paper
needle and sewing cotton
fabrics for patches
ruler, pencil and rubber

To make regular patches of the right size, you first need to make a template. This is the exact shape of your patch cut in card. The hexagon (six-sided) shape is not difficult and very pleasing to use (diagram 1). The hexagon shape is drawn out on cardboard. Take the pair of compasses, draw a circle roughly the size of your patch. Do not alter the compasses, and placing the leg on the drawn circle, mark off two points on the circle to either side of the point you are standing on. Repeat by putting the leg onto one of these marks. Repeat twice more and you should find 6 equidistant points on the circle. Join them up and you have a hexagon. Cut out the hexagon and use this to cut as many hexagons in brown paper as you need for your patchwork. You must have one for each patch. Cut the fabric about 6 mm (0·2 in) wider than the hexagon, place the paper lining on the wrong side in the middle and pin (diagram 2). Making a small tuck at each corner, fold the fabric

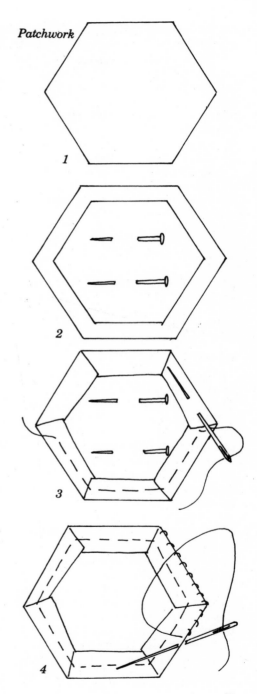

Patchwork

1

2

3

4

over and baste all around (diagram 3, p. 71). When all the patches are ready, you can begin to stitch them together. Hold two right sides facing together, and oversew one edge (diagram 4, p. 71). Avoid the paper lining and keep the corners exact. When you have joined all the patches together, take out the basting thread and the paper lining. Press the patchwork on the wrong side, so that the edges lie flat, pointing towards the centre of the patch. You can appliqué your work onto a larger piece of cloth or you can line it with a pre-shrunk washable fabric. Cut the lining material 1 cm (0·4 in) wider than your finished patchwork, turn the edges over and clip in places to adjust the corners. Oversew the edges all around (unless you are making a cushion) holding the wrong sides together.

PROJECT IDEAS

You could make a patchwork table cloth or pram-cover by using appliqué to attach little sets of hexagons on to a plain-coloured, thicker cotton and edging the cover with patchwork squares. Use embroidery stitches to sew the patchwork on the cloth. Try making some of the patchwork motifs lighter, some darker, some with lighter patches outside and a darker one in the middle. An example is given in diagram 5.

If you are using felt for your patchwork, you might like to try 'Irish patchwork'. You do not have to cut extra seam allowance with felt but, to join the patches, you first blanket-stitch all around each patch and then double-crochet the

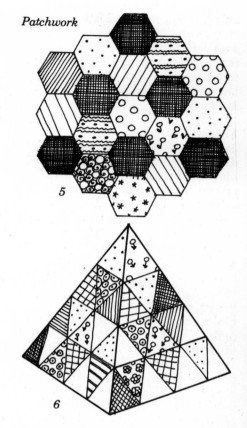

Patchwork

5

6

edges together, using the top of the blanket stitch as the foundation row of your crochet.

Patchwork does not need to be flat. You can of course use different thicknesses of material and different shapes and make something called 'crazy patchwork'. But you can also make three-dimensional objects with patches. Using triangles, you can make four triangular pieces, which can be joined together to make a tetrahedron (diagram 6), with six squares you can make a cube, and with twelve pentagons you could even make a little ball!

PRESSING FLOWERS

You will need
some sheets of white blotting paper
or thick absorbent sugar paper
large heavy books
bricks or other heavy weights

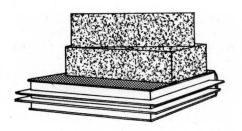

Flowers and leaves are best
gathered on a dry day, after the
dew has evaporated. A thick, fleshy
plant or a flower with many petals
are best separated carefully and
dried in pieces. Arrange the flowers
and leaves on the blotting paper as
soon as you can after picking,
remembering to include stems as
well. Smooth out the surfaces, so
that the pieces dry the way you
want to see them later. Cover with
another sheet of blotting paper and
place these sheets in a heavy book.
It is better to take a book with
paper that is glossy because the
moisture from the drying flowers
and leaves will not be absorbed by
shiny surfaces. Place bricks and
other heavy objects on top and
keep in a dry place for at least six
weeks. Peeping before that time
has passed is not allowed!
Remember NOT to overcrowd the
blotting paper and NOT to press
the sheets down so heavily that the
moisture cannot escape. You might
find, otherwise, that the plants
have gone mouldy.

MOUNTING

You will need
rubber solution glue
cards of different sorts
adhesive transparent plastic
scissors
paintbrush

The type of card you use depends
on what you are making. You can
use thin cards for greetings cards
or for covering match-boxes or for
making bookmarks, thicker card
for pictures to hang on the wall or
for mats. Cut the card to the size
required and first arrange your
dried petals, leaves and stems as
you wish for your design. Then,
using the tiniest dab of glue on the
back, stick the pieces down. A
paintbrush is useful here, because
you can push the petals or leaves
about with the brush end and dab
the glue on with the other end.
Now, cut the shape of the card in
the sticky backed plastic, and
mount the plastic on the card over
the dried arrangement, by tearing
off the backing of the plastic a
little at a time and smoothing the
plastic carefully down into place.
Trim off any uneven edges.

There are so many ways to use
dried flowers – you will probably
have lots of other ideas yourself.
You could try embedding them in
plastic to make paperweights,
using a 'Plasticraft' kit or other
similar type. You could mount
flowers on a strip of ribbon instead
of card for bookmarks. You could
even make an album of dried flower
arrangements and cover the front
with a special flower design.

House Plants

Houseplants come in a wonderful range of colours, shapes and sizes and many of them are easy to grow. So don't be deterred if you do not have green-fingers. You can have amazing success provided you stick to the basic rules.

Before dealing with plant care, however, you must decide whether you want a tall or trailing plant, one with or without flowers, a plant to occupy permanently a particular position or one just to provide a shorter-term decoration. Each type of plant must be cared for differently.

SELECT SOMETHING SIMPLE

A house plant is one which lives its entire life indoors. These fall into two groups: flowering and foliage plants, the latter are grown for their almost endless variety of leaf-shapes. Of course, an indoor collection can well include all sorts of pot plants. Often, these are given as gifts. They are, however, only temporary visitors which, after flowering, should be removed and, in some cases, planted in the garden.

Beginner's Guide

For any beginner deciding to buy a house plant, here are four simple-to-grow favourites.

Spider Plant (*Chlorophytum*)

Despite its creepy name, it is a very popular foliage plant with arching, striped, grass-like leaves. It is good value, too, because it produces plantlets at the end of long runners. You can plant each of these into a pot of compost. Once rooted, detach them from the mother plant. The Spider Plant is an ideal eye-catcher whether suspended or placed on a cupboard or table. Just remember it likes a well-lit position, though not in direct sunlight.

Swiss Cheese Plant (*Monstera Deliciosa*)

For a little extra cost, you can buy this big, climbing plant which brings a true touch of the tropical into your house. Its large, shiny leaves develop deep cuts and holes – hence, the plant's name. Again, this plant does not like direct sunlight. It prefers a medium light and a warm, draught-free, moist atmosphere.

Busy Lizzie (*Impatiens*)

If you like flowering house plants, this one provides pretty pink, red or white flowers and blooms for most of the year. Ideally, it should be placed in a sunny spot, this helps it to flower well.

Shrimp Plant (*Beloperone Guttata*)

Another plant that likes a sunny window-sill, this one takes its name from the shrimp-like flowers.

If you are searching for a tough, easy-to-keep trailer or climber, the Ivy (*Hedera*) family offers a superb choice. Spring flowers, for contrast, can be grown simply by planting bulbs or corms in pots to provide delightful, temporary indoor plants. Sunny Daffodils will cheer a room.

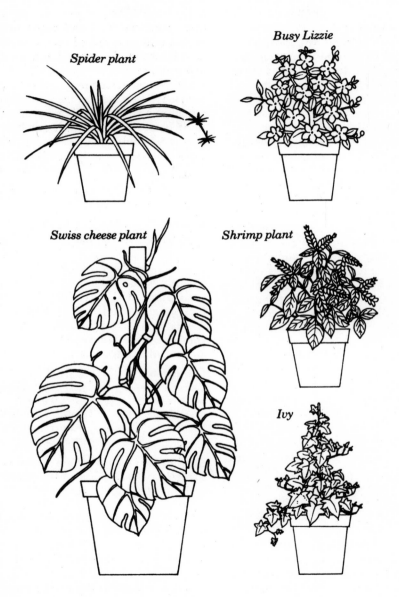

Spider plant

Busy Lizzie

Swiss cheese plant

Shrimp plant

Ivy

HOW TO KEEP YOUR PLANT HEALTHY

Plants are similar to people and have individual likes and dislikes. Some prefer sunny spots, others where there is good but indirect lighting. The two golden rules to help keep them healthy are never over-water or place them near draughts. These are the major killers.

There are five main points relating to plant care and growth: light, food, air, warmth and water. Get this balance right and you will see your plants flourish. In the garden, nature provides this. House plants, however, must rely on you.

Obviously, requirements vary from plant to plant. So when you buy one, study the recommended instructions carefully. Don't treat all plants the same and remember that winter provides a rest season when you should allow much longer intervals between watering. Never let the soil dry out completely or, on the other hand, become so sodden that the roots cannot survive.

As a general guide, water your plants two or three times a week in summer and only once a week or even less in winter.

Swift changes of temperature are harmful. Try to keep your plant in a room where it does not exceed 25°C (75°F) and where the temperature is normally moderate and constant. Usually, foliage plants prefer a little more warmth than do the flowering types.

Most plants do not like a very dry atmosphere. Central heating in a house can cause this. To compensate, stand plants in a dish of moist gravel or pebbles. Spray the leaves with water, too, or put your plant in the kitchen or bathroom, where steam increases the air's moisture content. When your plant is in its growing season, feed it with a fertilizer. Again, do not overdo this.

There are countless books available on the precise care and needs of particular house plants. So if in doubt, always check first.

Nonetheless, rest assured that provided you stick to the simpler plants, such as the few mentioned here, they will grow happily with only the basic care and attention.

WHAT TO WATCH FOR

There are all sorts of tell-tale signs to warn of trouble with your plant. If you keep a keen look out and act quickly when these signs appear, your plant will stay safe. It's rather like being a doctor who must identify the symptoms to apply a remedy. Here is a brief guide for some conditions.

Condition	Solution
Leaves turning yellow, and falling off	If several leaves are affected, watch for over-watering, dry air or draughts
Slow or no growth	If during the growing season, watch for over-watering, underfeeding, or perhaps the plant is becoming too pot-bound
Spindly plant with pale leaves	If during the growing season, watch for

	inadequate light or insufficient feeding
Mildew	Watch for poor conditions, over-watering
Leaf rot	Again, watch for poor conditions or over-watering in winter
Brown edges and marks on leaves	Watch for over-watering, draughts, sun-burn and hot, dry air.

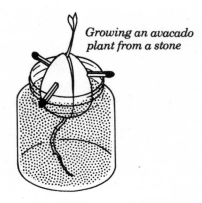

Growing an avacado plant from a stone

A bottle garden

WASTE NOT, WANT NOT

Creating something from nothing can add a little extra fun to raising house plants. Pips from everyday fruits like lemons, grapefruit and oranges can be grown quite easily. Germinate them in shallow, moist compost. Then move the young plants to bigger pots, as they develop. In the case of the lemon pip, you may even end up picking your own fruit, provided the plant gets plenty of sunshine.

Life from a stone

Watching an avocado pear stone grow into a plant can be very interesting. One method of starting the process is to suspend the stone, pierced with small cocktail sticks or matchsticks for support, in water. When roots appear, plant the stone in a pot of compost. You will be surprised with the final result.

SPECIAL HOUSE PLANT DISPLAYS

If you find that your interest in house plants really develops, there are many ways of making your plants appear even more attractive. Hanging baskets are popular. So, too, are miniature gardens, with smaller plants carefully designed in a shallow dish. The idea is to create a life-like garden complete with pool, path and even a model building. There are other suggestions, too.

The bottle garden

Use a large glass bottle or carboy which must be washed out and dried. Pour gravel into the bottom for drainage. Then add a layer of moss. Using a plastic or paper funnel, carefully pour in the soil, consisting of two parts loam to one each of peat and sand. Also, mix in a little charcoal. Now you are all set to arrange the plants.

It is best to use small, slow-growing plants and not too many or it will easily look over-crowded when the plants begin to grow. Use two slim pieces of wood to plant them. To make it easier, you can tie spoons to the ends of the sticks. Use a long-spouted can for watering and continue to water occasionally, unless you seal the bottle and let the plants create their own moisture.

A Dish Garden

As its title suggests, you simply use a shallow dish or container. Just make sure it is sufficiently deep to allow the plant roots to establish themselves properly. Add your soil to a layer of moss which lies on a bed of gravel. Then pick your plants – either foliage, flowering or both – to produce the design you want. You can even make a miniature jungle by carefully selecting and adding pieces of dead wood or stones of the right shape and size. Whenever a plant grows too large for the dish, simply replace it with a smaller one.

Dish gardens are especially attractive

ANIMALS
AND PETS

Scottish wild cat

Lion

Domestic cat

Cats

There is something very cosy and homely about the cat, one of the most popular of household pets. This cosiness is the reason why for some time certain cats were bred especially to be nursed by ladies to keep their laps warm. This same popularity reveals itself in the old nursery rhyme 'I love little pussy, her coat is so warm'. Though, amusingly, there follows the immediate warning about, 'If you don't tease her, she'll do you no harm'. A very timely reminder!

The history of the cat family can be traced back to prehistoric times, over millions of years, but there is still an uncertainty as to the exact ancestry of the domestic species.

According to one source, the cat originated in Persia. The very nickname 'puss' is possibly a corruption of 'pers'. It is more likely, however, that puss's true ancestor was the cat tamed and then worshipped by the ancient Egyptians, the African wildcat, *Felis ocreata*. This was very different from the striped tabby wildcat of Europe, considered by others to be the true ancestor. Argument over which came first still goes on today.

The wild and large cats
In the same general family as the cat (Felidae) are the lion, tiger, lynx, leopard, jaguar and many

Panther

Lynx

Cheetah

others you will be able to name. The word 'Cat' is usually applied only to the smaller species, but there are similarities in all members of the family. The mouth of puss has characteristics of a jungle hunter. It is perfectly created for cutting and eating meat and the rough tongue, like a rasp, is used to draw out the juices. The same speed and stealth are used to capture and destroy prey – always that same springing movement to bring down or bowl-over the victim. This helps to explain why some people consider cats cruel and are not among cat-lovers, though what better way is there of keeping down rats and mice? Factories and farms rely heavily on puss's hunting ability. A most useful pet indeed.

Their agility

Since the cat is more of a jumper than a runner, its legs are light and delicate. The power comes from its very muscular and strongly developed hips. While running it draws in its claws, which no longer act as a protection for the feet – unlike those of the dog. Of course, those same claws help it to climb and descend, apart from their very formidable use in fighting or capturing prey.

The looseness of the skin permits the cat's rippling, muscular grace of movement. This, combined with the small head and strong, supple spine, enhances the cat's agility and speed. In the middle of each foot is a large springy ball or pad divided into five parts, with a similar pad at the base of each toe.

(Look closely at the tracks of any cat in soft mud to examine the distinct pattern.) These are specially designed to break the force of a fall, rather like landing on sponge rubber or elastic. As you know, a cat, however dropped, almost always manages to land on its feet.

The whiskers, set above and at the sides of the mouth, are also an aid for survival. Each is connected to a delicate nerve. These whiskers enable a cat to tell whether or not a hole or gap is wide enough to admit the width of its body, and are particularly useful when the cat is crossing difficult terrain or moving through undergrowth. They act as an important sensory organ at night as well.

From the above description it is easy to see why the cat is often referred to as having 'nine lives'. Its great powers of resistance tend to make it a natural survivor. Its supersensitive hearing and awareness of even distant vibration account for what sometimes appears to be a 'sixth sense'.

Legends and myths

The cat has many unusual and mysterious features. Its eyes are particularly interesting, for they are specially adapted for seeing well in the dark. This is made possible because of a reflecting surface at the back of the eye that catches and makes the most of every single bit of light. The brilliant and rather glaring green colour is due to this reflection of the light. During daylight the pupils narrow down to mere slits. It is no wonder then that the cat was once regarded as an emblem of the moon and, from time immemorial, has always been associated with witches.

Witches were thought to have the power to change into cats. In Greek mythology the Fates changed Galinthia into one, and the goddess Hecate chose a cat form when Typhon compelled all gods and goddesses to disguise themselves in animal form.

Unfortunately these beliefs, particularly in olden days, resulted in cats being feared and treated cruelly in various counties of England. The old saying 'not enough room to swing a cat' referred to one of these cruel actions. It was even mentioned by Shakespeare. When the fear of witches disappeared, the other fears and the cruelty disappeared also. It is interesting, however, that it is only in Britain that black cats are thought to be lucky!

Breeds of cats

The domestic short-haired cats have interbred over many years to produce more varieties than any other breed. Cats produced from selected breeding are much sought after and can be very expensive.

The Persian cat is probably the most fancied. Championships generally go to a blue furred variety with deep orange or amber eyes. It is a dignified, 'soft-voiced' cat with short and compact legs and body.

The Siamese cat probably first came to Europe a little more than 50 or so years ago. Generally the body is sandy or fawn-coloured and the slanted eyes are deep blue. It is often regarded as rather difficult to train and inclined to be treacherous, though some would prefer the word 'mischievous'. These cats have great acrobatic agility and will quite naturally do tricks which other breeds could not perform without training.

In all there are many popular breeds of show cats, though the Persian and Siamese are probably the most popular.

The Manx cat does not have a tail and originated from the Isle of Man. Even so, it is sometimes called the Cornish cat and one source gives its origin as Japan. It is unlikely, however, that any Manxman would agree with this. It is a gentle pet, very easy to train and manage, and naturally trusting.

The Scottish Wildcat deserves a special mention because it is totally wild. For sheer ferocity and savagery, per pound of weight, it is unequalled. It resembles a large and rather powerfully built tabby cat, and is about 0·6 m (2 ft) long, with the tail adding another 0·3 m (1 ft). The wild cat lives on game, rabbits, hares, small birds and watercourses. It is untamable and can travel at such a speed that few of its victims ever escape. It is on record that a Scottish Wildcat once attacked and killed a man. Both were found dead, still gripping each other, on the porch of a church. It is generally known as the European Wild Cat, *Felis silvestris*.

Interesting facts
Cats are generally clean and fastidious and have an incredible

Persian

Siamese

Manx

'homing' instinct. Unlike that other favourite pet, the dog, they can return to the wild with comparative ease. Their attachment to a particular owner is not as great. It is often said that no one owns a cat but that a cat owns people.

In the past the fur of cats was used for the trimmings of coats and cloaks. Its skin was also highly desirable. Catgut was used, then, for the finer strings of violins and also for the strings of tennis rackets. A smaller kind of fiddle was consequently known as a 'kit'. Another link with the violin is that cats were once trained to dance and perform to its music, but this died out in the 19th century. The old nursery rhyme, 'Hey diddle diddle, the cat and the fiddle . . .' probably stems from that source. Though white cats with blue eyes were wrongly considered to be deaf.

'Making someone a cat's-paw'
This originated from the old fable about the artful monkey who retrieved roasted chestnuts from the embers of a fire by using the paw of a luckless cat which happened to be nearby. It appears to have some foundation in fact, for a similar situation is on record in Dr John Careri's book *A Voyage Round the World* (1695). In this case, the nut was a coconut, but the artful monkey's part was the same.

'Letting the cat out of the bag'
A favourite old trick of countrymen going to market in former times was to offer for sale a sucking-pig carried in a tied sack or, as it was called, poke. An unwary buyer, talked into a quick 'bargain', would purchase the sack before opening it – when he would find a very angry cat inside, instead of a pig. By that time the sharp-witted salesman would be elsewhere. So the saying, 'letting the cat out of the bag', came to mean an unlucky or premature disclosure. It also explains why one should never buy 'a pig in a poke', meaning that you should always investigate first before making a purchase.

Dogs

The dog is such a popular pet that almost from the beginning of time it seems to have been linked with man. It is almost as if some strange chemical attraction drew them together. One can almost imagine a wild, rather wolflike creature approaching a cave where primitive man sat, and gazing at him not with attack in mind but rather with an instinctive desire to make friends. Perhaps, on the other hand, some early man found a litter of wild dog pups, took them home and carefully reared them, producing the first domesticated dogs. One way or another, a kind of affinity does seem to exist.

Generally speaking, the dog was used for companionship, in various working roles and quite often as an object of adoration. The loyalty and affection it returns are accepted as unparalleled in the animal kingdom. The early Egyptians and Syrians revered and worshipped the dog. Their sculptures and images of it have been found dating from the beginning of history. Red Indian tribes regarded the dog as one of the sacred forms of their deities. So it is perhaps not surprising that in world folklore dogs have often been credited with mysterious knowledge and an insight into the spiritual realm. For example, the German philosopher and occultist Cornelius Agrippa, regarded as a magician, had a dog companion suspected of being a spirit incarnate.

Origin of the dog

Charles Darwin believed that the domestic dog originated from two species of wolf as well as various canine species and the jackal. The wolf-descent theory was widespread but it is now generally accepted that both wolf and dog may have had a common ancestor many millions of years ago and that the four earliest breeds of dog descended from this ancestor.

The term, dog, referring to our domestic pet, may also be extended to cover foxes, wolves, jackals and other allied species. However, certain differences are apparent, particularly in the shape of the pupil of the eye.

Uses of the dog

The range of activities is wide. The ancient Greeks used dogs on the battlefields as well as in hunting.

Foxhound

Chow

Cairn terrier

Basenji

Corgi

Poodle

Chihuahua

Dalmatian

Aerdale

The Romans classified theirs into three types: guard-dogs, hunting-dogs and sheep-dogs. In England, during the Middle Ages, dogs were used chiefly for sport, some of it, unfortunately, cruel. Bulldogs, then known as butcher's hounds, were used for bull-baiting as well as for catching cattle. Earlier still, Britain was renowned for her mastiffs. According to one source they played a significant part in the Gallic Wars. Dogs have been used constantly in exploration, Columbus took dogs with him when he discovered America and several polar expeditions used dog teams to tow sleds.

On the European continent, not too long ago, dogs were commonly used to pull small carts of various kinds; while in England, 'turnspit' dogs were used to turn the spits used for roasting meat. A kind of treadmill was specially designed for this purpose. There is a humorous story of how one dog refused to work the spit when he decided it was another dog's turn, and such instances are actually on record. Many folk would agree that, as well as being intelligent, dogs have a sense of humour.

Dogs have been used in war, have been known to save people from drowning, and have been used as trackers and as guides for the blind. One famous St Bernard named 'Barry' is recorded as having saved 40 lives.

Much depends on the keen natural senses of the dog. He is a sniffer, relying on air and ground scents as much as on keen sight and hearing. The wet nose is particularly sensitive in this

Dachshund

Bulldog

Scots terrier

Spaniel

respect. The dog learns a great deal from a scent – whether he likes or dislikes a person, whether that person is afraid. So his nose is often more important than his eyes when he is seeking something. Special breeds can follow a scent trail several hours old. The dogs used by police and custom officials come in this group. In contrast, the greyhound hunts by sight, perhaps because of its amazing speed.

Breeds of dog

The Kennel Club lists over 100 breeds but, across the world, the total must be around 400. Those imported into the U.K. include the Dachshund, Doberman Pinscher, Rottweiler, Boxer and the Alsation from Germany, poodles from France, the Japanese Spaniel and others too numerous to mention.

Certain breeds tend to be used for particular working tasks. Alsatians are generally chosen as police dogs and as guide dogs for the blind. This is because they are not only excellent 'seeing' dogs but have a reasoning power along with their natural intelligence. Such an ability can never be substituted by even the very best training. For example, the French Poodle is highly intelligent and can be trained easily, yet it lacks this ability to reason. It would obey the order of a blind master equally blindly and might lead him straight in front of a bus. A particular breed of dog is chosen and sometimes specially bred for a particular task.

Wild dogs

We have already mentioned the

wolf, fox and jackal. The other types of dog may be divided into four main groups: American (North and South), African, Asiatic and Australian. From the Americas come the coyote (North), the Crab-eating dog (South) and the Bushdog of Brazil. The African group includes the hyena and Cape hunting-dog; the Asiatic includes the pariah dog, the dhole and the Raccoon dog of North China and Japan. The Australian wild dog is also known as the dingo, being unique in that it is the only wild carnivore living there today. It is found nowhere else in the world. All wild dogs belong to the general family of Canidae, one section of flesh-eating mammals.

Dogs in literature

Dogs are named and characterized in the works of Marlowe, Shakespeare, Chaucer, Sir Walter Scott, Homer, Sir Isaac Newton and others. The same interest in dogs applies to famous owners who revered their special pets to such an extent that the names of the cherished dogs are still recorded today with the names of their owners. In song, story and painting, owners sought to immortalize them. Two French dramas were based on dogs: *Le Chien de Montargris* by Guilbert de Pixérécourt, and *Le Chien D'Aubry*.

Superstitions and legends

The dog, as an omen of death or disaster, crops up in folklore under several different names and in varying places. The dreaded 'Black Shuck' of Britain, a kind of Hell Hound, goes back at least to Anglo-Saxon times. Even today, though not always black, a similar creature is mentioned and feared in rural areas. Conan Doyle's *The Hound of the Baskervilles* seems almost certainly inspired by such a legend. The Devil was sometimes depicted as hunting with a pack of grisly hounds.

From Biblical times it was believed that the howling of a dog signified death; the ancient Gaels believed that the victim would be the dog's master. The Chinese say that the blood of a dog will reveal a person who has made himself invisible. An old Latin quotation states: 'When dogs wallow in dust, expect foul weather.' Even today, we say of a sullen or sulky person, 'He has the Black Dog on his shoulder.' The guardian of Hades, in Greek mythology, was the terrible many-headed dog monster, Cerberus.

Interesting facts

In view of the fact that the dog is generally considered man's best friend, it is surprising that many unfavourable expressions (some intended as insults) are linked with this favourite pet. For instance, we have: you dog!, you cur!, whelp, insolent puppy, a dog's trick, a dog's life, dog sick, dog cheap, and many more. Perhaps the reason for this is that, particularly in the East, dogs are street scavengers.

In contrast, many wayside plants and flowers have 'dog' as part of their more common names. A glance through a dictionary will give some idea of the number. We also have 'Dog-days', referring to that period when the Dogstar (Sirius) rises and sets with the Sun.

Sizes of dogs
These vary greatly. The heaviest is
the St Bernard, which can weigh
around 113 kg (250 lb). The tallest
are the Great Dane and Irish
Wolfhound, both reaching 1 m (39 in)
at the shoulder. The smallest breeds
are the short-haired
Chihuahua, Toy Poodle and
Yorkshire Terrier. The fastest dogs
are the Greyhound and Arabian
Saluki.

Horses

The horse, like the dog, is
sometimes called man's best friend.
Horses have been helping man for
4,000 years. Before that they were
hunted for food by the primitive
tribes of Europe and Asia. Then,
gradually, man began to capture
and tame them. They were trained
to work and carry riders.

The horse has played a very
important part in our history. Just
think how this noble beast has
served us by pulling chariots and
ploughs, bearing knights and
soldiers into battle, and opening up
the Wild West with cowboys.
Horses are also used for sports
such as racing, jumping and polo.
And there are many other ways in
which man's best friend earns his
title.

Most of the 65 million horses in
the world today are kept for riding
– everything from police horses to
children's ponies. The 300 breeds
range from the tiny Falabella, an
Argentine pony no bigger than a St
Bernard dog and usually kept as a
pet, to the mighty English Shire
horse which is so powerful that
only an elephant is stronger.

The first horses
The horse's earliest ancestors,
Eohippus, lived 55 million years
ago. He was a strange, striped
animal standing just 20 cm (8 in)
high. *Eohippus* made his home in

Eohippus   *Mesohippus*

swampy forests and ate leaves, not grass. Each of his front feet had four toes and his hind feet three.

This little creature was replaced, 15 million years later, by *Mesohippus*. As the earth's climate became drier and the prehistoric forests shrank, *Mesohippus* moved on to the plains. He had three toes on each foot and ate grass.

Then, after another 15 million years, came *Merychippus*. He was bigger than the other two and had a longer neck. To help him escape danger in the open, he had long legs, strong muscles and could run fast on his middle toes. The side toes became less and less important and eventually disappeared. *Pliohippus* was the first horse with only one toe, and the toe was protected by a hard nail, or hoof.

Pliohippus evolved about five million years ago and is the direct ancestor of *Equus caballus* – the horse we all know.

Running wild

Nowadays, there are very few wild horses left in the world. One type, named Przewalski's Horse after the explorer who discovered it in 1881, can still be found in Mongolia. The famous and beautiful white horses that roam the Camargue in southern France are only half wild; as are the black Mérens mountain ponies of southwest France.

Britain's Welsh Mountain and Exmoor ponies are also semi-wild. The Exmoor is a particularly ancient breed and was used by Queen Boadicea when she fought against the Roman army.

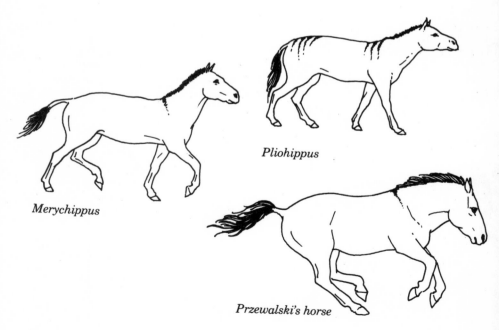

Merychippus

Pliohippus

Przewalski's horse

There are, however, other members of the horse family that still live in the wild. The black and white striped zebra lives free in the African savannahs, and the donkey is another wild species that is related to the horse.

Kings of horses

If horses had a king, he would be an Arab. This handsome horse is one of the world's oldest and purest breeds. He is a very fast animal. All racehorses which can run at up to 69 km/h (43 mph) have some of his blood in their veins. Indeed, most modern breeds, including circus, rodeo and jumping horses, are related to the Arab.

Four-footed giants

The world's biggest and strongest horses are draught horses. They are descended from the great horses of the Middle Ages which used to carry armoured knights into battle. During the 18th and 19th centuries, draught horses hauled ploughs across fields, barges along canals and heavy loads of timber or coal on roads. Today, however, machines have taken over and few of the four-footed giants are still working. At times you can see them pulling British brewery drays (carts) stacked with barrels of beer for public houses. They are also a popular attraction at horse shows.

Britain is lucky enough to have three fine breeds of draught horse. They are the Shire (tallest of all horses), the Suffolk Punch and the Clydesdale. France has the Breton

Equus Caballus

Pony

Donkey

Zebra

Draught and the Percherons, Holland has the Dutch Draught, Denmark has the Jutland (once ridden by Vikings), Sweden has the Ardennes and Italy has the Italian Draught. It would be a sad day if these magnificent creatures ever died out.

Ponies
After the giants, let's look at the pygmies of the horse family – the ponies. These small horses stand no higher than 1·4 m (4 ft 8 in). Some are much shorter. The much-loved Shetland pony from Scotland is only 0·9 m (3 ft) tall, while the Argentine Fallabella, mentioned earlier, stands less than 0·7 m (2 ft 4 in) high. Ponies are used as working animals in many countries because they are strong and hardy. In Norway, for example, the Fjord pony pulls heavy loads up the snowy mountains, while on the great cattle ranges of South America the sturdy Criollo is a cowboy's pony. Furthermore, as ponies are intelligent, good-natured and small, they are ideal for children to ride.

Among the best-known breeds are the Pony of the Americas, the Australian pony, England's friendly New Forest pony, South Africa's tough Basuto, Japan's fast Hocaido, Austria's long-living Haflinger and the Iceland pony which has been kept for work and food since the days of the Vikings.

Points of a horse
The following diagram shows the various parts of the horse. These parts are called points. The points of a horse add up to its conformation, the way it is put together. A horse may have a good or bad conformation. Features such as an extra-large head or a hollow back would give the creature a bad conformation.

Colours and markings
What colour was the last horse you saw? Compare your answer with the descriptions below, which give the correct names for different coloured horses.

- **Cream** – Creamy coat, mane and tail with pinkish eyes
- **Chestnut** – Reddish-brown body, mane and tail
- **Strawberry Roan** – Chestnut mixed with white hairs
- **Palomino** – Golden with pale mane and tail
- **Dun** – Sandy with black mane and tail
- **Piebald** – Large patches of black and white
- **Skewbald** – Brown and white patches
- **Grey** – Mixed black and white hairs
- **Brown** – Dark brown with dark brown mane and tail
- **Bay** – Brown body with black mane, tail and legs
- **Black** – All black

Many horses have what are called markings. These may be white marks on the head, body or legs. The following illustration shows some of them. A horse with no markings is known as whole-coloured.

Coaches and carriages
Horse-drawn vehicles existed as

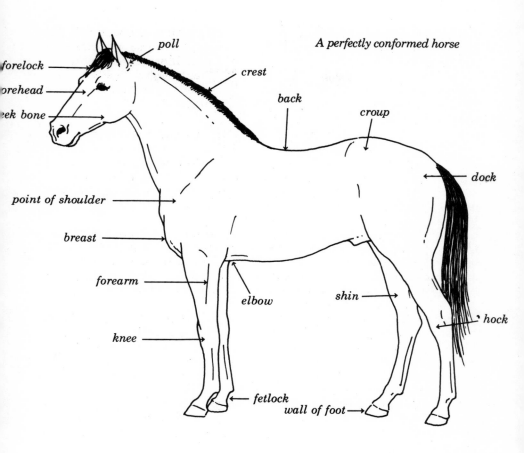

A perfectly conformed horse

forelock

forehead

eek bone

poll

crest

back

croup

dock

point of shoulder

breast

forearm

elbow

shin

hock

knee

fetlock

wall of foot

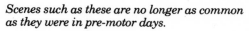

Scenes such as these are no longer as common as they were in pre-motor days.

long ago as 2000 BC. It was, however, much later, during the 18th century, that coaches and carriages became popular. Then, there were state coaches for royalty, mail coaches for letters, stagecoaches for travellers, and carriages for the gentry. All were drawn by special horses such as the English Cleveland Bay, the Czechoslovakian Kladruber and the Dutch Gelderland.

Today, coaches and carriages are hardly ever seen in the street except on ceremonial occasions or as tourist attractions. On the other hand they are still widely used for sporting events. An event called driving involves different kinds of vehicles and different numbers of horses. There can be one, a pair, or a team of four or six horses. Another exciting event is trotting.

The horses race round a track pulling light carriages known as gigs or sulkies. In this race the horse is not allowed to gallop.

Riding and jumping

Riding is fun. There are lots of things to learn before you start. For example, you must know how to mount, dismount, sit, balance and hold the reins. An expert at a riding school will teach you. Later when you can control your horse as it walks, trots, canters and gallops (the four different paces), you may decide you want to learn jumping.

Many people, as they get better at riding and jumping, go in for competitions such as show-jumping and eventing. Eventing consists of three tests: dressage, cross-country and, of course, show-jumping.

Riders sit on leather saddles, like the one pictured here with the names of the various parts. The saddle is kept in place by the girth, a strap which fastens round the horse's belly.

More about horses

'Don't look a gift horse in the mouth.' Perhaps you have heard this saying. It means that if someone gave you a horse as a present, it would be rude of you to look inside the animal's mouth. Why? Because by examining its teeth, you could tell its age. Soon after a horse is born, it develops small, white milk (baby) teeth. Large adult teeth start growing at three years. By the time a horse is five, it has a full mouth of permanent teeth. The older a horse is the more worn its teeth become.

To protect their feet from hard surfaces such as roads, horses are fitted with metal shoes. Horses need new shoes after six to eight weeks. This is not because the old ones are worn out but because the outside, or wall, of the hoof is continually growing. The wall grows fast and can easily outgrow the shoe, causing lameness. So a blacksmith takes off the old shoe, cuts away the extra growth and attaches a new shoe. The horse feels no pain.

How do you measure a horse's height? Which is the nearside of a horse and which is the offside? Both questions are answered in the diagrams below.

Horses of different ages and sexes have special names as you can see from this list:

- **Stallion** – A male horse over four years of age, used for breeding
- **Mare** – A female over four
- **Colt** – A male between one and four
- **Filly** – A female between one and four
- **Foal** – A horse up to one year

The awkward one

Like people, horses can be either easy or difficult to get along with. There is, however, one of our four-footed friends which is noted for its extreme stubbornness. It is the mule, which is a cross between a horse and a donkey. Mules are sterile and cannot breed. So every mule that is born has a horse and a donkey for parents. Mules are agile animals that can carry heavy packs through rugged terrain such as mountains. If a mule decides not to move, however, there is nothing you can do to change its mind!

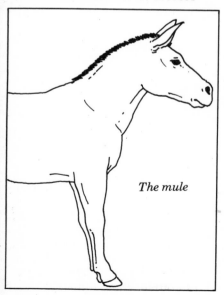

The mule

THE ARTS

Who Wrote That?

General Literature

Alice-All-by-Herself, Elizabeth Coatsworth (b. 1893)
Anne of Green Gables, Lucy M. Montgomery (1874–1942)
Ballet Shoes, Noel Streatfeild (b. 1895)
Blue Boat, The, William Mayne (b. 1928)
Bobbsey Twins, The, Laura Lee Hope
Borrowers, The, Mary Norton (b. 1900)
Broom Stages, Clemence Dane
Children of Green Knowe, The, Lucy M. Boston (b. 1892)
Christmas Carol, A, Charles Dickens (1812–70)
Circus is Coming, The, Noel Streatfeild (b. 1897)
Clunie, Hugh Charteris
Cowboy Small, Lois Lenski (1893–1974)
Darkie & Co., Howard Spring (1889–1965)
David Copperfield, Charles Dickens (1812–70)
Family at Misrule, The, Ethel Turner (1872–1958)
Family from One End Street, The, Eve Garnett
Famous Five, The (Secret Seven etc.), Enid Blyton (1897–1968)
Five Proud Riders, Ann Stafford
Girl of the Limberlost, A, Gene Stratton-Porter (1868–1924)
Golden Shore, The Elinor Lyon (b. 1921)
Good Wives, Louisa M. Alcott (1832–88)
Grass Rope, A, William Mayne (b. 1928)
Green Dolphin Country, Elizabeth Goudge (b. 1900)
Green Mansions, W. H. Hudson (1841–1922)
Hans Brinker; or the Silver Skates, Mary Mapes Dodge (1831–1905)
Harlequin Corner, Pamela Brown (b. 1924)
Hartwarp books, The, John Pudney (1909–77)
Heidi, Johanna Spyri (1827–1901)
House in Turner Square, The, Ann Thwaite (b. 1932)
House of the Pelican, The, Elizabeth Kyle
Impractical Chimney Sweep, The, Rosemary Anne Sisson (b. 1923)
I Will Tell You of a Town, Alastair Reid (b. 1926)
Jo's Boys, Louisa M. Alcott (1832–88)
Lark in the Morn, The, Elfrida Vipont (b. 1902)
Linda in Cambridge, Winifred Donald
Little Lord Fauntleroy, Frances Hodgson Burnett (1849–1924)
Little Princess, A, Frances Hodgson Burnett (1849–1924)
Little Tim and the Brave Sea Captain, Edward Ardizzone (1900–79)
Little Women, Louisa M. Alcott (1832–88)
Lorna Doone, R. D. Blackmore (1825–1900)
Lovely Summer, The, Barbara Ker Wilson (b. 1929)

Marianne and Mark, Catherine Storr (b. 1913)
Marlows and the Traitor, The, Antonia Forest
Martin Pippin in the Daisy Field, Eleanor Farjeon (1881–1965)
Mary-Mary books, Joan G. Robinson (b. 1910)
Mary Plain books, Gwynedd Rae (b. 1892)
Milly–Molly–Mandy books, Joyce Lankester Brisley (b. 1896)
Minnow on the Say, Ann Philippa Pearce (b. 1920)
Mystery at Witchend, Malcolm Saville (b. 1901)
Not Scarlet but Gold, Malcolm Saville (b. 1901)
Paddington Bear books, Michael Bond (b. 1926)
Parcel of Trees, A, William Mayne (b. 1928)
Path-Through-the-Woods, Barbara Ker Wilson (b. 1929)
Penny books, Stephen A. Tring
Pigeon Post, Arthur Ransome (1884–1967)
Polly & Oliver books, David Scott Daniell (1906–65)
Pollyanna books, Eleanor Hodgman Porter (1868–1920)
Prize Essay, The, Kathleen Wallace
Punchbowl Farm books, Monica Edwards (b. 1912)
Railway Children, The, E. Nesbit (1858–1924)
Rebecca of Sunnybrook Farm, Kate Douglas Wiggin (1856–1923)
Redcap Runs Away, Rhoda Power (1890–1957)
Romany books, G. Bramwell Evens (1884–1943)
Ryan's Fort, Patricia Lynch (1898–1972)
Sampson's Circus, Howard Spring (1889–1965)
Saturdays, The, Elizabeth Enright (1909–68)
Secret Garden, The, Frances Hodgson Burnett (1849–1924)
Showboat Summer, Pamela Brown (b. 1924)
Silver Curlew, The, Eleanor Farjeon (1881–1965)
Stig of the Dump, Clive King (b. 1924)
Story of Holly and Ivy, Rumer Godden (b. 1907)
Sue Barton books, Helen Dore Boylston (b. 1895)
Summer with Spike, The, Barbara Willard (b. 1909)
Susan and Bill books, Malcolm Saville (b. 1901)
Swish of the Curtain, The, Pamela Brown (b. 1924)
Teddy Robinson books, Joan G. Robinson (b. 1901)
Thimble Summer, Elizabeth Enright (1909–68)
Thumbstick, The, William Mayne (b. 1928)
We Couldn't Leave Dinah, Mary Treadgold (b. 1910)
We Didn't Mean to Go to Sea, Arthur Ransome (1884–1967)
What Katy Did books, Susan Coolidge (1835–1905)
Wintle's Wonders, Noel Streatfeild (b. 1897)
Wooroo, Joyce Gard (b. 1911)

Animal Stories

At the Back of the North Wind, George MacDonald (1824–1905)
Bambi, Felix Salten (1869–1945)

Black Beauty, Anna Sewell (1820–78)
Born Free, Joy Adamson (1910–80)
Call of the Wild, Jack London (1876–1916)
Dog Toby, Richard Church (1893–1972)
I Wanted a Pony, Diana Pullein-Thompson
Jungle Book, The, Rudyard Kipling (1865–1936)
Just So Stories, Rudyard Kipling (1865–1936)
Linda and the Silver Greyhound, Winifred Donald
Mousewife, The, Rumer Godden (b. 1907)
National Velvet, Enid Bagnold (b. 1889)
One Hundred and One Dalmations, Dodie Smith
Orlando books, Kathleen Hale (b. 1898)
Rufty Tufty books, Ruth Ainsworth (b. 1908)
Snow Goose, The, Paul Gallico (1897–1976)
Soapbox Derby, Rosemary Weir (b. 1905)
Tarka the Otter, Henry Williamson (b. 1897)
Uncle Remus books, Joel Chandler Harris (1848–1908)
Watership Down, Richard Adams (b. 1920)
White Fang, Jack London (1876–1916)
White Stag, The, Kate Seredy (1899–1975)
Whoo, Whoo, the Wind Blews, Diana Ross (b. 1910)
Wind in the Willows, The, Kenneth Grahame (1859–1932)
Wish for a Pony, Monica Edwards (b. 1912)

School Stories

Abbey Girls, The, Elsie Oxenham (d. 1960)
Autumn Term, Antonia Forest
Beyond the Blue Mountains, L. T. Meade (1854–1914)
End of Term, Antonia Frost
Exciting Term, An, Angela Brazil (1869–1947)
Jeanette's First Term, Alice Lunt
Manor House School, The, Angela Brazil (1869–1947)
Rebel of the School, L. T. Meade (1854–1914)
School on the Lock, The, Angela Brazil (1869–1947)
School under Snowdon, Mabel Esther Allan (b. 1915)

Fantasy and Fairy Stories

Alice's Adventures in Wonderland, Lewis Carrol (1832–98)
Blue Fairy Book, The, Andrew Lang (1844–1912)
Book of Discoveries, A, John Masefield (1878–1967)
Box of Delights, The, John Masefield (1878–1967)
Cuckoo Clock, The, Mrs M. L. Molesworth (1839–1921)
Dragon of the Hill, The, Joyce Gard (b. 1911)
Enchanted Castle, The, E. Nesbit (1858–1924)
English Fairy Tales, Joseph Jacobs (1854–1916)
Five Children and It, E. Nesbit (1858–1924)

Granny's Wonderful Chair, Frances Browne (1816–c.1879)
Happy Prince and Other Stories, The, Oscar Wilde (1854–1900)
Hobbit, The, J. R. R. Tolkien (1892–1973)
Invisible Man, The, H. G. Wells (1866–1946)
King of the Golden River The, John Ruskin (1819–1900)
Lion, the Witch and the Wardrobe, The, C. S. Lewis (1898–1963)
Little Grey Men, The, 'B. B.' (b. 1905)
Lord of the Rings, The, J. R. R. Tolkein (1892–1973)
Lost World, The, Sir Arthur Conan Doyle (1859–1930)
Magic City, The, E. Nesbit (1858–1924)
Magic Finger, The, Roald Dahl (b. 1916)
Magic Walking Stick, The, John Buchan (1875–1940)
Mary Poppins books, Pamela L. Travers (b. 1906)
Midnight Folk, The, John Masefield (1878–1967)
Moon of Gomrath, The, Alan Garner (b. 1934)
Oz books, L. Frank Baum (1856–1919)
Peter Pan and Wendy, Sir James Barrie (1860–1937)
Phoenix and the Carpet, The, E. Nesbit (1858–1924)
Princess and the Goblin, The, George MacDonald (1824–1905)
Puck of Pook's Hill, Rudyard Kipling (1865–1936)
Rose and the Ring, The, William Makepeace Thackeray (1811–63)
Story of the Amulet, The, E. Nesbit (1858–1924)
Three Royal Monkeys, The, Walter de la Mare (1873–1956)
Through the Looking Glass, Lewis Carroll (1832–98)
Time Garden, The, Edward Eager (b. circa 1900–64)
Tom's Midnight Garden, Ann Philippa Pearce (b. 1920)
Twelve and the Genii, The, Pauline Clarke (b. 1921)
Weirdstone of Brisingamen, The, Alan Garner (b. 1934)
Witch Family, The, Eleanor Ruth Estes (b. 1906)
Wizard of Earthsea, A, Ursula Le Guin (b. 1929)

Adventure Stories

Adventures of Huckleberry Finn, The, Mark Twain (1835–1910)
Adventures of Tom Sawyer, The, Mark Twain (1835–1910)
Coral Island, The, R. M. Ballantyne (1825–94)
Gulliver's Travels, Jonathan Swift (1667–1745)
Hornblower books, C. S. Forester (1899–1966)
Kidnapped, Robert Louis Stevenson (1850–94)
King Solomon's Mines, Sir Henry Rider Haggard (1856–1925)
Moby Dick, Herman Melville (1819–91)
Pilgrims of the Wild, 'Grey Owl' (1885–1937)
Prisoner of Zenda, The, Anthony Hope (1863–1933)
Robinson Crusoe, Daniel Defoe (1660–1731)
Scarlet Pimpernel, The, Baroness Orczy (1865–1947)
Swiss Family Robinson, W. H. G. Kingston (1814–80)
Treasure Island, Robert Louis Stevenson (1850–94)

Twenty Thousand Leagues Under the Sea, Jules Verne (1828–1905)

Uncle Tom's Cabin, Harriet Beecher Stowe (1811–96)

Humorous Stories

Bad Child's Book of Beasts, The, Hilaire Belloc (1870–1953)

Book of Nonsense, A, Edward Lear (1812–88)

Charlie and the Chocolate Factory, Roald Dahl (b. 1916)

Dr Doolittle books, Hugh Lofting (1886–1947)

Father Christmas, Raymond Briggs (b. 1934)

Helen's Babies, John Habberton (1842–1921)

Magic Pudding, The, Norman Lindsay (1879–1969)

My Friend Mr Leakey, J. B. S. Haldane (1892–1964)

Nonsense Novels, Stephen Leacock (1869–1944)

North Winds Blow Free, Elizabeth Howard

Now We are Six, A. A. Milne (1882–1956)

Old Possum's Book of Practical Cats, T. S. Eliot (1888–1965)

Professor Branestawm books, Norman Hunter (b. 1899)

Three Men in a Boat, Jerome K. Jerome (1859–1927)

Wind on the Moon, The, Eric Linklater (1899–1974)

Winnie-the-Pooh, A. A. Milne (1882–1956)

Wombles books, Elisabeth Beresford (b. circa 1890)

Worzel Gummidge books, Barbara E. Todd (d. 1976)

Historical Stories

Children of the New Forest, The, Captain Marryat (1792–1848)

Daisy Chain, The, Charlotte M. Yonge (1823–1901)

Eagle of the Ninth, The, Rosemary Sutcliffe (b. 1920)

Fearless Treasure, The, Noel Streatfeild (b. 1897)

Hereward the Wake, Charles Kingsley (1819–75)

House of Arden, The, E. Nesbit (1858–1924)

Knight Crusader, Ronald Welch

Land the Ravens Found, The, Naomi Mitchison (b. 1897)

Lantern Bearers, The, Rosemary Sutcliffe (b. 1920)

Load of Unicorn, The, Cynthia Harnett (b. 1893)

Men of the Hills, Henry Treece (1911–66)

Otto of the Silver Hand, Howard Pyle (1853–1911)

Peacock House, The, Gillian Avery (b. 1926)

Traveller in Time, A, Alison Uttley (1884–1976)

Wool-pack, The, Cynthia Harnett (b. 1893)

Word to Caesar, Geoffrey Trease (b. 1909)

Myths and Legends

Heroes of Greece and Troy, Roger Lancelyn Green (b. 1918)

Mystery at Mycenae, Roger Lancelyn Green (b. 1918)

Sword in the Stone, The, T. H. White (1906–64)

Tales of Troy and Greece, Andrew Lang (1844–1912)

Tanglewood Tales, Nathaniel Hawthorne (1804–64)

Music

SYMPHONIES, CONCERTOS, INSTRUMENTS AND ORCHESTRAS

The word symphony is derived from the ancient Greek word *symphonia*, literally meaning 'harmonious sound'. In musical terms it has come to mean a composition for full orchestra. Traditionally a symphony consisted of four contrasting but closely related movements.

Until the time when Haydn and Mozart began to dominate the musical world, that is, prior to the middle of the 18th century, symphony still retained its archaic meaning of 'harmony' or 'consonance of sounds' (sounding together). A variety of compositions, termed symphonies, were then written to be performed by a number of musical instruments. Haydn and Mozart were largely responsible, by their innovations, for altering the meaning of the word symphony, and from then on it was used to describe an orchestral sonata.

Beethoven, in the early years of the 19th century, broke the rules which had developed to turn the design of symphonies into a set formula. He raised the standard of classical symphonies to new heights of perfection. As generally happens to innovators, he was derided in many quarters for these changes.

The next stage in the development of the symphony came with the rise in popularity of the romantic composers – first Berlioz and then Liszt. Berlioz introduced a specific idea, making his symphonies relate a musical tale and contain a theme throughout. The *Fantastic Symphony* is a typical example of his style. Liszt enlarged on this development to a greater extent. In his *Faust* symphony, for example, we are presented with a symphonic poem rather than the generally accepted form of the 'classical' symphony.

Further developments occurred when Franck and Tchaikovsky, during the second half of the 19th century, used the symphony to express their own particular philosophies in musical form.

Since the late 19th century, composers such as Borodin and Sibelius have usually based their works on an initial theme, letting a symphony or movement develop from it naturally. This was a far cry from the concepts of the classical originators of the symphony. Nevertheless, during the last century, the original approach to the composition of symphonies was maintained, with excellent results, by Mendelssohn and Brahms. The latter based his four symphonic works on the styles of Beethoven and Mendelssohn.

Concertos, overtures and symphonic poems

In the first instance, there was not a great deal of difference between a symphony and a concerto. Both were performed by playing several instruments together. Concertos for

The positions of the instruments in a symphony orchestra

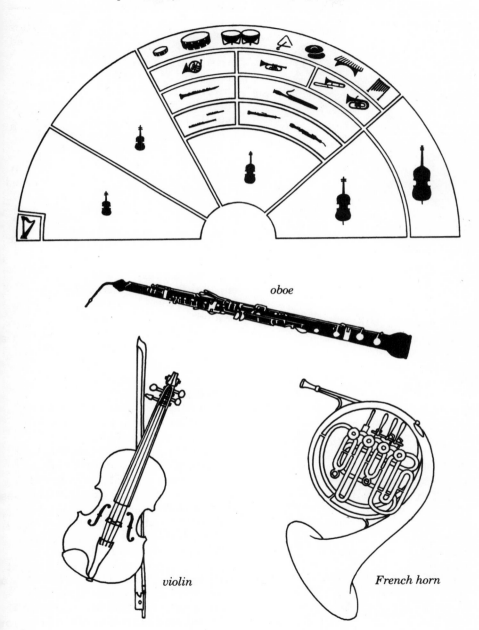

oboe

violin

French horn

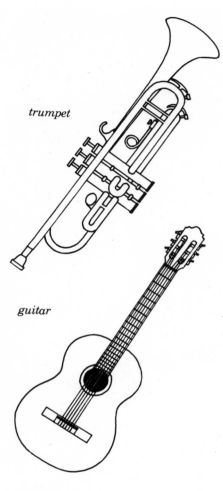

trumpet

guitar

Accordian

string orchestras were composed by Corelli, Bach and Handel in the first part of the 18th century.

Nowadays, a concerto is described as a composition designed for one or more solo instruments accompanied by an orchestra. More often than not, however, it concentrates on just one solo instrument and there are usually three movements.

An overture generally follows the design of a symphony's first movement. It is an orchestral form which frequently acts as the introduction to an opera. Sometimes an overture is performed as a concert piece. Beethoven's *Coriolan* is a good example.

Symphonic poems date from the mid-19th century, when this new musical form was introduced by Liszt. Liszt tried to convey a sequence of ideas or emotional moods, suggested in the music by transformations of the principal theme that he had chosen.

Instruments
A summary of the instruments used in an orchestra ought to start with the piano. It is probably more popular than any other instrument because of its outstanding ability to reproduce not only melody but also wide-ranging harmony without any accompaniment.

Before the appearance of the earliest kind of piano, the virginal, spinet, clavichord and harpsichord had been in use as keyboard instruments. Despite the fact that the first pianos date back to the start of the 18th century, it was not until the end of the century that they began to become popular. More often than not, to the regret of some people, music composed for the earlier instruments is nowadays frequently played on a modern piano.

Beethoven, who had a deep understanding of a piano's flexibility, wrote many sonatas and concertos for it. The instrument's popularity increased further as, in succession, Schubert, Chopin, Schumann, Brahms and Liszt all composed for the piano. As a result of these composers' works and the advances in technique they made, the piano's mechanism was perfected by the end of the 19th century, presenting the modern pianist with the fine instrument we all know today.

Another instrument which deserves special mention is the violin. A great quantity of music has been specially written for it by famous composers. This stringed instrument, a smaller form of the even older viol, has been in use since remote times, and the modern version is virtually the same as that played in the 16th century. During the 17th century, violin construction was perfected to a degree never since equalled, and Antonio Stradivari (1644–1730), of Cremona, is regarded as the supreme master of all time in the art of making violins. His instruments are worth vast sums of money today.

Other orchestral musical instruments, listed alphabetically, are as follows:

Bassoon Uses a double reed, and is the lowest in pitch of the woodwind instruments.

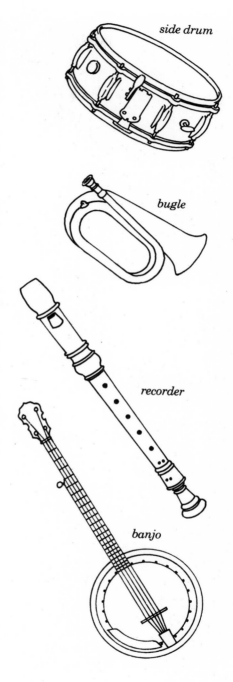

side drum

bugle

recorder

banjo

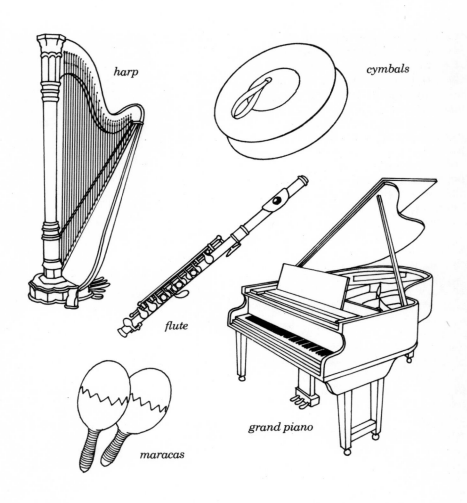

harp

cymbals

flute

grand piano

maracas

Cello Placed between the viola and double bass, this four-stringed instrument has a bass range and is played with a bow.
Clarinet In use since the mid-18th century, this woodwind instrument has a single reed.
Cymbal A brass percussion instrument shaped rather like a plate. Two cymbals are struck together.
Double bass Played with a bow,

this is the largest member and has the lowest pitch of the violin family.
Drums Percussion instruments. Sound is produced by hitting a skin tightly stretched across a hemisphere or hollow cylinder. The largest, the bass drum, is placed upright and hit on its side. The kettledrum can be tuned by turning handles on its rim to tighten or relax the skin. The person who

plays the kettle drums in an orchestra is known as the timpanist.

English horn Otherwise known as the *cor anglais*, this is a woodwind instrument with the double reed of the oboe family.

Flute Blown sideways, this woodwind instrument is played through a hole and not a reed. Some modern flutes are manufactured with metal.

French horn This is a brass instrument with coiled tubes. Valves were introduced during the 19th century.

Harp An ancient instrument, the harp is played by plucking strings that are stretched, parallel, across its frame. A set of pedals is used to alter the instrument's basic scale, C flat major.

Oboe This woodwind instrument is a descendant of the old hautboy. It has a double reed. It has been in use for some 400 years and has had its present form since the 18th century.

Trombone A brass instrument which has a slide to adjust the length of its tube and thereby alter the pitch.

Trumpet Another ancient instrument, the trumpet is made of metal and has three valves.

Piccolo A small flute. It is an octave higher than the ordinary flute.

Tuba Equipped with three or four valves, the tuba is the deepest-pitched brass instrument.

Viola This is slightly larger than a violin and is tuned a 5th below.

Xylophone Consisting of a series of wooden bars, this percussion instrument is played with sticks.

MUSICAL TERMS

Accelerando increasing in tempo
Adagio at a slow pace
Ad lib (*ad libitum*) strict time need not be observed
Affettuoso affectionately, with tenderness
Agitato in agitated manner
Allegretto rather less fast than Allegro
Allegro at a quick pace
Andante fairly slow pace
Animato lively
Calando becoming quieter and slower
Cantabile in a singing manner
Con brio with spirit, dash
Con fuoco with fire
Crescendo getting louder
Da capo return to the beginning of the first section
Diminuendo getting softer
Dolce sweet
Forte strong, loud
Fortissimo very loud
Fugato in the manner of a fugue
Grave slow tempo
Grazioso gracefully
Largamente spaciously
Largo slow
Legato with notes smoothly connected
Lento slowly
Maestoso stately
Marcato with each note strongly marked
Molto much, e.g. Allegro Molto, very quickly
Piano soft
Pianissimo very soft
Piu more, e.g. Piu Lento, more slowly
Presto quick
Rallentando getting slower
Rubato performing a piece without strict rhythm for purposes of expression
Scherzando in a jesting manner
Sforzando forced, strongly accented
Tremolando tremulously
Tremolo tremulous effect in singing or in playing bowed instruments
Vivace in a lively manner

The Cinema

Academy of Motion Picture Arts and Sciences Awards (Oscars)

The *Academy Awards* or *Oscars* are given each spring for outstanding merit in filmmaking during the preceding year. Winners receive a statuette made of bronze covered with gold plate. The statuette was named in 1931 after an Academy librarian said it reminded her of her Uncle Oscar.

AWARD FOR BEST ACTOR

1927–28 Emil Jannings (*The Way of All Flesh, The Last Command*)

1928–29 Warner Baxter (*In Old Arizona*)

1929–30 George Arliss (*Disraeli*)

1930–31 Lionel Barrymore (*A Free Soul*)

1931–32 Fredric March (*Dr Jekyll and Mr Hyde*), Wallace Beery (*The Champ*)

1932–33 Charles Laughton (*The Private Life of Henry VIII*)

1934 Clark Gable (*It Happened One Night*)

1935 Victor McLaglen (*The Informer*)

1936 Paul Muni (*The Story of Louis Pasteur*)

1937 Spencer Tracy (*Captains Courageous*)

1938 Spencer Tracy (*Boys Town*)

1939 Robert Donat (*Goodbye, Mr Chips*)

1940 James Stewart (*The Philadelphia Story*)

1941 Gary Cooper (*Sergeant York*)

1942 James Cagney (*Yankee Doodle Dandy*)

1943 Paul Lukas (*Watch on the Rhine*)

1944 Bing Crosby (*Going My Way*)

1945 Ray Milland (*The Lost Weekend*)

1946 Fredric March (*The Best Years of Our Lives*)

1947 Ronald Colman (*A Double Life*)

1948 Laurence Olivier (*Hamlet*)

1949 Broderick Crawford (*All the King's Men*)

1950 José Ferrer (*Cyrano de Bergerac*)

1951 Humphrey Bogart (*The African Queen*)

1952 Gary Cooper (*High Noon*)

1953 William Holden (*Stalag 17*)

1954 Marlon Brando (*On the Waterfront*)

1955 Ernest Borgnine (*Marty*)

1956 Yul Brynner (*The King and I*)

1957 Alec Guinness (*The Bridge on the River Kwai*)

1958 David Niven (*Separate Tables*)

1959 Charlton Heston (*Ben-Hur*)

1960 Burt Lancaster (*Elmer Gantry*)

1961 Maximilian Schell (*Judgment at Nuremberg*)

1962 Gregory Peck (*To Kill a Mockingbird*)

1963 Sidney Poitier (*Lilies of the Field*)

1964 Rex Harrison (*My Fair Lady*)

1965	Lee Marvin (*Cat Ballou*)	1946	Olivia de Havilland (*To Each His Own*)
1966	Paul Scofield (*A Man for All Seasons*)	1947	Loretta Young (*The Farmer's Daughter*)
1967	Rod Steiger (*In the Heat of the Night*)	1948	Jane Wyman (*Johnny Belinda*)
1968	Cliff Robertson (*Charly*)	1949	Olivia de Havilland (*The Heiress*)
1969	John Wayne (*True Grit*)	1950	Judy Holliday (*Born Yesterday*)
1970	George C. Scott (*Patton*)		
1971	Gene Hackman (*The French Connection*)	1951	Vivien Leigh (*A Streetcar Named Desire*)
1972	Marlon Brando (*The Godfather*)	1952	Shirley Booth (*Come Back, Little Sheba*)
1973	Jack Lemmon (*Save the Tiger*)	1953	Audrey Hepburn (*Roman Holiday*)
1974	Art Carney (*Harry and Tonto*)		
1975	Jack Nicholson (*One Flew Over the Cuckoo's Nest*)	1954	Grace Kelly (*The Country Girl*)
		1955	Anna Magnani (*The Rose Tattoo*)
1976	Peter Finch (*Network*)	1956	Ingrid Bergman (*Anastasia*)
1977	Richard Dreyfuss (*The Goodbye Girl*)	1957	Joanne Woodward (*The Three Faces of Eve*)
1978	Jon Voight (*Coming Home*)	1958	Susan Hayward (*I Want to Live!*)
1979	Dustin Hoffman (*Kramer vs Kramer*)	1959	Simone Signoret (*Room at the Top*)

AWARD FOR BEST ACTRESS

		1960	Elizabeth Taylor (*Butterfield 8*)
1927–28	Janet Gaynor (*Seventh Heaven, Street Angel, Sunrise*)	1961	Sophia Loren (*Two Women*)
1928–29	Mary Pickford (*Coquette*)	1962	Anne Bancroft (*The Miracle Worker*)
1929–30	Norma Shearer (*The Divorcee*)		
1930–31	Marie Dressler (*Min and Bill*)	1963	Patricia Neal (*Hud*)
1931–32	Helen Hayes (*The Sin of Madelon Claudet*)	1964	Julie Andrews (*Mary Poppins*)
		1965	Julie Christie (*Darling*)
1932–33	Katharine Hepburn (*Morning Glory*)	1966	Elizabeth Taylor (*Who's Afraid of Virginia Woolf?*)
1934	Claudette Colbert (*It Happened One Night*)	1967	Katharine Hepburn (*Guess Who's Coming to Dinner*)
1935	Bette Davis (*Dangerous*)		
1936	Luise Rainer (*The Great Ziegfeld*)	1968	Katharine Hepburn (*The Lion in Winter*), Barbra Streisand (*Funny Girl*)
1937	Luise Rainer (*The Good Earth*)		
1938	Bette Davis (*Jezebel*)	1969	Maggie Smith (*The Prime of Miss Jean Brodie*)
1939	Vivien Leigh (*Gone with the Wind*)	1970	Glenda Jackson (*Women in Love*)
1940	Ginger Rogers (*Kitty Foyle*)		
1941	Joan Fontaine (*Suspicion*)	1971	Jane Fonda (*Klute*)
1942	Greer Garson (*Mrs Miniver*)	1972	Liza Minnelli (*Cabaret*)
1943	Jennifer Jones (*The Song of Bernadette*)	1973	Glenda Jackson (*A Touch of Class*)
1944	Ingrid Bergman (*Gaslight*)	1974	Ellen Burstyn (*Alice Doesn't Live Here Anymore*)
1945	Joan Crawford (*Mildred Pierce*)	1975	Louise Fletcher (*One Flew Over the Cuckoo's Nest*)

1976	Faye Dunaway (*Network*)		*Youth*)
1977	Diane Keaton (*Annie Hall*)	1963	Melvyn Douglas (*Hud*)
1978	Jane Fonda (*Coming Home*)	1964	Peter Ustinov (*Topkapi*)
1979	Sally Field (*Norma Rae*)	1965	Martin Balsam (*A Thousand Clowns*)

AWARD FOR BEST SUPPORTING ACTOR

1936	Walter Brennan (*Come and Get It*)
1937	Joseph Schildkraut (*The Life of Émile Zola*)
1938	Walter Brennan (*Kentucky*)
1939	Thomas Mitchell (*Stagecoach*)
1940	Walter Brennan (*The Westerner*)
1941	Donald Crisp (*How Green Was My Valley*)
1942	Van Heflin (*Johnny Eager*)
1943	Charles Coburn (*The More the Merrier*)
1944	Barry Fitzgerald (*Going My Way*)
1945	James Dunn (*A Tree Grows in Brooklyn*)
1946	Harold Russell (*The Best Years of Our Lives*)
1947	Edmund Gwenn (*Miracle on 34th Street*)
1948	Walter Huston (*The Treasure of Sierre Madre*)
1949	Dean Jagger (*Twelve O'Clock High*)
1950	George Sanders (*All About Eve*)
1951	Karl Malden (*A Streetcar Named Desire*)
1952	Anthony Quinn (*Viva Zapata!*)
1953	Frank Sinatra (*From Here to Eternity*)
1954	Edmond O'Brien (*The Barefoot Contessa*)
1955	Jack Lemmon (*Mister Roberts*)
1956	Anthony Quinn (*Lust for Life*)
1957	Red Buttons (*Sayonara*)
1958	Burl Ives (*The Big Country*)
1959	Hugh Griffith (*Ben-Hur*)
1960	Peter Ustinov (*Spartacus*)
1961	George Chakiris (*West Side Story*)
1962	Ed Begley (*Sweet Bird of*

1966	Walter Matthau (*The Fortune Cookie*)
1967	George Kennedy (*Cool Hand Luke*)
1968	Jack Albertson (*The Subject Was Roses*)
1969	Gig Young (*They Shoot Horses, Don't They?*)
1970	John Mills (*Ryan's Daughter*)
1971	Ben Johnson (*The Last Picture Show*)
1972	Joel Grey (*Cabaret*)
1973	John Houseman (*The Paper Chase*)
1974	Robert De Niro (*The Godfather, Part II*)
1975	George Burns (*The Sunshine Boys*)
1976	Jason Robards (*All the President's Men*)
1977	Jason Robards (*Julia*)
1978	Christopher Walken (*The Deer Hunter*)
1979	Melvyn Douglas (*Being There*)

AWARD FOR BEST SUPPORTING ACTRESS

1936	Gale Sondergaard (*Anthony Adverse*)
1937	Alice Brady (*In Old Chicago*)
1938	Fay Bainter (*Jezebel*)
1939	Hattie McDaniel (*Gone with the Wind*)
1940	Jane Darwell (*The Grapes of Wrath*)
1941	Mary Astor (*The Great Lie*)
1942	Teresa Wright (*Mrs. Miniver*)
1943	Katina Paxinou (*For Whom the Bell Tolls*)
1944	Ethel Barrymore (*None But the Lonely Heart*)
1945	Anne Revere (*National Velvet*)
1946	Anne Baxter (*The Razor's Edge*)
1947	Celeste Holm (*Gentleman's*

Agreement)
1948 Claire Trevor (*Key Largo*)
1949 Mercedes McCambridge (*All the King's Men*)
1950 Josephine Hull (*Harvey*)
1951 Kim Hunter (*A Streetcar Named Desire*)
1952 Gloria Grahame (*The Bad and the Beautiful*)
1953 Donna Reed (*From Here to Eternity*)
1954 Eva Marie Saint (*On the Waterfront*)
1955 Jo Van Fleet (*East of Eden*)
1956 Dorothy Malone (*Written on the Wind*)
1957 Miyoshi Umeki (*Sayonara*)
1958 Wendy Hiller (*Separate Tables*)
1959 Shelley Winters (*The Diary of Anne Frank*)
1960 Shirley Jones (*Elmer Gantry*)
1961 Rita Moreno (*West Side Story*)
1962 Patty Duke (*The Miracle Worker*)
1963 Margaret Rutherford (*The V.I.P.'s*)
1964 Lila Kedrova (*Zorba the Greek*)
1965 Shelley Winters (*A Patch of Blue*)
1966 Sandy Dennis (*Who's Afraid of Virginia Woolf?*)
1967 Estelle Parsons (*Bonnie and Clyde*)
1968 Ruth Gordon (*Rosemary's Baby*)
1969 Goldie Hawn (*Cactus Flower*)
1970 Helen Hayes (*Airport*)
1971 Cloris Leachman (*The Last Picture Show*)
1972 Eileen Heckart (*Butterflies Are Free*)
1973 Tatum O'Neal (*Paper Moon*)
1974 Ingrid Bergman (*Murder on the Orient Express*)
1975 Lee Grant (*Shampoo*)
1976 Beatrice Straight (*Network*)
1977 Vanessa Redgrave (*Julia*)
1978 Maggie Smith (*California Suite*)
1979 Meryl Streep (*Kramer vs Kramer*)

AWARD FOR BEST PICTURE

1927–28 *Wings*, Paramount
1928–29 *Broadway Melody*, MGM
1929–30 *All Quiet on the Western Front*, Universal
1930–31 *Cimarron*, RKO
1931–32 *Grand Hotel*, MGM
        Special: *Mickey Mouse*, Walt Disney
1932–33 *Cavalcade*, 20th Century-Fox
1934 *It Happened One Night*, Columbia
1935 *Mutiny on the Bounty*, MGM
1936 *The Great Ziegfeld*, MGM
1937 *Life of Emile Zola*, Warner
1938 *You Can't Take It With You*, Columbia
1939 *Gone With the Wind*, Selznick International
1940 *Rebecca*, Selznick International
1941 *How Green Was My Valley*, 20th Century-Fox
1942 *Mrs Miniver*, MGM
1943 *Casablanca*, Warner
1944 *Going My Way*, Paramount
1945 *The Lost Weekend*, Paramount
1946 *The Best Years of Our Lives*, Goldwyn, RKO
1947 *Gentleman's Agreement*, 20th Century-Fox
1948 *Hamlet*, Two Cities Film, Universal International
1949 *All the King's Men*, Columbia
1950 *All About Eve*, 20th Century-Fox
1951 *An American in Paris*, MGM
1952 *Greatest Show on Earth*, Cecil B. De Mille, Paramount
1953 *From Here to Eternity*, Columbia
1954 *On the Waterfront*, Horizon-American Corp. Columbia
1955 *Marty*, Hecht and Lancaster's Steven Productions UA
1956 *Around the World in 80 Days*, Michael Todd Co. UA
1957 *The Bridge on the River Kwai*, Columbia
1958 *Gigi*, Arthur Freed Production,

MGM
1959 *Ben-Hur*, MGM
1960 *The Apartment*, Mirisch Co. UA
1961 *West Side Story*, United Artists
1962 *Lawrence of Arabia*, Columbia
1963 *Tom Jones*, Woodfall Prod. UA-Lopert Pictures
1964 *My Fair Lady*, Warner Bros.
1965 *The Sound of Music*, 20th Century-Fox
1966 *A Man for All Seasons*, Columbia
1967 *In the Heat of the Night*, United Artists
1968 *Oliver*, Columbia
1969 *Midnight Cowboy*, United Artists
1970 *Patton*, 20th Century-Fox
1971 *The French Connection*, 20th Century-Fox
1972 *The Godfather*, Paramount
1973 *The Sting*, Universal
1974 *The Godfather, Part II*, Paramount
1975 *One Flew Over the Cuckoo's Nest*, United Artists
1976 *Rocky*, United Artists
1977 *Annie Hall*, United Artists
1978 *The Deer Hunter*, EMI
1979 *Kramer vs Kramer*, Columbia

AWARD FOR BEST DIRECTOR

1927–28 Frank Borzage, *Seventh Heaven*, Lewis Milestone, *Two Arabian Knights*
1928–29 Frank Lloyd, *The Divine Lady*
1929–30 Lewis Milestone, *All Quiet on the Western Front*
1930–31 Norman Taurog, *Skippy*
1931–32 Frank Borzage, *Bad Girl*
1932–33 Frank Lloyd, *Cavalcade*
1934 Frank Capra, *It Happened One Night*
1935 John Ford, *The Informer*
1936 Frank Capra, *Mr Deeds Goes to Town*
1937 Leo McCarey, *The Awful Truth*
1938 Frank Capra, *You Can't Take It With You*
1939 Victor Fleming, *Gone with the Wind*
1940 John Ford, *The Grapes of Wrath*
1941 John Ford, *How Green Was My Valley*
1942 William Wyler, *Mrs Miniver*
1943 Michael Curtiz, *Casablanca*
1944 Leo McCarey, *Going My Way*
1945 Billy Wilder, *The Lost Weekend*
1946 William Wyler, *The Best Years of Our Lives*
1947 Elia Kazan, *Gentleman's Agreement*
1948 John Huston, *Treasure of Sierra Madre*
1949 Joseph L. Mankiewicz, *A Letter to Three Wives*
1950 Joseph L. Mankiewicz, *All About Eve*
1951 George Stevens, *A Place in the Sun*
1952 John Ford, *The Quiet Man*
1953 Fred Zinnemann, *From Here to Eternity*
1954 Elia Kazan, *On the Waterfront*
1955 Delbert Mann, *Marty*
1956 George Stevens, *Giant*
1957 David Lean, *The Bridge on the River Kwai*
1958 Vincente Minnelli, *Gigi*
1959 William Wyler, *Ben-Hur*
1960 Billy Wilder, *The Apartment*
1961 Jerome Robbins, Robert Wise, *West Side Story*
1962 David Lean, *Lawrence of Arabia*
1963 Tony Richardson, *Tom Jones*
1964 George Cukor, *My Fair Lady*
1965 Robert Wise, *Sound of Music*
1966 Fred Zinnemann, *A Man for All Seasons*
1967 Mike Nichols, *The Graduate*
1968 Sir Carol Reed, *Oliver*
1969 John Schlesinger, *Midnight Cowboy*
1970 Franklin J. Schaffner, *Patton*
1971 William Friedkin, *The French Connection*

Drawing and Painting

Drawing

When you first started drawing you probably derived great satisfaction and enjoyment from drawing matchstick figures. Simple lines represented a body and limbs, while dots for eyes and a line for the mouth transformed a plain circle into a face. By experimenting you probably soon realised it was possible to give your little matchstick-man feelings. To show happiness or sadness you merely curved the mouthline up or down.

This ability to transform simple lines into works of art is the whole secret of drawing. From the intriguing half-smile of the celebrated Mona Lisa to the cheeky grin of your favourite cartoon character, all are achieved by mastery of the drawn line. As well as a representation of real objects, drawing is also an expression of the imagination.

Broken lines can suggest rain; wavy lines water. To appreciate fully the art of drawing, you must learn to enjoy lines! Study the linework of past masters of draughtsmanship, such as Leonardo da Vinci, Holbein, Rembrandt and Dürer. If you are unable to visit art galleries, search in your local library for books containing reproductions of the works of these artists.

Train yourself to look at things with a critical eye. Constantly remind yourself to analyse what you are seeing. When you look at a box, for instance, you do not see lines but edges (such as where the box ends and the background begins). Although you do not literally see lines you can depict exactly what you do see by using lines. Light and shade can be represented by the skilful use of lines. Known as *chiaroscuro*, this technique gives form and depth to the drawing, which, though only two-dimensional, appears to the eye to be in relief (that is, standing out from the surface).

An important element, if your drawing is to be convincing, is the ability to suggest foreshortening. A

113

famous and very effective World War I recruitment poster, captioned 'Your Country Needs You!' shows Lord Kitchener pointing a finger directly ahead. No matter how far to either side of the poster the viewer moves, that commanding finger still points directly at the viewer! This dramatic effect is achieved by making the arm appear shorter and the hand bigger in relation to the head – just as it would if Lord Kitchener was really standing before the viewer and pointing at the viewer in person.

Foreshortening is really part of the principle of perspective, which is the art of representing objects as they appear to the eye from different viewpoints. You must have noticed, when standing on a bridge and looking along railway lines or a motorway, that the tracks or carriageways appear to meet in the distance? While you know perfectly well that telegraph poles in a line are really the same size, your eye persists in telling you that the pole nearest to you is both taller and fatter than those farther away!

These everyday examples underline the importance of an awareness of perspective. Develop the technique of perspective drawing by practising constantly. One simple and very useful exercise is to draw a box from as many different angles as possible.

Figure-drawing demands a basic knowledge of anatomy (the structure of the human body). It is well worth buying a good anatomy book, which will repay study and remain a useful source of reference.

Draw from life as much as possible. Try sketching the model in different poses and observe how muscles are thrown into relief when under tension.

The need for discipline in your drawing cannot be too strongly stressed. Indeed, until you have mastered the technique of drawing it is unwise to take the next step to painting. Many effects – clouds and seascapes, for instance – will be wholly dependent on the skill and ability to handle perspective you have acquired while learning to draw.

It is an excellent idea to keep a sketchbook permanently with you, not only to record figures, objects and places but also to note details you may need when later incorporating sketches into finished illustrations or paintings.

Water-colour painting
Whatever your first choice of subject – simple still life (fruit,

114

Drawing a box from many angles helps develop perspective

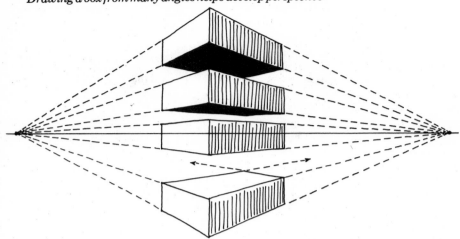

flowers, even vegetables) or that most popular of all water-colour subjects, landscape painting – you will need to equip yourself with a few basic items. The most essential are:

drawing board (size A3 or A4)
block paints (good quality, in box or tin with mixing trays)
water-colour paints in tubes
water-colour brushes
water-colour paper (experiment to find which type suits you best)
charcoal or soft pencils (2B, 3B or 4B)
soft rubber
sponge
blotting-paper
two bottles of water
drawing-pins or clips

For landscape painting, you will need also an easel, folding or telescopic, and a stool or folding camp-seat.

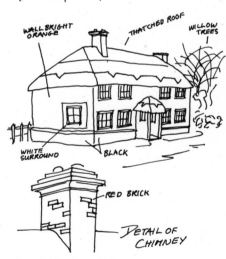

A typical sketchbook page

Your supply of paints (contents of paint-box plus tubes) should include the following colours: light yellow, middle cadmium, yellow ochre, orange madder, vermilion, light red, crimson lake, Indian red, ultramarine, cobalt, Prussian blue,

115

A home-made brush case

emerald, pale green, raw umber, burnt umber, and black or dark grey. Experiment with mixing these basic colours for a greater range. (For example:
ultramarine + crimson lake = violet; Prussian blue + emerald = viridian.) Remember that, in general, red and yellow shades give a warm effect while blues and greens convey a cool quality.

Brushes should be carefully looked after. They are best kept in a case, or in a home-made wallet (flaps at both ends will protect the points and elastic bands can be used to hold the brushes in position).

It is generally accepted that the best time of day for painting

outdoors is the afternoon, when the sun is past its height and the view is broken up into areas of light and shading. Many landscape artists prefer the daylight of spring, autumn or winter to that of high summer, which is often garish, flat and lacking in atmosphere.

The easel should be capable of being tilted horizontally (to prevent uncontrolled running of colour-washes), and should be adjustable in height to a sitting or standing working position. Your paper should be securely fixed to the board by means of drawing pins or clips. Charcoal and pencils are used to sketch in essential outlines in the first stages but do learn to draw with the brush, too.

116

Once you are comfortably settled, with the right equipment, try to construct your picture in the following sequence:

1   **Lightly indicate the outlines;**
2   **Begin with the dark colours;**
3   **Add the middle tones;**
4   **Add the light tones;**
5   **Pull the picture together by adding light or dark, washing away or pushing back areas, as necessary.**

Perhaps the most essential requirement in all water-colour painting is the ability to lay a flat wash successfully. You can practise this technique by mixing a pale colour (say, for the sky) with plenty of water and quickly sweeping a brushful from left to right across the top of your paper: this allows the colour to settle gently downwards. (Do not slope the board too steeply or the wash will run down too quickly.) While the first wash is still wet, mix a stronger tone of the same colour using slightly less water (it should still be very fluid) and run a brushful across under the first wash. This allows the colours to merge naturally.

Continue with washes, varying the strength of the colours, until you have a satisfactory sky. Let the final wash almost dry, then run in the first of a darker colour for mountains or distant landscape, with peaks or church spire piercing the lowest sky-wash.

This is the basic technique of water-colour painting. Practice will soon teach you how to achieve the exact effect you desire. All kinds of satisfying effect are possible, from the gentle haze of a misty landscape to the spectacular industrial scene, with belching chimneys and the red glow of furnaces. Dramatic results can be obtained by sweeping a sponge across part of a wet wash. The sponge can also be used to remove washes, or to spot out unsatisfactory patches. Blotting-paper, too, is effective when dabbed gently on a wet wash. And you might experiment with wetting the paper before you start work and allowing it nearly to dry before you apply the first colour-wash.

The secret is restraint: don't overwork the washes or attempt to touch up here and there. Do less, rather than more, to gain the desired result: for example, it is enough to let the paper show through, when you want to show white clouds, or snow. The overall effect should be clean, translucent and fresh – so remember to use clean water and to clean your brushes between colour-washes.

A final thought: painting that lacks the touch of emotion and individual creativity is not art. Never attempt to imitate the photographer – try, instead, to put something of yourself into the picture. (Though remember, with painting as with any other art, only when you have learned the rules can you break them!)

Anything worth doing brings its share of disappointment and frustration. If you persevere with your technique and practise your art, however, you will soon find yourself doing just what the title of this article suggests – drawing and painting for pleasure!

HISTORY

Major Historical Events

A world chronology of major events
Prehistory spans the time from when the world was formed until man began to write. Rocks, fossils and artifacts alone tell the story of these early times, until someone between 5000 to 4000 BC when recorded history began.

4000–3000 BC	Foundation of Susa (today called Sousse, in Tunisia). Civilization well established in Sumeria. Cuneiform writing introduced. Start of civilization in Egypt, where some early pyramids are built and a first calendar compiled.
3000–2000 BC	The great Egyptian Empire dominates this period, which includes the Great Pyramid age.
2000–1000 BC	Flourishing civilizations in Mesopotamia, Crete (the Minoans), Ugarit (North Syria), and the spread of the Phoenicians with their sea-power and trade. The Jews are in bondage in Egypt, followed by their exodus and invasion of Palestine.
1000–900 BC	Beginning of the Chou Dynasty in China. Kingdom of David and Solomon. Achaeans occupy Greece.
900–800 BC	The Greek city-states make their appearance. The Assyrians begin to record events chronologically.
800–700 BC	Rome founded. Period of the great Hebrew prophets. Southern Italy colonized by Greeks.
700–600 BC	The rise and fall of the Assyrian Empire. Destruction of Nineveh.
600–500 BC	The Athenians receive their laws from Solon. Buddha (died 480) teaches in India, and Confucius (died 479) in China.
500–400 BC	Great Age of Greece, with Pericles in power, the Parthenon under construction, and such outstanding figures as Aeschylus, Phidias, Herodotus, Euripides and Sophocles.
400–300 BC	The Gauls occupy Rome. Philip II of Macedon defeats the Greek city-states. After his assassination, he is succeeded by Alexander who defeats the Persians, captures Tyre, and occupies Egypt and the Punjab.
300–200 BC	Rise of Rome, with colonial expansion along the west coast of the Mediterranean. Hannibal challenges the power of Rome and is finally defeated in 207. The kingdom of Ch'in conquers all Chinese lands and, in 214, the Great Wall of China is completed, by joining together a number of existing walls.
200–100 BC	Roman Empire grows steadily across the eastern Mediterranean coast, and into Asia and Africa; Carthage is destroyed in 146. China also spreads her power and control.
100 BC–AD 1	Julius Caesar conquers Gaul and mounts expeditions to Britain in 55 and 54. Following the assassination of Caesar in 44, Octavian triumphs over all his adversaries and becomes Emperor Augustus

119

and supreme ruler of the Roman Empire. The birth of Jesus Christ marks the end of this century; the year 6 is often reckoned to be the actual year of His Nativity at Bethlehem.

AD 1–100 Crucifixion of Jesus Christ, circa 29, following which the Christian message is carried far afield in Europe. Roman expansion continues and includes the conquest of Britain. An eruption of Mt Vesuvius destroys Pompeii in 79. Expedition from China reaches the Persian Gulf in 97.

AD 100–200 The accession of Hadrian, in 197, sees the Roman Empire commanding more power and territory than at any other time; by the end of the century Rome's decline begins.

AD 200–300 In 212, Rome confers citizenship on every free inhabitant of its Empire. China suffers the first of many invasions which last over a period of 300 years and her power and control begin to decline.

AD 300–400 The decline of the Roman Empire gathers momentum until in 395, on the death of Emperor Theodosius the Great, it is divided into East and West.

AD 400–500 The collapse of Rome, in 476, follows the invasion of Spain by the Visigoths, raids into Gaul and Italy by Attila the Hun, and the pillaging of Rome itself by Vandals in 455.

AD 500–600 The Byzantines reconquer North Africa and, later in 552, Italy. Christianity continues to spread. A mission is founded at Iona by St Columba (543) and St Augustine crosses the sea to Kent (597). Muhammad is born in 570.

AD 600–700 The rise of the T'ang Dynasty in China introduces system of administration which is destined to last for some 1,300 years. Beginnings of Islamic expansion in 622; Arabia entirely Muslim by the time of Muhammad's death in 632, followed by the capture of Jerusalem (638), Persia (641), Alexandria (643) and Carthage (698). The Slavs completed their occupation of the Balkans by 650.

AD 700–800 Muslim occupation of southern Spain. Beginning of the wide-flung raids and settlements by the Vikings. At the century's end, Charlemagne is crowned as Holy Roman Emperor.

AD 800–900 Following the death of Charlemagne, in 814, and the break-up of his empire, the Muslims seize much of southern Italy. The Vikings scourge many lands, from England and France to Russia. In eastern Europe the first Bulgar Empire is founded and the Magyars reach Hungary, whilst in the west Alfred the Great brings stability to much of England.

AD 900–1000 The century starts with Ghana's powerful empire in west Africa. Norsemen continue to dominate the seas around Europe, and discover both Greenland and North America (Leif Ericsson in 1000). Many rulers of northern Europe accept Christianity, including kings of Denmark, Poland, Kiev and Sweden.

AD 1000–1100 Rise of Norman power in western Europe, particularly in Italy, and then in England, after the conquest in 1066; Domesday Book compiled in 1086. The Turks take Jerusalem in 1075 but the city falls again during the First Crusade in 1099.

AD 1100–1200 A century of crusades to Palestine. The third of these is led by the kings of England and France and the Holy Roman Emperor, Frederick Barbarossa. The Mediterranean becomes an important centre of trade. In 1161 explosives are used in battles during internal wars in China.

AD 1200–1300 The period of Mongol power across much of Asia, beginning with the proclamation of Temujin as Gengiz Khan in 1206; the Golden Horde sweep through Russia in 1237 and reach central Europe four years later. China ruled by Kublai Khan in 1260. The signing of the Magna Carta by King John, in England, leads to the establishment of the first real Parliament in 1265 by Simon de Montfort. Crusades to the Holy Land come to an end with the fall of Acre in 1291.

AD 1300–1400 Hundred Years' War, between England and France, begins in 1338. The Black Death appears in Europe in 1348 and sweeps westward from country to country.

AD 1400–1500 Joan of Arc inspires the French in their war with England. She is burnt at the stake in 1439. With the capture of Constantinople by the Turks the East Roman Empire comes to an end (1453). Printing from movable type is introduced in Germany (1454); Caxton operates his press in 1476 at Westminster. In 1492 the Spaniards finally oust the Muslims from their land. The age of great explorations and discoveries begins in 1488 with the rounding of the Cape of Good Hope by Diaz; Christopher Columbus discovers the West Indies in 1492; John Cabot finds Newfoundland in 1497; Amerigo Vespucci maps part of South America's coast in 1499; and Pedro Cabral discovers Brazil in 1500.

AD 1500–1600 Start of the Reformation in 1517, as Martin Luther openly renounces Roman Catholicism; Henry VIII of England breaks away in 1534. Another century of momentous seaborne discoveries and the foundation of trade and settlements all over the globe by such great navigators as Balboa, Magellan, Drake and Raleigh. Spain's threat to England is removed by the defeat of the Armada in 1588, and her hold over the Low Countries is broken by the rebellion of the Dutch people.

AD 1600–1700 Union of England and Scotland in 1603. Peak of Shakespeare's enormous contribution to world drama. Thirty Years' War commences in 1618. The Pilgrim Fathers colonize New England in 1620. English Civil War begins in 1642; Cromwell becomes Protector in 1653. Great advances in the field of science, dominated by such leading names as Galileo and Newton.

AD 1700–1800 A century of wars and revolutions, both in Europe and in other areas of the world which are being competitively colonized by the great European powers. In 1701 the War of the Spanish Succession breaks out; in 1756 the Seven Years' War begins; in 1775 the American War of Independence starts; and in 1789 the French Revolution starts, leading to the rise of Napoleon Bonaparte and the wars resulting from his military campaigns. Robert Clive succeeds in defeating Indian uprisings and finally establishes British rule throughout India. Industrial and commercial advances, particularly in textiles, take place in Britain; whilst in Europe outstanding philosophers include Spinoza, Descartes, Diderot, Voltaire, Kant and Goethe; and great composers such as J.S. Bach, Handel, Mozart and Beethoven.

AD **1800–1900**   Early years of the century are dominated by the Napoleonic Wars, ending with the French Emperor's defeat at Waterloo in 1815. Later, Britain and her empire grow to an immense size and strength, whilst many countries merge into their modern form, such as Germany, Greece and Italy, and others become independent, notably the South American republics. As well as a series of colonial conflicts in Africa and Asia, three important wars take place: the Crimea War (1854), the American Civil War (1861–5), and the Franco-Prussian War (1870). The 19th century is also noted for the industrial revolution and the development of new kinds of machinery, equipment and methods of transport. Towards the end of the century, major social reforms gradually ease the misery and poverty of working people, and trade unions are granted recognition. Culturally, the period sees the appearance of a host of eminent composers and authors, many of the former being German or Austrian, and of the latter British. Great international undertakings include the building of important canals: Suez (1869), Manchester (1894) and Kiel (1895).

AD **1900–**   The pace of scientific investigation and technological advancement accelerates enormously: motor-driven road transport; conquest of the air and space; radio and television; modern methods of heating and lighting; devices for the mass production of a vast range of products – all these, and many more, are basically 20th century achievements. Despite wonderful advances in medical knowledge and skill human suffering has probably been on a greater scale than in any previous century as a result of the two World Wars (1914–18 and 1939–45), and the political upheavals and minor conflicts arising out of them. Some particularly outstanding dates in a variety of fields are: 1903, Orville and Wilbur Wright make the first controlled flight in a machine heavier than air; 1909, Henry Ford begins the era of low-price cars with his Model T chassis; 1917, revolution breaks out in Russia; 1926, General Strike in Britain; 1933, Hitler appointed German Chancellor; 1945, atomic bombs dropped on Hiroshima and Nagasaki, Japan; 1945, birth of the United Nations; 1947, Independence of India and Pakistan; 1949, North Atlantic Treaty becomes effective, and the Chinese People's Republic is established; 1969, landing of the first men on the Moon by the Americans in Apollo rocket.

The Seven Wonders of the Ancient World

The pyramids of Egypt	The biggest, the Great Pyramid of Cheops, was originally 147 m (481 ft) high and 230 m (756 ft) square at the base. The oldest pyramid is that of Zoser, at Saggara, built about 3000 BC.
The Hanging Gardens of Babylon	These were terraced gardens adjoining the palace of Nebuchadnezzar near Bagdad. They were irrigated by means of large storage tanks on the uppermost terraces.
The tomb of Mausolus	This was built by the king's widow at Halicarnassus, in Asia Minor, about 350 BC. Our word 'mausoleum' is derived from it.
The temple of Diana at Ephesus	This was a great marble temple erected about 480 BC.
The Colossus of Rhodes	Set up about 280 BC, this bronze statue of Apollo, around 32 m (105 ft) high, stood with legs astride the harbour entrance at Rhodes.
The statue of Zeus at Olympia	Made of marble inlaid with ivory and gold, this statue was made by the sculptor Phidias about 430 BC.
The Pharos of Alexandria	Built about 250 BC, this was a marble watchtower and lighthouse on the island of Pharos in Alexandria Harbour.

Famous Queens

ADELAIDE (1792–1849) In 1818, Adelaide married the Duke of Clarence, later to reign as King William IV of Great Britain. She was a devoted wife and succeeded in raising standards of morality at Court to a considerable degree. All Queen Adelaide's children died as infants, and it was as a result of this that Victoria succeeded King William.

ALEXANDRA (of England) (1844–1826) A daughter of King Christian IX of Denmark, Alexandra married Queen Victoria's son Edward, then Prince of Wales, in 1863. She became Queen when her husband succeeded to the throne, as King Edward VII, in 1901. Greatly admired by her people, Alexandra devoted much of her time to charities and is well-known for the 'Rose Day' named after her. Her eldest son, the Duke of Clarence, died in 1892, and it was George, her second son, who eventually succeeded Edward VII to the throne.

ALEXANDRA (of Russia) (1872–1918) Married Tsar Nicholas II (Nikolai) in 1894 and became Tsarina. Alexandra had five children – Alexei, Olga, Tatiana, Maria and Anastasia. Aloof, withdrawn, stiff and haughty, she seldom carried out her public duties as empress, and was consequently unpopular. One reason for this was her constant anxiety about her son, Tsarevitch Alexei, who suffered from haemophilia and was often close to death. Alexandra befriended the mysterious and sinister 'holy man' Rasputin, who claimed to be able to cure Alexei's disease, inherited from his mother's side of the family. She perished with her husband and children, probably by being shot on the orders of Russia's revolutionary government in July, 1918.

ANNE (1665–1714) A daughter of King James II and cousin of King William III (of Orange), Anne became queen of Great Britain, in her own right, in 1702. Last of the Stuart monarchs, she was married to Prince George of Denmark, but all their children died young. Her reign is noted for the number of men of letters living at that time (sometimes termed Britain's Augustan Age), and also for the great victories won by the Duke of Marlborough (John Churchill) during the War of the Spanish Succession. Anne made the Duke's wife, Sarah, her friend and favourite for a long period; as the queen lacked self-confidence and seldom showed any initiative, Sarah Churchill wielded enormous influence at Court, until she eventually fell out of favour.

ANNE BOLEYN (1507–36) The second wife of King Henry VIII and mother of the future Queen Elizabeth I (q.v.). Formerly maid-in-waiting to Catherine of Aragon (q.v.), Anne enthusiastically supported her future husband's introduction of the Reformation, but her insolence caused a bitterly hostile faction to grow up. Henry eventually became disappointed at her inability to provide him with a male heir to the throne, and when her enemies accused Anne of adultery, she was beheaded on a charge of treason.

ANNE OF CLEVES (1515–57) King Henry VIII's fourth wife, Anne was chosen principally for political reasons because her brother, the Duke of Cleves, ruled a territory occupying a very important position on the lower Rhine. Henry, however, also looked forward to the marriage as he had been told that Anne was beautiful. Too late, he discovered that his new wife was exceedingly plain (she was sometimes

Queen Anne

Catherine II

referred to as 'the Flemish Mare'), and
soon took steps to divorce her.
Provided with a pension in 1540, Anne
seems to have accepted the situation
without rancour and settled down to a
quiet life in England.

BEATRIX (1938–   ) Eldest daughter
of ex-Queen Juliana (q.v.) and queen of
the Netherlands since her mother's
abdication, on retirement, in 1980.
Born at Soestdijk Palace, she spent the
war years abroad with her family, and
then, as Crown Princess, married Claus
von Amsberg in 1966. She has three
sons, Willem-Alexander (1967), Johan
Friss (1968) and Constantijn (1969).

BOADICEA (or BOUDICCA)
(AD 62) Queen of the Iceni, an East
Anglian people, Boadicea led a revolt
against Roman rule in England, largely
because of the illtreatment of her
family, following the death of her
husband. The Celtic army, led by
Queen Boadicea, stormed
Camulodunum (Colchester),
Verulamium (St Albans) and
Londinium (London) in AD 61,
reportedly killing some 70,000 Romans.
The governor, Suetonius, however,
soon brought up his trained Roman
legions and defeated Boadicea's brave
but ill-trained Britons. The queen

avoided being captured by the Romans
by taking poison in AD 62.

CATHERINE OF ARAGON
(1485–1536) An attractive young lady of
24 when King Henry made her his first
wife in 1509, Catherine of Aragon was
described as being 'of a lively and
gracious disposition'. Moreover, she
proved to be a devoted wife, and an
accomplished dancer, musician and
English-speaker. After 18 years of
marriage, however, Henry, already
disturbed that Catherine's only living
child was a girl – later to become
Queen Mary I (q.v.) – and worried
about the succession, became
passionately fond of Anne Boleyn
(q.v.), who, however, refused to be his
mistress. Henry finally succeeded in
divorcing Catherine in 1533.

CATHERINE THE GREAT (1729–96)
Empress Catherine II of Russia was
responsible for the considerable
expansion of her country's boundaries
as a result of the victories of her
famous generals, Potemkin and
Suvarov. By the treaty of Jassy, she
obtained the fortress of Oczakov, and
the region between the rivers Dnieper
and Bug, on the Black Sea. She
succeeded her husband, Peter III, when
he was murdered and was a capable

Catherine de Medici

Elizabeth I

ruler for some time. Later, however, Catherine nearly ruined Russia with the costs of her licentious excesses, and became known as the 'Semiramis of the North'.

CATHERINE HOWARD (?–1542)
Unlucky fifth wife of King Henry VIII, whom he married in 1540 immediately following the divorce from Anne of Cleves (q.v.). Two years later, the king had Catherine beheaded.

CATHERINE DE MEDICI (1519–89)
The wife of Henry II of France, Catherine was a woman who commanded great power and influence, particularly when acting as regent during the minority of Charles IX, her son. Two more of her sons became kings of France – Francis II and Henry III. Catherine had a great appreciation of literature and art, but she was a cruel woman. Her hostility to the French Protestants (or Huguenots) led to the infamous Bartholomew Massacre in Paris, on St Bartholomew's Day, 1572, when she organized the slaughter of a large number of them.

CATHERINE PARR (1512–48) King
Henry VIII's sixth and last wife, whom he married in 1543. Catherine, the widow of Lord Latimer, made an excellent wife for the king during his last four years.

CLEOPATRA (69–30 BC) The daughter
of Ptolemy XII of Egypt, Cleopatra became joint ruler with a younger brother, Ptolemy XIII, at the age of 17. She later lost her authority and withdrew to Syria. Supported by Julius Caesar, Cleopatra succeeded in regaining the throne, Ptolemy XIII having been killed in the war and his successor, Ptolemy XIV, put to death by poisoning on her orders. Cleopatra then lived in Rome with Caesar until his assassination in 44 BC, when she returned to Egypt and declared her son by Caesar, Caesarion, joint monarch with her.

During the wars that followed Caesar's death, Cleopatra became the mistress of Mark Antony, but Octavian (later known as Augustus) declared war on them. After their naval defeat at Actium, in 31 BC, Antony committed suicide. Cleopatra failed to win Augustus over with her charms and, to avoid the ignominy of capture by the Romans, ended her life by poisoning, traditionally by means of an asp bite on her bosom. So, at only 39 years of age, this imperious, ambitious and intellectual queen died.

ELIZABETH I (1533–1603) Protestant Elizabeth followed her Roman Catholic half-sister Mary I (q.v.) to the throne of England in 1558. Intensely patriotic, courageous and strong-minded, she exerted a powerful influence on her country and, indeed, Europe generally. Elizabeth ruled well and presided over a period when England became a great power at sea, established colonies in the New World, and also shone in the literary sphere, notably because of the works of Shakespeare. Queen Elizabeth never married but had a number of Court favourites.

ELIZABETH II (1926–   ) The present queen of Great Britain and Northern Ireland – and monarch of several Commonwealth nations, besides acting as Head of the Commonwealth – Elizabeth came to the throne in 1952. She married her consort, Prince Philip, Duke of Edinburgh, in 1947; they have three sons, Charles, Prince of Wales (1948), Prince Andrew (1960) and Prince Edward (1964), and one daughter, Princess Anne (1950).

EUGENIE (1826–1920) As the wife of Napoleon III, Eugenie kept a brilliant Court but was forced to escape, in disguise, from Paris to England during the Franco–Prussian War. Joined by her husband, she lived in exile at Chislehurst, Kent, until his death, and then at Farnborough, in Hampshire.

ISABELLA OF CASTILE (1451–1504) She reigned over a united Spain jointly with her husband, Ferdinand V, and over a period of 30 years saw the country attain great power and authority. During their reign, Spaniards discovered America and began to establish an empire there. They also succeeded in ridding Spain of the Moors (Muslims).

JANE GREY (1537–54) The unfortunate daughter of the Duke of Suffolk and great-granddaughter of King Henry VII, Lady Jane Grey became the tool of power-seekers. She was declared queen of England upon the death of Edward VI, to maintain the Protestant succession. Queen Mary I (q.v.), the rightful monarch, soon vanquished the Queen Jane faction by ousting her sixteen-year-old rival from the throne after a reign of only ten days. Jane and her husband, Lord Guildford Dudley, were executed some six months later.

JANE SEYMOUR (?–1537) Within a few days of the execution of Anne Boleyn (q.v.), King Henry VIII married Jane Seymour (1536), his third wife. She bore him his long-awaited son, Edward, in 1537 but unfortunately died within a few days of the birth.

JEZEBEL (died c.843 BC) The daughter of the priest-king Ethbaal, ruler of the cities of Tyre and Sidon, Jezebel married the ruler of Israel, King Ahab (ruled c.874–853 BC). She persuaded him to introduce the worship of the Tyrian god, Baal-Melkart, and tried to destroy anyone who opposed her. She had most of the prophets of Yahweh killed, and thus incurred the wrath of the prophet Elijah.

After Ahab had died in battle with the Syrians, Jezebel lived on for another ten years and her son Jehoram ruled. Elijah's successor, Elisha the prophet, had a military commander called Jehu anointed as king of Israel which led to a civil war. Jehu killed Jehoram and then went to Jezebel's palace. Jezebel, expecting him, adorned herself for the occasion and taunted him from a window. Jehu ordered her servants to throw her out of the window. Her body was never buried, as had been prophesied, because dogs devoured most of her remains.

JOSEPHINE (1763–1814) Napoleon Bonaparte married the widowed Josephine, formerly the wife of Vicomte Alexandre Beauharnais, in

Josephine

Maria Theresa

1796. She became empress when her husband was made Emperor Napoleon I of France in 1804. In 1809, however, Napoleon divorced Josephine, and it was her successor, Maria Louise, who bore him the son he desired to maintain the succession.

JULIANA (1909–   ) The daughter of Queen Wilhelmina (q.v.) of the Netherlands, Juliana succeeded her mother in 1948, when Wilhelmina decided to abdicate and retire from public life. Regarded with great affection by the Dutch people, Juliana helped her country enormously through the years of reconstruction after World War II. She followed the example of her mother by abdicating in 1980, in favour of her daughter Beatrix (q.v.), and went into well-earned retirement.

MARGRETHE II (1940–   ) She succeeded her father, King Frederick IX, in 1972, inheriting the throne of Denmark by virtue of a special act passed in 1953. It revised the country's law pertaining to royal succession and entitled her to become the first woman to reign over the country as monarch in her own right. Much travelled, Queen Margrethe was educated at Danish universities, Cambridge, the

London School of Economics and the Sorbonne, in Paris; her particular interest is archaeology.

MARIA THERESA (1717–80) This famous empress succeeded to the throne of Austria and its wide dominions in 1740 as a result of a special sanction executed by her father, Charles VI. Being a woman of remarkable ability and great strength of character, Maria Theresa succeeded, with the aid of allies such as Britain, in defeating those who challenged her right to rule during the War of the Austrian Succession. During her reign she did an enormous amount to enhance the prestige of the Austrian Empire.

MARIE ANTOINETTE (1755–93) The ill-fated daughter of Emperor Francis I of Austria, Marie Antoinette married King Louis XVI of France. She greatly enjoyed the gaiety of the French Court and became hated by the downtrodden mass of French people. Marie Antoinette was guillotined during the French Revolution which began in 1789.

MARY I (1516–58) Succeeding her half-brother, Edward VI, in 1553, this elder daughter of King Henry VIII reversed

Marie Antoinette

Nefertiti

her father's establishment of Protestantism in England. Almost a fanatical Roman Catholic, Queen Mary imprisoned, persecuted and burned at the stake hundreds of reformers whom she regarded as heretics. She married Philip of Spain in 1554 but had no children.

MARY II (1662–94) A daughter of King James II, Mary ruled Britain jointly with her husband and cousin, William IV (a Dutch prince known as William of Orange). She came to the throne in 1689 after her father fled into exile.

MARY STUART (1542–87) Mary, Queen of Scots, returned to Scotland after the death of her husband, the dauphin of France, and was recognized for some time as queen. Her marriage to Lord Darnley ended in his murder by Bothwell who then married Mary. The Scottish nobles were angered by these events and rebelled against the queen, who was forced to abdicate and eventually fled to England to seek Elizabeth I's (q.v.) protection. Elizabeth, however, imprisoned the exiled queen and, 19 years later, had her beheaded on a charge of conspiracy.

MATILDA (or Maud) (1102–67) After the death of her husband, Henry V

(Holy Roman Emperor), Matilda returned to England in 1125 and married Geoffrey of Anjou three years later. On the death of her father, King Henry I, in 1135, Matilda struggled to assert her claim to the throne, based upon the barons' pledge to recognize her as Henry's sole legitimate child. She lost the civil war to Stephen in 1142 and fled. Matilda's son, however, inherited the throne, as Henry II, on the death of King Stephen.

NEFERTITI (14th century BC) She was the wife of Pharaoh Akhnaton, 18th Dynasty King of Egypt. Akhnaton declared that the only god, Aton, was visible as the Sun's disk. He quarrelled with the priest of Amun, at Thebes, and then removed the capital to a new site, Tel-el-Amarna, and dedicated it to Aton. A fine sculptured head of Queen Nefertiti was discovered at Tel-el-Amarna and is now at the West Berlin Museum.

SHEBA, QUEEN OF (10th century BC) The Queen of Sheba ruled over a land in southern Arabia, now known as Yemen. It was rich by virtue of its control over an important trade route, particularly that of incense. The story of the Queen of Sheba's visit to King Solomon, the third king of Israel, is

Queen Victoria

Queen Wilhelmina

related in the Bible (1 Kings 10) and in the Koran. Known to Arab writers as Bilqis, she is reputed to have been the founder of the royal house of Ethiopia which was recently overthrown.

SOPHIA (or SOFIA) (1938–) The consort of King Juan Carlos I of Spain, whom she married in 1962. She has one son, Crown Prince Felipe (1968), and two daughters, Princess Elena (1963) and Princess Christina (1965). Sophia is the daughter of late King Paul of Greece and Queen Frederica; her brother is Constantine XII, ex-king of the Hellenes. A linguist, Queen Sophia has studied in Greece and Madrid, and at Salem College, Baden, in Germany.

VICTORIA (1819–1901) Queen of Great Britain and Ireland, and Empress of India, Victoria was only 18 when she came to the throne in 1837. She succeeded her uncle, King William IV. During her long and illustrious reign, the strength and power of Britain and

the Empire increased enormously. Queen Victoria married Prince Albert of Saxe-Coburg-Gotha in 1840 and was criticized for virtually retiring from public life for many years after her consort's death in 1861. However, the Queen's influence and authority continued to be felt throughout the nation. Her closing years were marked with great public respect for her, and with the celebrations of her golden and diamond jubilees.

WILHELMINA (1880–1962) She became queen of the Netherlands in 1890 but her mother, Queen Emma, acted as regent until 1898. She reigned until 1948 (from overseas during World War II) and was held in great esteem by the Dutch people. After re-establishing the monarchy in the Netherlands following the war, Wilhelmina decided to abdicate and retired with the title of Princess of the Netherlands. She was succeeded by her daughter, Queen Juliana (q.v.).

MYTHOLOGY

Anubis

Hathar

Isis

Ra

DICTIONARY OF MYTHOLOGY

ANCIENT EGYPTIAN MYTHOLOGY

Ammon or **Amun** The chief god of upper Egypt, later identified with the Sun god Ra.

Anubis The son of Nephthys and Ra (or Osiris), his duty was to weigh the soul of a deceased person. If the soul was below standard it was eaten by a horrible monster. Anubis was represented with the head of a jackal.

Apis, or **Hapi** A sacred black bull worshipped at Memphis. The spirit of the god Osiris was thought to be living in the bull.

Atum Originally a local deity of Heliopolis, the Atum myth became merged with that of the Sun god Ra, giving rise to the deity Atum-Ra.

Bast or **Bastet**, Cat-headed goddess, the daughter of Isis. She was the goddess of the city of Bubastis in lower Egypt and of the kindly rays of the Sun as opposed to the fierce, harmful rays whose goddess was Sekhmet, Bast's sister.

Bes or **Bisu** God of recreation, represented as a dwarf with a large head, goggle eyes, protruding tongue, bow legs and bushy tail. Bes was often associated with children and childbirth.

Hathor or **Athor** Goddess of the sky and wife of Horus also considered to be the goddess of festivity, dance and love. She became identified with Isis. Hathor was sometimes represented with the head of a cow.

Horus The son of Osiris and Isis, the god of light who overcame darkness – he was believed to be the life-giving power of the Sun. A scorpion sent by the wicked god Set stung him to death, but he was revived by Isis with the help of the god Thoth.

Isis The sister-wife of Osiris and mother of Horus, Isis was the goddess of the Earth and of the Moon. She also ruled in the underworld where she meted out rewards and punishments.

Keb or **Seb** A son of Shu and Tefnut (or of Ra), Keb was the god of the Earth and its vegetation. He was represented with the head of a goose.

Mut or **Maut** The wife of Ra or Amun and called the mother of the gods and mistress of the sky. Mut was represented with the head of a lioness or of a vulture (the symbol of maternity).

Nephthys or **Nebt-Het** A goddess of the dead, sister of Isis and wife of Isis' brother Set.

Nut Daughter of Shu and Tefnut, Nut was married to her own brother, Keb. She became the mother of Osiris, Isis, Set and Nephthys. Like Mut, she was called the mother of the gods, and was associated with childbirth and nursing.

Osiris Son of Keb and Nut, brother-husband of Isis and father of Horus, Osiris was the principle of Good. His foe was his brother Set, the god of evil and darkness who finally killed him and cut his body into 14 pieces. Isis collected all the pieces except one and buried them. According to one myth the pieces joined together again and the body became alive. Thus Osiris became the god of resurrection and life eternal, the lord of the underworld and judge of the dead.

Ptah, **Neph**, **Num** or **Nu** The maker of the Sun, the Moon and the Earth and everything in or on it including men and gods. He was represented as a potter at his wheel, often with a ram's head.

Ra or **Re** God of the Sun, Ra was represented as a hawk, or as a man with a hawk's head, on top of which was the red disc of the Sun or a snake (symbol of supreme power). His emblem was the scarab beetle.

Sekhmet or **Sekhet** Wife of Ptah and sister of Bast, Sekhmet was the fierce goddess of war and destroyer of the enemies of the Sun god, Ra. She was considered to be the eye of Ra and was placed as the uraeus serpent on Ra's head. Sekhmet was represented as a lioness or as a woman with a lioness' head on which was placed the solar disc and uraeus.

Set or **Seth** Regarded as either the brother or son of Osiris. Once a sky god, represented by a falcon he was both a partner and rival of Horus. When the cult of Osiris gained in popularity the myth developed that Seth was his murderer.

Shu Twin brother and husband of Tefnut, Shu was the god of light, air and the supporter of the sky.

Tefnut Twin sister of Shu and mother of Keb, Tefnut was the goddess of the waters above the heavens.

Thoth The god of learning, wisdom and of writing. In the underworld, Thoth kept accounts of the weight of souls, handing them to Osiris who judged them. Thoth was also god of the Moon, at which time he was represented with a crescent and disc. He was usually depicted with the head of an ibis.

CLASSICAL MYTHOLOGY

Acheron The river across which the dead are carried by Charon.

Achilles A strong and handsome Grecian hero of the Trojan war. One of the legends concerning him was that Thetis, his mother, dropped him in the river Styx as a baby to make him immortal, but she forgot to immerse his heel by which she was holding him. Achilles later died from a death-wound in the heel.

Actaeon A hunter, who was changed into a stag by Artemis because he had seen her bathing.

Adonis A beautiful youth beloved by Aphrodite. Jealous Hephaestus transformed himself into a boar which Adonis followed in the hunt, and the boar killed him.

Aesculapius or **Asclepius** The god of medicine.

Agamemnon Commander in chief of

the Greeks during the Trojan war.

Alcmene Wife of Amphitryon. Zeus, disguised as her husband who was then away on a journey, seduced her. To Alcmene then was born Heracles.

Amazons A race of warlike females said to have come from the Caucasus and to have settled in Asia Minor.

Amphitrite Wife of Poseidon.

Andromeda Daughter of Cepheus, king of Ethiopia, and Cassiopia. She was offered as a sacrifice to a sea monster that was sent by Poseidon to lay waste to the country, but Perseus slew the monster and saved her.

Antigone Daughter of Oedipus. She accompanied her blind father when he was forced to leave Thebes.

Aphrodite The goddess of love and beauty, the daughter of Zeus and a female Titan, Dione.

Apollo Son of Zeus and Leto, twin brother of Artemis. Apollo was the god of music, song and poetry, of agriculture and the pastoral life. Originally he was a god of light, who thus made plants grow and fruits ripen. Apollo never married.

Arachne A maiden who challenged Athena in a test of weaving skill. The girl's work was flawless and the angry Athena changed her into a spider.

Ares The god of war. Ares was the son of Zeus and Hera. He loved, and was beloved by, Aphrodite.

Argonauts Sailors of the ship *Argo* who were the heroes who sailed with Jason to fetch the golden fleece.

Argus The 100-eyed guardian of the cow into which Io, beloved of Zeus, had been transformed by the wrath of Hera.

Ariadne Daughter of Minos, king of Crete, who helped Theseus find his way out of the maze known as the Labyrinth after killing the Minotaur.

Artemis Unmarried daughter of Zeus and Leto, twin-sister of Apollo, goddess of hunting and the Moon. Artemis often sent affliction and death to mankind but sometimes cured or

Athena

alleviated suffering.

Atalanta The most swift-footed of mortals. Atalanta required her suitors to beat her in a foot-race and if they failed they forfeited their lives. A suitor, Melanion, dropped three golden apples given to him by Aphrodite, during his race with Atalanta. Atalanta stopped to pick up the apples and lost the race.

Athena, **Athene** or **Pallas Athena** Unmarried daughter of Zeus and Metis. Before birth Athena swallowed her mother and afterwards sprang from the head of Zeus in complete armour. She was the goddess of wisdom and of war, and the protector of Athens. She was also the goddess of weaving and agriculture.

Atlas A Titan who, along with the other Titans, made war on Zeus. On being conquered he was condemned to hold up the heavens.

Bellerophon Son of the Corinthian king Glaucus, he was sent to kill the monster known as the Chimera, which he did with the help of the winged horse Pegasus.

Callisto A nymph beloved by Zeus who changed her into a she-bear. During a hunt, Hera caused Artemis to slay Callisto whereupon Zeus placed her among the stars.

Cassiopia The mother of Andromeda.

Diana

She also was placed among the stars.

Castor Brother of Pollux. *See* Dioscuri.

Centaurs Half men and half horses, they inhabited Mount Pelion in Thessaly.

Cepheus King of Ethiopia, husband of Cassiopia and father of Andromeda. He was placed among the stars after his death.

Cerberus A monstrous dog with several heads who guarded the entrance of Hades.

Chaos The empty space that existed prior to the creation of the world.

Charon The being usually described as an old man who conveyed the spirits of the dead across the rivers of the underworld in his boat. For this service he was paid with a coin placed in the mouth of every corpse.

Chimera A fire-breathing monster whose body consisted of the fore-parts of a lion, the middle part of a goat and the hind parts of a dragon. She was killed by Bellerophon.

Chiron The wisest of the Centaurs. Hercules accidentally killed Chiron with a poisoned arrow when Chiron was fighting with the other Centaurs. Zeus placed him among the stars as Sagittarius.

Clytemnestra The unfaithful wife of Agamemnon. She murdered her husband on his return from Troy and was killed in revenge by her son Orestes.

Cronus Youngest of the Titans, a son of Ouranus (Heaven) and Gaea (Earth). Cronus dethroned his father and out of the drops of his blood sprang the Gigantes while from the foam gathering around his limbs in the sea Aphrodite was formed.

Cyclops A race of gigantic shepherds in Sicily each of whom had one eye in the centre of his forehead. They devoured human beings. The chief among them, Polyphemus, was blinded by Odysseus.

Daedalus To escape from Minos, king of Crete, Daedalus made wings for his son Icarus and himself which he fastened with wax. Unfortunately Icarus flew too close to the Sun, the wax melted and he fell to his death.

Danaë Daughter of Acrisius, king of Argos, and the mother of Perseus by Zeus. Zeus visited her in a shower of gold while she was imprisoned in a tower by her father.

Daphne A nymph who, pursued by Apollo, prayed for aid and as a result was transformed into a laurel tree.

Demeter or **Cores** A daughter of Cronus and Rhea, sister of Zeus and mother of Persephone. She was protectoress of agriculture and all the fruits of the earth. When her daughter was carried off by Hades she would not allow the earth to produce any fruits. Zeus sent Hermes to fetch Persephone back but she had eaten part of a pomegranate in the lower world and was therefore obliged to spend a third of each year in Hades.

Deucalion Son of Prometheus and king of Phthia in Thessaly. When Zeus decided to destroy mankind because of its iniquity Deucalion and his wife Pyrrha were saved on account of their piety. They built a ship which floated safely on the flood-waters which destroyed the rest of the human race.

Dione A female Titan, beloved by Zeus by whom she became the mother of the godess Aphrodite.

Dionysus The son of Zeus and a maiden, Semele. He was the god of wine.

Dioscuri The twin sons of Zeus, Castor and Pollux. Pollux was immortal but Castor was subject to old age and death. Pollux was allowed by Zeus to share his brother's fate. He lived alternately one day in the underworld and one day in the heavens with the gods. Castor and Pollux appear as stars in the constellation Gemini (The Twins).

Echo A nymph who used to engage Hera's attention by talking to her while Zeus sported with other nymphs. When Hera discovered the trick she punished her by changing her into an echo. Because of her unrequited love for Narcissus, Echo pined away, leaving nothing but her voice.

Electra Daughter of Agamemnon and Clytemnestra, sister of Iphigenia and Orestes. After her mother murdered her father Electra saved the life of Orestes. She incited him to avenge their father's death.

Elysium A happy land where favoured heroes went instead of going through death. Also part of the underworld where the shades of the blessed had their abode.

Endymion A youth of extraordinary beauty who perpetually slept.

Eos Goddess of the dawn.

Eros Son of Aphrodite, and the god of love. He is represented as a small boy, beautiful but wanton, with a bow and arrows.

Eumenides, **Erinyes** *see* the Furies.

Europa Daughter of a Phoenician king whose beauty caught the eye of Zeus. The god changed himself into a bull who was so tame that Europa was tempted to climb upon its back. The bull carried her off as far as Crete where she became the mother of Minos.

Eurydice The wife of Orpheus. He tried, without success, to rescue her from the underworld.

Fates (Moerae) The goddesses of fate, three in number. They are described either as old, hideous women or as grave maidens. One, sometimes all three, carry a spindle and they are said to cut off the thread of life when it comes to an end.

Furies, The (Eumenides, Erinyes) Three avenging deities represented as winged monsters with serpents twined in their hair and blood dripping from their eyes. The Furies lived in the depths of Tartarus. They punished the living and the dead for their crimes.

Gaea or **Ge** The personification of the Earth and the first being that sprang from Chaos. She gave birth to Ouranus (Heaven) and Pontus (Sea), and was the mother of the Titans by Cronus.

Galatea A sea nymph beloved by Polyphemus the Cyclops.

Ganymede The most beautiful of all mortals who was carried off by the gods to fill the cup of Zeus. Ganymede is placed among the stars as Aquarius.

Gigantes Giants who sprang from the blood of the mutilated Ouranus. They had legs like serpents and feet formed of reptiles' heads.

Gorgons Three frightful female creatures, Stheno, Euryale and Medusa. They had wings, claws, enormous teeth and serpents on their heads instead of hair. Medusa alone was mortal. She was once a maiden whom Athena had changed into a Gorgon. Anyone who looked at her was changed to stone.

Graces, The (Charites) Goddesses of fertility, charm and beauty they were daughters of Zeus and Hera. Three in number, their names were Aglaea (Brightness), Euphrosyne (Joyfulness) and Thalia (Bloom).

Hades Son of Cronus and Rhea, brother of Zeus and Poseidon, Hades was god of the underworld and of metals. His wife was Persephone, daughter of Demeter. He stole her from the upper world.

Harpies Wind spirits often represented

as winged maidens or as birdlike monsters with the heads of maidens. The Harpies were said to have snatched away people who had disappeared.

Hebe The goddess of youth, a daughter of Zeus and Hera. She married Heracles after he became a god.

Hecate A goddess of the Moon, the Earth and the underworld and one of the Titans. She is represented with three bodies and three heads. A teacher of sorcery and witchcraft, at night she sent forth phantoms from the underworld.

Helen Daughter of Zeus and Leda, sister of Castor and Pollux and a renowned beauty. She married Menelaus but was seduced by Paris who carried her off to Troy. The Trojan war was the result.

Helios God of the Sun, Helios was the son of Hyperion and Thea and brother of Selene (the Moon) and Eos (Dawn).

Hephaestus The god of fire and of the blacksmith's art, son of Zeus and Hera. He was born lame and weak and so was disliked by his mother who threw him down from Olympus.

Hera A daughter of Cronus and Rhea, sister and wife of Zeus, Hera was goddess of marriage and of the birth of children. Jealous and quarrelsome, she persecuted the children of Zeus born of mortal mothers and hence was the enemy of Dionysus and Heracles among others.

Heracles The most famous Greek legendary hero, Heracles was the son of Zeus and Alcmene and a descendant of Perseus. Zeus swore that the next son born in the line of Perseus should become ruler of Greece but by a trick of Hera another child, Eurystheus, was born first and became king. When Heracles grew up he had to serve him. Eurystheus imposed on Heracles the twelve famous labours, including slaying the Nemean lion, cleansing the Augean stables, fetching the golden apples of the Hesperides and bringing

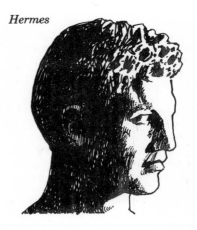

Hermes

back Cerberus from the underworld.

Hermes Son of Zeus and Maia, the daughter of Atlas, Hermes was the messenger of the gods. He himself was the god of prudence, cunning, trickery and theft, the alphabet, numbers, astronomy, music, gymnastics, weights and measures, commerce and riches, and of good luck. He also protected travellers. Hermes is represented with a winged hat, a staff bearing either ribbons or serpents and winged sandles.

Hesperides The guardians of the golden apples which Gaea gave to Hera at her marriage to Zeus.

Hestia A daughter of Cronus and Rhea who swore to remain a virgin. Hestia was the goddess of the fire burning on the hearth.

Horae Daughters of Zeus and Themis, the Horae were goddesses of the seasons.

Hyades Seven nymphs entrusted by Zeus to care for his infant son Dionysus. They were afterwards placed among the stars.

Hydra A gigantic monster with many heads, the centre one being immortal. The destruction of Hydra was one of the 12 labours of Heracles.

Hygiea Daughter or wife of Aesculapius and goddess of health.

Hymen God of marriage, represented

as an extremely handsome youth.

Hyperion A Titan, son of Ouranus and Gaea, father of Helios, Selene and Eos. He was sometimes identified with Helios himself.

Hypnus The god of sleep.

Iapetus A Titan, father of Atlas, Prometheus and Epimetheus.

Icarus The son of Daedalus (*q.v.*).

Io Daughter of the king of Argos. She was changed by Zeus, who loved her, into a cow to hide her from his jealous wife Hera. Hera, undeceived, put her in charge of Argus who was subsequently slain by Hermes at the command of Zeus. Hera then tormented Io with a gadfly which drove her from land to land. Eventually she found rest on the banks of the Nile and bore Zeus a son, Epaphus.

Iphigenia Daughter of Agamemnon and Clytemnestra. Her father killed a hart in a grove sacred to Artemis, angering the goddess who thereupon becalmed the Greek fleet which was about to sail for Troy. To placate Artemis, Iphigenia was offered as a sacrifice to her, but Artemis put a hart in Iphigenia's place and carried the maiden away.

Irene Goddess of peace, one of the Horae.

Iris Personfication of the rainbow, a sister of the Harpies.

Jason Leader of the Argonauts who set off to fetch the golden fleece in the possession of the king of Colchis and which was guarded by a dragon.

Leda Mother of Castor and Pullux, Clytemnestra and Helen. Zeus, the father, visited Leda in the guise of a swan.

Lethe A river in the underworld from which the dead drank to obtain forgetfulness.

Leto Daughter of the Titan Coeus and Phoebe, mother of Apollo and Artemis by Zeus.

Maia A daughter of Atlas and the eldest and most beautiful of the Pleiades sisters. She was the mother of the god Hermes by Zeus.

Medea Daughter of the king of Colchis and skilled in magic. She assisted Jason in obtaining the golden fleece. Medea afterwards became Jason's wife but he deserted her and in revenge she murdered their two children.

Medusa *see* Gorgons.

Menelaus Younger brother of Agamemnon and husband of Helen.

Midas King of Phrygia, renowned for his riches. As a reward for his kindness a satyr agreed to grant him a wish. Midas wished that everything he touched should turn to gold.

Minos The son of Zeus and Europa, and king of Crete. Minos made war against the Athenians and ordered them to send a yearly tribute of seven youths and seven maidens to be fed to the Minotaur.

Minotaur Cretan monster, half man, half bull, kept in the maze called the Labyrinth.

Mnemosyne Memory, the daughter of Ouranus and mother of the Muses by Zeus.

Moerae *see* The Fates.

Morpheus The son of Hypnus and god of dreams.

Muses, The Nine daughters of Zeus and Mnemosyne, goddesses of the different arts and sciences. They were: Clio of history; Euterpe of lyric poetry; Thalia of humorous and idyllic poetry; Melpomene of tragedy; Terpsichore of dance and song; Erato of love poetry and mimicry; Polymnia of sacred poetry; Urania of astronomy, and Calliope of epic poetry.

Narcissus A beautiful youth who fell deeply in love with his own reflection in a pool and pined away. He was changed into the flower that bears his name.

Nemesis Goddess of fertility, and who meted out retribution to mortals for their wrongdoing.

Nymphs Lesser female divinities divided into groups according to the part of nature they were associated with: Oceanides, the oceans; Nereides, the Mediterranean sea; Naiades, fresh water (rivers, lakes and springs); Oreades, mountains and grottoes; Napaeae, glens; gryades and Hamadryades, trees.

Oceanus God of the water which was believed to surround the Earth. He was the husband of Tethys and father of the river gods and water nymphs.

Odysseus Grecian hero of the Trojan war. After the destruction of Troy he set off on a journey full of adventure which is related in Homer's Odyssey.

Oedipus Son of Laius, king of Thebes who, learning from an oracle that he would die by the hands of his own son, exposed Oedipus on a mountainside at birth. The baby, however, was found by a shepherd who reared him as his own son. Oedipus later killed his father and then married his mother not knowing that they were his real parents. When he discovered what he had done he put out his own eyes.

Olympus A high snow-covered peak which was the residence of the Grecian gods.

Orestes Son of Agamemnon and Clytemnestra.

Orion A giant and a hunter. He fell in love with a maiden, Merope, but her exasperated father deprived him of his sight with the help of Dionysus. Orion recovered his sight by exposing his eyes to the Sun's rays. On his death he was placed among the stars.

Orpheus A poet who received his lyre from Apollo and was instructed in its use by the Muses. Wild beasts, and even trees and rocks, were charmed by his music. When his wife Eurydice died from a serpent bite he followed her to Hades. He was allowed to have his wife back provided he did not look back upon her until they arrived in the upper world. To make sure she was following Orpheus did look behind him, and so lost her. His lyre can be found among the stars.

Ouranus Personification of Heaven.

Called the son, sometimes the husband, of Gaea (Earth). Ouranus hated his children and always confined them to Tartarus as soon as they were born. As a result, he was overthrown by his son Cronus.

Pan God of shepherds and their flocks, a son of Hermes. Pan is represented as a man with horns and a goat's hind legs, sometimes playing the syrinx.

Pandora The first woman on Earth. She had a jar, or box, containing every kind of evil. When it was opened the evils spread all over the world – only Hope remained.

Pegasus A winged horse which sprang from the blood of Medusa when her head was struck off by Perseus. He is found among the stars.

Penelope Wife of Odysseus, king of Ithaca.

Persephone The daughter of Zeus and Demeter, she was carried off by Hades who made her his wife.

Perseus The son of Zeus and Danaë, Perseus was the hero who cut off the head of the Gorgon Medusa.

Phaeton A son of Helios (the Sun). On being allowed to drive his father's chariot of the Sun across the sky he came too close to the earth and almost set it on fire. Zeus immediately killed him with a flash of lightning.

Phoebe Another name for Artemis as goddess of the Moon.

Phoebus Another name for Apollo as a Sun god.

Pleiades The daughters of Atlas and companions of Artemis. Pursued by Orion the hunter, they prayed to be rescued from him. The gods changed them into doves and set them among the stars.

Pollux Brother of Castor. *See* Dioscuri.

Polyphemus *see* Cyclops.

Poseidon A son of Cronus and Rhea, brother of Zeus and Hades, Poseidon was god of the sea.

Prometheus The son of the Titan Iapetus and a brother of Atlas, he stole fire from heaven and taught mortals all

Zeus

the useful arts. Zeus chained him to a rock where he was exposed to eternal torture. Every day an eagle fed on his liver which was always restored again during the nights.

Proteus An old man who could foretell the future. At midday he would rise from the sea and this was the only time he could be caught by anyone wanting to know the future. He would, however, cunningly change himself into all manner of different forms to avoid having to tell what he knew.

Psyche The personification of the human soul. Psyche was the daughter of a king. She aroused the jealousy of Aphrodite because of her beauty. The goddess ordered Cupid to cause Psyche to marry the most despicable of all men. But Cupid himself fell in love with her and visited her in the dark of night. One night she approached him carrying a lamp but, unfortunately, a drop of hot oil fell on Cupid who awoke and fled.

Rhea or **Cybele** Goddess of the Earth, daughter of Ouranus and Gaea. The wife of Cronus, she became the mother of Hestia, Demeter, Hera, Hades, Poseidon and Zeus.

Satyrs Beings, part man and part beast, associated with Dionysus. They represented the powers of nature.

Selene Moon goddess, sister of Helios (the Sun), and later identified with Artemis.

Semele A maiden beloved by Zeus, mother of Dionysus.

Styx The river which flows seven times around the underworld.

Tantalus A king who incurred the wrath of the gods. His punishment in the underworld was to suffer from a raging thirst whilst in the middle of a lake whose waters always receded from him when he tried to drink.

Tartarus Another name for Hades, or the lowest depth of Hades which was reserved for the rebel Titans.

Tethys Daughter of Ouranus and Gaea, wife of Oceanus and mother of the Oceanides.

Themis Daughter of Ouranus and Gaea, wife of Zeus and mother of the Horae and the Fates.

Theseus Grecian hero who slew the Cretan Minotaur.

Titans Offspring of Ouranus (Heaven)

ROMAN EQUIVALENTS OF SOME CHARACTERS IN GREEK MYTHOLOGY

Aurora	=	Eos
Bacchus	=	Dionysus
Ceres	=	Demeter
Cupid	=	Eros
Diana	=	Artemis
Fauns	=	Satyrs
Fortuna	=	Tyche
Hercules	=	Heracles
Iuventas	=	Hebe
Juno	=	Hera
Jupiter	=	Zeus
Latona	=	Leto
Mars	=	Ares
Mercury	=	Hermes
Minerva	=	Athena
Neptune	=	Poseidon
Pax	=	Irene
Pluto	=	Hades
Proserpina	=	Persephone
Saturn	=	Cronus
Sol	=	Helios
Tellus	=	Gaea
Ulysses	=	Odysseus
Uranus	=	Ouranus
Vesta	=	Hestia
Vulcan	=	Hephaestus

and Gaea (Earth), 12 in number.
Triton Son of Poseidon and Amphitrite who dwelt in a golden palace on the sea floor.
Tyche Goddess of good luck.
Typhon A monster with 100 heads and terrible voices. The father of fierce winds, Typhon was struck by a thunderbolt from Zeus and was confined to Tartarus.
Zeus Son of Cronus and Rhea, brother of Poseidon, Hades, Hestia, Demeter and Hera (to whom he was married), and the greatest Olympian god.

TEUTONIC MYTHOLOGY

Aesir One of two main groups of deities which included Odin, Frigg, Tyr, Thor, Balder, Bragi, Idun, Jörd, Heimdall and Loki. The rival tribe of gods was the Vanir.
Asgard The land of the gods.
Balder A son of Odin and Frigg, Balder was beautiful and just, the favourite of the gods. The blind god Höd deceived by the evil god Loki, killed Balder with an arrow made of mistletoe, the only thing that could hurt him.
Bifrost Bridge The rainbow bridge which was the only link between Midgard (the Middle Earth) and Asgard (the dwelling place of the gods).
Bragi A son of Odin, god of poetry and husband of the goddess Idun.
Donar see Thor
Fenrir A monstrous wolf, son of the evil god Loki and a giantess, Angerboda. The god Tyr bound Fenrir to a rock with magical chains. He would remain there until Doomsday when he would then break the bonds and fall upon the gods and, according to some myths, swallow the Sun.
Frey or **Freyr** Son of the fertility god Njord, ruler of rain and sunshine. His wife was Gerd, daughter of a giant.
Frigg, **Freyja** or **Frija** Wife of Odin, mother of Balder. Friday is derived from her name.
Heimdal The watchman of the gods.

Hel Goddess of Niflheim, the world of the dead.
Idun Wife of Bragi and guardian of the apples the gods ate to preserve their youth.
Jörd Goddess of the Earth, mother of Odin.
Loki Evil trickster god, who was punished by being bound to a rock. Loki was the father of the giantess Angerboda, bringer of distress, Hel, the goddess of death, Jörmungard, an evil serpent, and Fenrir the wolf.
Midgard The Middle Earth, the abode of mankind.
Niflheim The cold, misty world of the dead, ruled by the goddess Hel.
Njörd or **Nerthus** God of the sea, father of Frey and Frigg.
Norns Supernatural beings similar to the Fates of classical mythology. They were usually represented as three maidens spinning or weaving the fate of men.
Odin or **Woden** War god and protector of heroes. Fallen warriors joined him in Valhalla.
Thor Son of Odin, god of thunder and lightning.
Tyr or **Tiw** A powerful sky god, also associated with war, government and justice. His hand was bitten off by Fenrir the wolf when he was chaining him to a rock.
Valhalla Odin's palace for slain warriors.
Valkyries Maidens who served Odin. They went to the battlefields where they chose the slain worthy to join Odin in Valhalla.
Vanir A group of deities responsible for wealth, fertility and commerce, and rivals of the Aesir. In a war with the Vanir, the Aesir suffered many defeats before granting equality to the Vanir. The Vanir sent their gods Njörd and Frey to reside with the Aesir and took in exchange Hoenir and Mimir. The poet-god Kvasin was born as a result of the peace ritual in which the two races mingled their saliva in a vessel.

THE WORLD OF SCIENCE

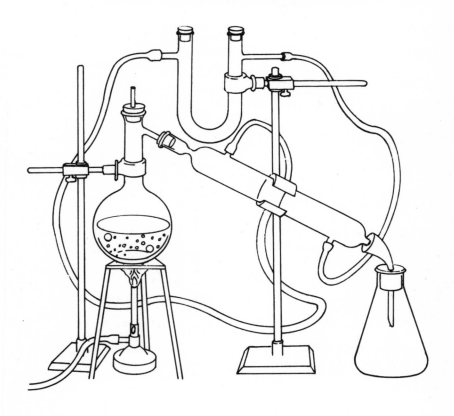

Inventors and Inventions

INVENTION	YEAR	INVENTOR
Adding machine	1642	Blaise Pascal (France)
Airplane	1903	Orville and Wilbur Wright (USA)
Airship (non-rigid)	1852	Henri Giffard (France)
(rigid)	1900	Graf Ferdinand von Zeppelin (Germany)
Aspirin	1899	Herman Dreser (Germany)
Autogyro	1923	Juan de la Cierva (Spain)
Bakelite	1907	Leo H. Backeland (Belgium/USA)
Ballpoint pen	1888	John J. Loud (USA)
Barometer	1644	Evangelista Torricelli (Italy)
Bathysphere	1930	William Beebe (USA)
Bicycle	1839	Kirkpatrick Macmillan (Britain)
Bicycle tyre (pneumatic)	1888	John Boyd Dunlop (Britain)
Bifocal lens	1780	Benjamin Franklin (USA)
Bunsen burner	1855	Robert Wilhelm von Bunsen (Germany)
Burglar alarm	1858	Edwin T. Holmes (USA)
Calculating machine	1823	Charles Babbage (Britain)
Carburettor	1876	Gottlieb Daimler (Germany)
Carpet sweeper	1876	Melville R. Bissell (USA)
Cash register	1879	James Ritty (USA)
Cellophane	1908	Dr Jacques Brandenberger (Switzerland)
Celluloid	1861	Alexander Parkes (Britain)
Cement	1824	Joseph Aspdin (Britain)
Chronometer	1735	John Harrison (Britain)
Clock (pendulum)	1656	Christiaan Huygens (Netherlands)
Electric battery	1800	Alessandro Volta (Italy)
Electric iron	1882	H. W. Seeley (USA)
Electric generator (DC)	1831	Michael Faraday (Britain)
Electric light	1878	Thomas Alva Edison (USA)
Electric motor (DC)	1873	Zénobe Gramme (Belgium)
(AC)	1888	Nikola Tesla (USA)
Electromagnet	1824	William Sturgeon (Britain)
Engine, Diesel	1890–2	Herbert Akroyd Stuart (Britain) and Rudolf Diesel (Germany)
Engine, Internal combustion (gas)	1860	Etienne Lenoir (France)
Engine, Jet	1930	Frank Whittle (Britain)
Engine, Steam (condenser)	1765	James Watt (Britain)
(piston)	1712	Thomas Newcomen (Britain)
Fountain pen	1884	Lewis E. Waterman (USA)
Gas lighting	1792	William Murdock (Britain)
Glider	1853	Sir George Cayley (Britain)
Gramophone (cylinder phonograph)	1877	Thomas Alva Edison (USA)
(disc)	1887	Emile Berliner (USA)
Gyrocompass	1911	Elmer A. Sperry (USA)

Gyroscope	1852	Jean Foucault (France)
Hot-air balloon	1783	Jacques and Joseph Montgolfier (France)
Hovercraft	1955	C. S. Cockerell (Britain)
Laser	1960	Dr Charles H. Townes (Britain)
Lift	1852	Elisha G. Otis (USA)
Lightning conductor	1752	Benjamin Franklin (USA)
Linoleum	1860	Frederick Walton (USA)
Locomotive, Steam	1804	Richard Trevithick (Britain)
Loudspeaker	1900	Horace Short (Britain)
Machine gun	1718	James Puckle (Britain)
Margarine	1869	Hippolyte Mège-Mouries (France)
Match	1827	John Walker (Britain)
Match (safety)	1855	J. E. Lundstrom (Sweden)
Microphone	1876	Alexander Graham Bell (USA)
Microscope, Compound	1590	Zacharies Janssen (Netherlands)
Miners' safety lamp	1816	Sir Humphry Davy (Britain)
Morphine	1806	Friederich Sertürner (Germany)
Motion-picture camera	1888	William Friese-Greene (Britain)
Motor car	1885	Karl Benz (German)
Motorcycle	1885	Gottlieb Daimler (German)
Neon lamp	1910	Georges Claude (France)
Nylon	1937	Dr Wallace H. Carothers (USA)
Parachute	1797	André-Jacques Garnerin (France)
Penicillin	1929	Sir Alexander Fleming (Britain)
Photography (on metal)	1826	J. Nicéphore Niépce (France)
(on paper)	1835	W. H. Fox Talbot (Britain)
(on film)	1888	John Carbutt (USA)
Pianoforte	1709	Bartolommeo Cristofou (Italy)
Pneumatic tyre	1845	Robert Thompson (Britain)
Power loom	1785	Edmund Cartwright (Britain)
Printing press	c.1455	Johann Gutenberg (Germany)
Propellor, Ship's	1837	Francis Smith (Britain)
Radar	1935	Sir Robert Watson-Watt (Britain)
Radio telescope	1931	Karl Jansky (USA)
Radio valve	1904	Sir Ambrose Fleming (Britain)
Rayon	1883	Sir Joseph Swan (Britain)
Razor Electric	1931	Col. Jacob Schick (USA)
Record, Long Playing	1948	Dr Peter Goldmark (USA)
Refrigerator	1850	James Harrison (Britain) and Alexander Catlin (USA)
Safety pin	1849	William Hunt (USA)
Sewing machine (domestic)	1851	Isaac M. Singer (USA)
Sextant	1730	John Hadley (Britain)
Slide rule	1621	William Oughtred (Britain)
Spinning frame	1769	Sir Richard Arkwright (Britain)
Spinning jenny	1764	James Hargreaves (Britain)
Spinning mule	1779	Samuel Crompton (Britain)
Stainless steel	1913	Harry Brearly (Britain)
Steam ship	1775	J. C. Périer (France)
Steam turbine	1894	Sir Charles A. Parsons (Britain)

144

Stethoscope	1816	René Laennec (France)
Submarine	1776	David Bushnell (USA)
Tank	1914	Sir Ernest Swinton (Britain)
Telegraph	1837	W. F. Cooke and Sir Charles Wheatstone (Britain)
Telephone	1876	Alexander Graham Bell (USA)
Telescope (refracting)	1608	Hans Lippershey (Netherlands)
(reflecting)	1669	Isaac Newton (Britain)
Television	1926	John Logie Baird (Britain)
Terylene	1941	J. R. Whinfield and J. T. Dickson (Britain)
Thermometer	1593	Galileo Galilei (Italy)
Torpedo	1868	Robert Whitehead (Britain)
Transistor	1948	John Bardeen, William Shockley and Walter Brattain (USA)
Typewriter	1808	Pellegrine Tarri (Italy)
Vaccination	1796	Edward Jenner (Britain)
Vacuum flask	1892	Sir James Dewar (Britain)
Welder, Electric	1877	Elisha Thomson (USA)
Wireless telegraphy	1895	Guglielmo Marconi (Italy)
X-ray	1895	Wilhelm von Röntgen (Germany)
Zip fastener	1891	Whitcomb L. Judson (USA)

Weather Forecasting

Meteorology concerns the study of all things which have a direct bearing on the world's weather, and the forecasting of what can be expected in the immediate future in any given area.

Worldwide observation stations keep a constant watch on all the atmospheric factors and weather movements, relying upon instrument readings of pressure, temperature, humidity, wind speeds and directions, clouds and so on. Earth satellites such as *Tiros* and *Nimbus* relay information, collected by special instruments, about atmospheric conditions all around the world. Computers are employed to assist in analyzing this information so that forecasts can be compiled and issued for the benefit of farmers, sailors, airmen and people in general. Modern forecasts have become very accurate, and even long-term analyses have a high degree of success.

Observations are also made locally. By recording temperature readings and using simple instruments such as the barometer, individuals can become reasonably accurate forecasters of the weather within their own immediate area. There is no reason to scorn all the traditional methods of weather-forecasting. Countrymen and seamen still use many of them quite successfully for short-term local forecasting. They watch the behaviour and movement of birds, look at the appearance of the sky and clouds (remember the saying 'a red sky at night is the shepherd's delight, a red sky in the morning is the shepherd's warning'), consider visibility (how clear and close, for example, a range of hills appears to be), measure the air's moisture content with seaweed, and study flowers (sensitive flowers will close up when it is dull, for instance).

The ordinary household barometer indicates broadly what is happening in the atmosphere and what can be expected of the weather. It measures the weight, or pressure, of the atmosphere. This is determined by changes in temperature, wind variations, and height above sea-level. The atmosphere is heavier in fine weather than it is in bad weather, and it is also heavier at sea-level than on a hill top. Aneroid barometers (from the Greek *a* and *neros* meaning 'without wet') are the most usual and useful; wet barometers use a liquid known as quicksilver (mercury).

Cyclones and anticyclones
As cyclones and anticyclones play such an important role in the

---

CLOUDS AND THE WEATHER

There are ten distinct types of cloud, as you can see in the accompanying illustration:

---

1 **Cirrus** Usually white and feathery. They are composed of ice-crystals and occur at a height of 6,100–7,600 m (20,000–25,000 ft).

---

2 **Cirrocumulus** Layers of small flaked or rounded clouds (a 'mackerel sky'), at 3,050–5,500 m (10,000–18,000 ft).

---

3 **Cirrostratus** A fine, whitish veil, forming haloes around the Sun or Moon, some 3,650 m (12,000 ft) high.

---

4 **Altocumulus** Grey or white flakes, or flattened round masses at 1,800–4,600 m (6,000–15,000 ft).

---

5 **Altostratus** A grey veil across the sky, sometimes thick enough to hide the Sun or Moon, at a height of 1,800–3,650 m (6,000–12,000 ft).

---

6 **Stratocumulus** Thick and dark, at 900–1,800 m (3,000–6,000 ft).

---

7 **Cumulus** Huge, rounded masses, with their lower surfaces almost level, at 760–900 m (2,500–3,000 ft).

---

8 **Cumulonimbus** Very big, rounded and towering masses, black or dark grey, often 300–1,370 m (1,000–4,500 ft) in height. They possess powerful up-currents and are a sign of bad weather and possibly thunderstorms.

---

9 **Nimbostratus** Grey, often dark, layers of clouds usually thousands of metres thick. They are composed of mixtures of ice crystals, raindrops and snowflakes, and occur below 2,000 m (6,500 ft).

---

10 **Stratus** Horizontal layers sometimes resting on higher ground as mist, but also up to 610 m (2,000 ft) in height.

Cumulus clouds

WIND FORCES – THE BEAUFORT SCALE

FORCE NO.	WIND DESCRIPTION	VISIBLE EFFECTS	SPEED km/h(mph)
0	Calm	Smoke rises vertically	Below 1·5 (1)
1	Light air	Smoke shows wind direction	1·5–5 (1–3)
2	Light breeze	Wind is felt on face, leaves rustle and wind-vanes move	6·5–11 (4–7)
3	Gentle breeze	Leaves and twigs move; light flag is extended	13–18 (8–12)
4	Moderate breeze	Dust and loose paper rise; small branches move	21–29 (13–18)
5	Fresh breeze	Small trees sway	30·5–38·5 (19–24)
6	Strong breeze	Large branches move and telegraph wires whistle	40–49·5 (25–31)
7	Moderate gale	Whole trees move; it is difficult to walk against the wind	51–61 (32–38)
8	Fresh gale	Tree twigs break off	62·5–73·5 (39–46)
9	Strong gale	Slight damage takes place; slates and chimney-pots can be blown down	75–86·5 (47–54)
10	Whole gale	Trees may be uprooted and considerable structural damage is done	88–101 (55–63)
11	Storm	Widespread damage occurs	102·5–120 (64–75)
12	Hurricane	A wind-force experienced in tropical revolving storms	Over 120 (75)

weather, it is essential for forecasters to recognize and understand them, as shown in Map A and Map B.

Winds, tempests and hurricanes

The Beaufort Scale table describes the various wind forces, and their speeds and effects.

Winds blowing toward the equator, from north and south, are deflected, because of the Earth's rotation, so that they become northeast and southeast winds respectively. These are called Trade Winds.

People living in certain regions of the world suffer from two forms of particularly violent wind – hurricanes and tornadoes. Formed by the violent entry of a large mass of cold air into a region of hot, moist air, a hurricane proceeds with a whirling movement. The wind races round in circles which frequently have a diameter of several hundred miles. Moving at a colossal speed, the hurricane tears across the ocean, leaving a trail of shipwreck and damage to coastal areas and islands in its wake.

Tornadoes occur on land and often can be even worse than hurricanes. A tornado is produced when cold air descends and hot air rises. This forms a spiral which contains a partial vacuum and moves at frightening speed across the country, destroying almost everything in its path.

Rain, blizzards and thunderstorms

When warm air, charged with water vapour collected from the sea, lakes and rivers, enters a cooler zone, some of the vapour is

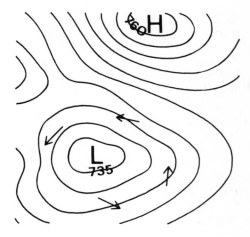

Cyclone

Isobar 760 (760 mm of mercury) indicates areas of high-pressure air. These flow inward in the direction of low pressure, encircled by isobar 735 (735 mm of mercury), but are deflected by the Earth's rotation. They become a swirling wind, represented by the anticlockwise arrow.

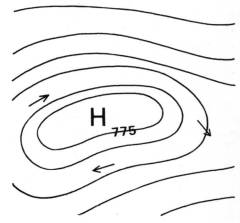

Anticyclone

In this case, the wind blows outwards from the centre of high pressure (isobar 775). It, also, is deflected but in this case in a clockwise direction, as indicated by the arrow.

148

forced out of the air and forms minute particles of water or ice. Many millions of these particles form a cloud and, if the process continues, the tiny drops join together and become rain.

If the condensation of the water vapour occurs at a temperature below freezing, a cloud of ice-particles is formed. Falling slowly towards the ground, the frozen droplets form into snowflakes and cover the earth with snow, if the temperature of the land is low enough.

When a snowfall is accompanied by strong winds, blizzard conditions prevail. The snowflakes are driven blindingly across the land, blanketing everything.

Thunderstorms take place when there is a great difference between electrical pressure either at the top and bottom of a cloud or between a cloud and the ground. Raindrops become electrically charged when they are formed, break up or evaporate. All of these processes take place in a thundercloud. Whenever the drops become charged, the air around the raindrops becomes oppositely charged. The charge in the raindrops is carried downwards, while the charge in the air rises. The difference in pressure created becomes unbearable and is stabilized by a flash of lightning.

The power of a big flash has been calculated at 10,000 million volts but it lasts only for approximately one thousandth of a second. The thunderous noise is produced by the lightning flash itself as the air rushes in to fill the gap and the sound echoes among the clouds.

Fog and mist
On land, fog is generally formed in valleys where the ground is cold and moist, and the air comparatively warm and windless. Often it takes the form of a ground mist, particularly in autumn, but thickens into fog during the winter months. The introduction of smokeless zones has reduced the frequency and degree of fog in many cities. This is particularly true of London where smoke-laden fogs of the past (referred to as 'pea-soupers') have virtually disappeared.

Fogs and mists at sea are formed like clouds. Warm air carrying moisture meets the cold sea and the water condenses into tiny drops which are too small to fall as rain. At sea, fog can be accompanied by some wind.

Special climatic features
There are a number of outstanding or unusual climatic features around the world which have a profound effect on the weather over vast areas.

In south and east Asia, for example, monsoons occur. They arise out of the great changes of temperature which take place over the land mass between summer and winter. Monsoons are regular and persistent winds which, for example, bring India heavy rainfall from June to October each year, after their long journey across the sea. The wet southwest monsoon is replaced by the dry and cold northeast monsoon during the October to March period, when the wind switches round to the opposite direction.

Another important feature is the Gulf Stream, which flows out of the warm Gulf of Mexico in a 'river' more than 48 km (30 miles) in width and almost 300 m (1,000 ft) in depth. The Gulf Stream flows towards the northeast and then divides, one part going towards Greenland, and the other to the Azores. In the mid-Atlantic it splits again. One part continues to the African coast, before swinging round to return to the Gulf of Mexico, while the other moves northeast past the coast of northwestern Europe.

The effect on northwestern Europe's weather is considerable. The warmth of the Gulf Stream helps to keep winter temperatures much higher, on average, than they would otherwise be. It is also responsible for sea fogs, however, when its warmth meets cold air from the north.

CHEMICAL NAMES FOR SOME COMMON SUBSTANCES

SUBSTANCE	CHEMICAL NAME
Alcohol	Ethyl alcohol (ethanol)
Alum	Aluminium potassium sulphate
Baking powder	Sodium bicarbonate
Black lead	Graphite (a form of carbon)
Boracic acid	Boric acid
Borax	Sodium borate
Brimstone	Sulphur
Caustic soda	Sodium hydroxide
Chalk	Sodium carbonate
Common salt	Sodium chloride
Cream of tartar	Potassium bitartrate
DDT	Dichlor-diphenyl-trichlorethane
Epsom salts	Magnesium sulphate
Glauber salts	Sodium sulphate
Hypo	Sodium Thiosulphate
Magnesia	Magnesium oxide

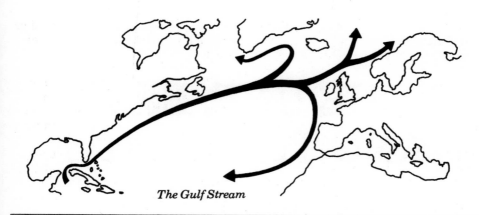

The Gulf Stream

Marsh gas	Methane
Plaster of Paris	Calcium sulphate
Plumbago	Graphite (a form of carbon)
Potash	Potassium carbonate
Quick-lime	Calcium oxide
Quicksilver	Mercury
Red lead	Triplumbic tetroxide
Sal-ammoniac	Ammonium chloride
Saltpetre (nitre)	Potassium nitrate
Salts of lemon	Potassium quadroxalate
Sal volatile	Ammonium carbonate
Spirits of salts	Hydrochloric acid
TNT	Trinitrotoluene
Vinegar	Dilute acetic acid
Washing soda	Crystalline sodium carbonate
White lead	Basic lead carbonate
Wood spirit	Methyl alcohol (methanol)

THE UNIVERSE
AND THE EARTH

Dimensions of the Universe

The mean distance between the Earth and the Sun is 150,000,000 km (93,000,000 miles). When measuring distances beyond the solar system, however, kilometres and miles are inconveniently small. The unit astronomers use is the *light-year*, the distance light travels in one year. Light travels at about 3,000,000 km (186,000 miles) per second. In one year it covers 9,470,000,000,000 km (nearly 6,000,000,000,000 miles).

The nearest star is 4·28 light-years away. Like our Sun, it is just one of many millions of stars in the galaxy which we call the Milky Way. On a clear night you can see our galaxy, which appears as a misty white band stretching across the heavens. What we see in fact is only part of the galaxy. The whole is like a huge disc that turns in space like a wheel. Our Sun lies near the edge of the disc, which takes 250 million years to revolve.

The distance across the Milky Way Galaxy is approximately 100,000 light-years, and the total number of stars in it is approximately 100,000 million. There are at least 100,000 million other galaxies in the universe, of which the nearest is around 160,000 light-years away.

THE EARTH

The Earth is divided into an inner core, an outer core, the mantle and the crust. The inner core is extremely dense and is composed of iron with probably some nickel. The temperature is thought to be between 4,000°C and 10,000°C at the very centre of the Earth. The outer core is molten and also composed of nickel and iron. The upper mantle is solid and its temperature is at least 1,000°C.

The crust, in proportion to the whole body of the Earth, is as thin as the skin on an apple. The thinnest part of the crust directly

SOME FACTS ABOUT EARTH

Estimated age of the Earth over 4,500 million years

Diameter of Earth at equator 12,757 km (7,927 miles)

Diameter of Earth at poles 12,714 km (7,900 miles)

Equatorial circumference 64,496 km (24,902 miles)

Meridianal circumference 64,387 km (24,860 miles)

Total surface area 510,100,000 sq km (196,950,000 sq miles)

Land area 148,950,000 sq km (57,510,000 sq miles)

Sea area 361,150,000 sq km (139,440,000 sq miles)

Weight of the Earth 5,970 million million million tonnes (5,876 million million million tons)

THE TWENTY BRIGHTEST STARS

NAME	VISUAL MAGNITUDE	DISTANCE IN LIGHT-YEARS
Sirius	− 1·43	8·6
Canopus	− 0·72	98
Alpha Centauri	− 0·27	4·3
Arcturus	− 0·06	36
Vega	+ 0·04	26
Capella	+ 0·05	45
Rigel	+ 0·08	600
Procyon	+ 0·37	11·4
Betelgeuse	+ 0·41 (variable)	600
Archernar	+ 0·47	65
Beta Centauri	+ 0·63	300
Altair	+ 0·77	16·6
Aldebaran	+ 0·86 (variable)	52
Alpha Crucis	+ 0·87	390
Spica	+ 0·91 (variable)	274
Antares	+ 0·92 (variable)	420
Pollux	+ 1·16	37
Fomalhaut	+ 1·19	22·6
Beta Crucis	+ 1·24	490
Deneb	+ 1·26	1,400

underlies the ocean floor and consists of basalt or rocks of similar density. The oceanic crust is about 6 km (3·7 miles) thick. The continental crust is 30–35 km (19–22 miles) thick. There is constant movement in the crust and occasionally new mountains are formed. Volcanoes are caused by magma (molten rock) rising from the deeper parts of the crust to the surface.

The main part of the Earth's atmosphere is about 160 km (100 miles) deep but very faint traces can be detected 8,000 km (5,000 miles) above the Earth's surface. At lower depths, up to 11 km (7 miles) above the surface, the atmosphere consists of 78% nitrogen, 21% oxygen, 0·03% carbon dioxide and 0.93% argon, with minute quantities of the inert gases neon, helium, krypton, xenon and radon. There is a variable amount of water vapour also.

Stellar magnitudes

The stars in the night sky differ in apparent brightness, and these differences are measured on the scale of stellar magnitudes. Roughly speaking, the brightest stars in the sky are of the first magnitude. All the other stars visible to the naked eye on a clear night are divided into five lower magnitudes, the very faintest belonging to the sixth. The stars of each magnitude are 2·5 times as bright as those of the next lower magnitude. Negative magnitudes are brightest. A star that has a magnitude of − 1 is ten times brighter than one of + 1·5.

PLANET	MEAN DISTANCE FROM SUN		EQUATORIAL DIAMETERS		LENGTH OF YEAR (SIDE-REAL PERIOD) IN EARTH TIME
	Km	Miles	Km	Miles	
Mercury	58,000,000	36,000,000	4,878	3,031	88 days
Venus	108,200,000	67,200,000	12,100	7,519	225 days
Earth	149,600,000	93,000,000	12,757	7,927	365 days
Mars	228,000,000	141,000,000	6,793	4,221	687 days
Jupiter	778,000,000	484,000,000	142,880	88,780	12 years
Saturn	1,427,000,000	887,000,000	120,000	74,600	$29\frac{1}{2}$ years
Uranus	2,870,000,000	1,780,000,000	50,800	31,600	84 years
Neptune	4,497,000,000	2,794,000,000	48,600	30,200	165 years
Pluto	5,900,000,000	3,658,000,000	5,500	3,400	$248\frac{1}{2}$ years

The Earth

Composition of the earth's crust

The outer shell or crust of the Earth is composed of a great variety of rocks. These rocks include relatively soft and loosely compacted materials such as clay, sand and gravel. There are also hard ones such as sandstone, limestone and granite. Rocks can be classified into three groups: igneous, sedimentary and metamorphic rocks.

Igneous rocks are those which have solidified out of hot, molten material (magma), e.g. basalt. *Sedimentary* rocks may be formed from the breakdown of existing rocks, from the shells of marine organisms or by chemical precipitation. These substances are deposited on land, or on sea or river beds. Sedimentary rocks cover most of the Earth's surface but constitute only about five per

155

The form of a perfect quartz crystal

cent of the crust. Examples are sandstone, shale, limestone and chalk. *Metamorphic* rocks are formed from igneous or sedimentary rocks by the action of heat and pressure, e.g. marble, slate and schist.

Rocks are composed of minerals. About 2,000 different minerals are found on the Earth, and each mineral is composed of chemical elements. A few elements, such as gold, are found in a free, uncombined state but most minerals are composed of a combination of elements. The commonest elements found in the Earth's crust are shown in the table.

Minerals composed of silicates (compounds of silicon and oxygen) make up more than 95 per cent of the Earth's crust and are usually combined with one or more of the metallic elements such as aluminium, calcium, iron, magnesium, potassium and sodium. One of the commonest of all silicates is the mineral quartz (SiO_2).

With few exceptions, minerals are crystalline, though the crystals are often microscopically small, or so bunched up that they have lost their perfect form. The regular external form characteristic of crystals is caused by the orderly arrangement of their atoms.

Gemstones

Some 120 minerals have been classified as gemstones, but only about 25 are in common use in jewellery. Those classified as precious stones are diamond, emerald, ruby, sapphire, black opal and pearl. Among those classified as semi-precious are amethyst, topaz, aquamarine, garnet, turquoise, jade and amber. There are other stones, less valued, which can be classified as ornamental stones.

Most gems occur as natural minerals. Many are found in igneous rocks, e.g. beryl, topaz and tourmaline. There are others which are found in metamorphic rocks, e.g. emerald, garnet and diamond. Quite often gemstones, including diamonds, are found in the gravels of river beds. There are some substances of organic origin that are classed as gems. Amber is a fossilized resin. Jet is a hard, shiny black fossilized wood. Coral is made by small sea animals, and pearls form inside oysters.

A gem is valued for its beauty and rarity, and for its size. Opaque and cloudy gems, such as opals, are valued for their colour. Transparent gems are valued for their brilliance, as well as their durability and colour. Many gems are composed of the colourful oxides of aluminium, beryllium and magnesium, sometimes with silica. Others are coloured by metal

 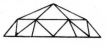

A diamond is cut so that slight movement of the stone produces scintillating flashes of rainbow colours.

oxides that are only present as impurities.

Diamond is the hardest of all minerals. It also refracts light more than any other precious stone. Variation in refraction for different colours (dispersion) accounts for the brilliant flashes of colour – the 'fire' – of a faceted diamond.

Diamonds are the most valued of all gems, apart from the deepest-red rubies. The largest diamond in the world was the Cullinan diamond, found in 1905 in the Premier mine in Transvaal, South Africa. It was purchased by the Transvaal government and presented to the reigning king, Edward VII. Originally weighing 3,106 carats (a carat is equal to 200 milligrams), the diamond was cut into 2 large stones, 7 medium and 96 smaller ones. The largest of the stones, weighing 530 carats, is the pear-shaped gem set in the English sceptre called the Star of Africa. It is also the largest cut diamond in the world. The second largest, the Cullinan II, is set in the Imperial State Crown.

Very few precious stones are set just as they are found. They are seldom perfect enough. To show their colour and sparkle to the full, they have to be polished and cut. Stones may be cut with a curved surface (a cabochon) or in facets. There are various names for different kinds of faceting. For example, a brilliant is usually cut with 58 facets, 33 above and 25 below, with a band running between the two halves which is the part gripped by the setting. Diamonds are generally cut this way.

Another very large diamond in the British Crown Jewels collection is the Indian diamond Koh-i-noor (Mountain of Light), which was given to Queen Victoria in 1850 by the East India Company. The largest coloured diamond is also from India; it is the vivid blue Hope Diamond (44·4 carats) belonging to the Smithsonian Institution in Washington D.C.

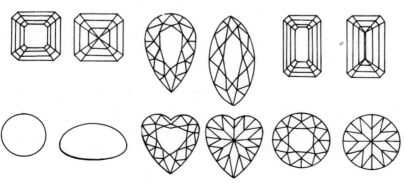

A selection of precious stone faceting

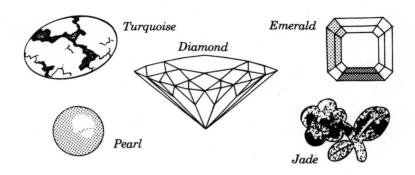

Turquoise

Diamond

Emerald

Pearl

Jade

GEMSTONES IN COMMON USE

Garnet Birthstone for January – symbolizes faithfulness. Garnets are silicates of various minerals (calcium, magnesium, titanium, iron, aluminium). The blood-red variety is an important gemstone.

Amethyst Birthstone for February – symbolizes sincerity. It is a violet-coloured quartz. The best specimens come from Brazil and the USSR.

Aquamarine Birthstone for March – symbolizes courage. A light blue-green form of beryl. (Beryl is composed of beryllium and aluminium silicates.) The best ones are from Brazil and the USSR.

Diamond Birthstone for April – symbolizes innocence. Diamonds are a crystallized form of carbon, the most prized ones being colourless. Principal source is South Africa.

Emerald Birthstone for May – symbolizes love. A rare green variety of beryl. The finest occur in Colombia, South America.

Pearl Birthstone for June – symbolizes health. Found mainly in oysters. Pearls are believed to be formed from secretions built up around specks of foreign matter in the shell.

Ruby Birthstone for July – symbolizes contentment. The ruby is a red variety of the aluminium oxide mineral, corundum. The best are deep red in colour and come from Burma.

Peridot Birthstone for August – symbolizes married happiness. A transparent variety of the green mineral olivine (a magnesium-iron silicate). The finest come from Australia, Brazil, Burma, Norway and Thailand.

Sapphire Birthstone for September – symbolizes clear thinking. A variety of corundum, sapphires are commonly deep blue, but they can occur in other colours. The finest come from Burma and Thailand.

Opal Birthstone for October – symbolizes hope. Opals are a non-crystalline form of quartz containing varying amounts of water. The most valuable types are called 'black opals' which, despite their name, flash with several different colours; they come from the Australian continent.

Topaz Birthstone for November – symbolizes fidelity. Found in granites and other igneous rocks, topaz is a silicate of aluminium and fluorine. The crystals are usually yellow, brown or, when heated, pink. Topaz is found mainly in Brazil, the USSR and the USA.

Turquoise Birthstone for December – symbolizes prosperity. A copper and aluminium phosphate mineral, blue or greenish-blue in colour. It is found in Iran, India, Tibet, Poland and the USA.

Alexandrite (Chrysoberyl) An oxide of beryllium and aluminium, alexandrite is dull green in daylight and blood-red in artificial light. It is found in Brazil, the USA, the USSR and Czechoslovakia.

Chalcedony A mixture of quartz and opal, often white and creamy with a waxy lustre. The orange-red variety is called cornelian (also called carnelian), the brown is sard. Chrysoprase is apple-green and is an alternative May birthstone to emerald. Bloodstone, which is green with red spots, is an alternative to Aquamarine for the March birthstone. Jasper is a red, brown or yellow variety of chalcedony, and sometimes a mixture of all three colours. Onyx and agate, two other varieties, are characterized by parallel bands of colour. Sardonyx, a reddish-brown and white banded agate, is an alternative to peridot, the August birthstone.

Jade An opaque, waxy or pearly mineral, it is usually green but can be white, yellow or pink. There are two kinds of jade. The rarer *jadeite* (a sodium aluminium silicate) comes from Burma, Tibet and China. *Nephrite* (a calcium magnesium silicate) is found in New Zealand, China and the USSR.

Lapis lazuli A rock rich in lazurite, an opaque, deep-blue mineral. It consists of a silicate of sodium and aluminium. Lapis lazuli has been used as an ornamental stone and as a gemstone since ancient times. When it is ground, the pigment ultramarine is obtained. Lapis lazuli is an alternative to sapphire, the September birthstone.

Moonstone Composed of albite, a form of feldspar, moonstone is white with a bluish sheen. It is an alternative to pearl which is June's birthstone.

Obsidian A volcanic glass, green or yellowish in colour.

Quartz gems Quartz is a common and usually colourless mineral. When found in pure, hexagonal crystals it is called rock crystals. It is an alternative to diamond for April's birthstone. Other varieties of quartz include amethyst (violet), citrine (yellow), rose quartz (pink), milky quartz and smoky quartz. Cat's eye and tiger's eye contain asbestos fibres.

Spinel An oxide of magnesium and aluminium, it sometimes reaches gem quality. The best red spinels come from Sri Lanka. Brown, green and blue ones also occur.

Tourmaline A double silicate of aluminium and boron, tourmaline is commonly black but when it occurs in other colours (green, red or blue) it is a gemstone. It forms long crystals, sometimes varicoloured. Chief sources are Brazil, Sri Lanka and the USSR.

Zircon An oxide of zirconium and silicon, zircon is found in igneous rocks. The clear brown crystals turn blue when heated and thereby make better gems.

THE WORLD'S LONGEST RIVERS

RIVER	MAIN LOCATION	LENGTH Kilo-metres	Miles	OUTFLOW
Nile	Egypt	6,650	4,132	Mediterranean Sea
Amazon	Peru, Brazil	6,437	4,000	Atlantic Ocean
Mississippi-Missouri	USA	6,020	3,741	Gulf of Mexico
Yenisey	Siberia	5,540	3,442	Arctic Ocean
Yangtze	Tibet, China	5,494	3,434	East China Sea
Ob-Irtysh	W. Siberia	5,410	3,362	Gulf of Ob, Arctic Ocean
Zaire	Equatorial Africa	4,700	2,914	South Atlantic Ocean
Hwang-ho (Yellow River)	China	4,640	2,883	Gulf of Pohai
Lena	Siberia	4,400	2,734	Arctic Ocean
Mackenzie	Canada	4,241	2,635	Beaufort Sea
Niger	W. Africa	4,180	2,600	Gulf of Guinea
St Lawrence-Great Lakes	Canada	4,023	2,500	Gulf of St Lawrence
Mekong	Tibet, China, Laos, Kampuchea, Vietnam	4,000	2,485	China Sea
Rio de la Plata-Parana	Brazil, Argentina, Uruguay	4,000	2,485	South Atlantic Ocean
Murray-Darling	Australia	3,780	2,350	Indian Ocean
Volga	USSR	3,690	2,293	Caspian Sea
Zambesi	S.E. Africa	3,540	2,200	Indian Ocean
Madeira	Brazil	3,200	1,988	Amazon River
Yukon	Canada, Alaska	3,200	1,988	Bering Strait
Rio Grande	USA, Mexico	3,040	1,885	Gulf of Mexico
Ganges-Brahmaputra	India	2,897	1,800	Bay of Bengal
São Francisco	Brazil	2,897	1,800	Atlantic Ocean
Indus	Pakistan	2,880	1,790	Arabian Sea

Salween	Tibet, Burma	2,880	1,790	Gulf of Martaban
Danube	Europe	2,850	1,770	Black Sea
Amur	Mongolia, China, Siberia	2,824	1,755	Pacific Ocean
Tigris-Euphrates	Syria, Iraq	2,740	1,700	Persian Gulf
Nelson	Canada	2,570	1,600	Hudson Bay
Kolyma	N.E. Siberia	2,560	1,591	Arctic Ocean
Tocantins	Brazil	2,560	1,591	Atlantic Ocean
Orinoco	Venezuela	2,368	1,471	Atlantic Ocean
Colorado	W. USA	2,320	1,441	Gulf of California

PRINCIPAL OCEANS AND SEAS OF THE WORLD

NAME	AREA		AVERAGE DEPTH		GREATEST DEPTH	
	Sq km	Sq miles	Metres	Feet	Metres	Feet
Pacific Ocean	160,000,000	63,986,000	4,280	14,040	11,033	36,198
Atlantic Ocean	81,663,000	31,530,000	3,926	12,880	9,188	30,143
Indian Ocean	73,427,000	28,350,000	3,962	13,000	7,000	22,968
Arctic Ocean	14,353,000	5,541,500	1,280	4,200	5,440	17,850
Mediterranean Sea	2,851,000	1,145,000	1,372	4,500	4,400	14,435
South China Sea	2,318,000	895,000	1,645	5,400	5,016	16,456
Bering Sea	2,274,000	878,000	507	1,665	4,091	13,422
Caribbean Sea	1,942,500	750,000	2,560	8,400	7,239	23,750
Gulf of Mexico	1,813,000	700,000	1,433	4,700	3,787	12,426
Sea of Okhotsk	1,507,000	582,000	914	3,000	3,847	12,621
East China Sea	1,243,000	480,000	186	610	3,200	10,500
Yellow Sea	1,243,000	480,000	49	160	106	348
Hudson Bay	1,222,500	472,000	134	440	457	1,500
Sea of Japan	1,049,000	405,000	1,474	4,835	3,109	10,200
North Sea	572,500	221,000	55	180	609	1,998
Red Sea	461,000	178,000	454	1,490	2,211	7,254
Black Sea	436,415	168,500	1,311	4,300	2,244	7,362
Baltic Sea	409,000	158,000	67	221	396	1,300
Persian Gulf	194,000	75,000	30	82	84	230

THE WORLD'S LARGEST LAKES

LAKE	AREA		LOCATION
	Sq km	Sq miles	
Caspian Sea (salt)	371,800	143,550	USSR and Iran
Superior	82,350	31,800	Canada and USA
Victoria	69,500	26,830	Kenya, Uganda and Tanzania
Aral Sea (salt)	65,500	25,300	USSR
Huron	59,600	23,010	Canada and USA
Michigan	58,000	22,400	USA
Tanganyika	32,900	12,700	Tanzania, Zaire and Zambia
Great Bear	31,800	12,275	Canada
Baykal	30,500	11,780	USSR
Malawi	29,600	11,430	Malawi, Mozambique and Tanzania
Great Slave	28,500	10,980	Canada
Erie	25,700	9,930	Canada and USA
Winnipeg	24,500	9,465	Canada
Ontario	19,500	7,520	Canada and USA
Ladoga (Ladozhskoye)	17,700	6,835	USSR
Balkhash	17,400	6,720	USSR
Chad	16,300	6,300	Chad, Cameroon, Niger and Nigeria
Onega	9,840	3,800	USSR
Eyre (salt)	9,585	3,700	Australia
Rudolf (salt)	9,065	3,500	Kenya
Titicaca	8,290	3,200	Peru-Bolivia
Athabasca	7,920	3,058	Canada
Nicaragua	7,770	3,000	Nicaragua
Reindeer	6,320	2,440	Canada
Torrens (salt)	6,215	2,400	Australia
Koko Nor (salt)	5,960	2,300	China
Issyk-Kul'	5,895	2,276	USSR
Vänern	5,570	2,150	Sweden

The Himalaya-Karakoram-Hindu Kush-Pamir Range of Asia includes the highest mountain of the world and has 104 peaks over 7,315 m (24,000 ft) above sea level. The Andes Range in South America, the second greatest, has 54 peaks over 6,096 m (20,000 ft).

THE WORLD'S HIGHEST MOUNTAINS

NOTABLE MOUNTAIN PEAKS	MOUNTAIN	HEIGHT		LOCATION
		Metres	Feet	
Highest mountain in the world	Mt Everest	8,847	29,028	Himalayas, Asia
Highest mountain in the USSR	Communism Peak	7,495	24,590	Tadzhik
Highest mountain in South America	Mt Aconcagua	6,960	22,834	Argentina (Andes Range)
Highest mountain in the USA	Mt McKinley	6,194	20,320	Alaska
Highest mountain in Canada	Mt Logan	6,050	19,850	Yukon
Highest active volcano	Cotopaxi	5,897	19,347	Ecuador
Highest mountain in Africa	Mt Kilimanjaro	5,895	19,340	Tanzania
Highest mountain in Europe	Elbruz	5,636	18,497	Caucasus, Georgian SSR
Highest mountain in Antarctica	Mt Vinson	5,140	16,863	Antarctica
Highest mountain in western Europe	Mt Blanc	4,807	15,771	France/Italy
Highest mountain in the USA (excluding Alaska)	Mt Whitney	4,418	14,494	California
Highest island mountain in the world	Mauna Kea	4,205	13,796	Hawaii
Highest mountain in New Zealand	Mt Cook	3,764	12,349	South Island
Highest mountain in Australia	Mt Kosciusko	2,228	7,310	Great Dividing Range
Highest mountain in UK	Ben Nevis	1,343	4,404	Scotland

GREAT DESERTS OF THE WORLD

DESERT	APPROX. AREA Sq km	Sq miles	TERRITORIES
Sahara	16,835,000	6,500,000	Algeria, Chad, Libya, Mali, Mauritania, Niger, Sudan, Tunisia, Egypt, Morocco.
Australian	1,550,000	600,000	Australia
Arabian	1,300,000	500,000	Saudi Arabia, S. Arabia, Syria, Yemen.
Gobi	1,040,000	400,000	Mongolia, Inner Mongolia (region of China)
Kalahari	520,000	200,000	Botswana
Kara-Kum	350,000	135,000	Turkmen SSR
Taklamakan	320,000	125,000	Sinkiang (region of China)
Namib	310,000	120,000	Namibia
Sonoran	310,000	120,000	Arizona, California, Mexico
Somali	260,000	100,000	Somalia
Thar	260,000	100,000	N.W. India, Pakistan

THE WORLD'S DEEPEST-KNOWN CAVERNS

CAVE	DEPTH Metres	Feet	LOCATION
Gouffre de la Pierre Martin	1,332	4,370	Basses-Pyrénées, France-Spain
Gouffre Jean Bernard	1,298	4,258	Savoy Alps, France
Gouffre Berger	1,141	3,743	Vercors, France
Kievskaya	1,080	3,543	USSR
Chourun des Aguilles	980	3,214	Dauphine Alps, France
Sumidero de Cellagua	970	3,182	Cantabria, Spain
Gouffre André Touya	950	3,116	W. pyrénées, France
Grotta di Monte Cuco	922	3,025	Perugia, Italy
Abisso Michele Gortani	920	3,018	Julian Alps, Italy

The largest-known cavern is the Big Room in the Carlsbad Caverns, New Mexico, USA. It is 1,438 m (4,720 ft) long, 100 m (328 ft) high and 200 m (656 ft) across. The most extensive known cave system is the Mammoth Cave-Flint Ridge system in Kentucky, USA, with a length of 292 km (181 miles). There may, of course, be larger, undiscovered caver

THE WORLD'S HIGHEST WATERFALLS

NAME	TOTAL DROP Metres	Feet	RIVER	LOCATION
Angel (highest fall 807 m, 2,648 ft)	979	3,212	Carrao	Venezuela
Tugela (5 falls, the highest being 410 m, 1,350 ft)	947	3,110	Tugela	Natal, S. Africa
Utigârd (highest fall 600 m, 1,970 ft)	800	2,625	Jostedal Glacier	Norway
Mongefossen	774	2,540	Monge	Norway
Yosemite (upper section 205 m, 1,430 ft; middle, Cascades, section 205 m, 675 ft; lower section 97 m, 320 ft)	739	2,425	Yosemite Creek	Yosemite National Park, Cal., USA
Østre Mardøla Foss (highest fall 296 m, 974 ft)	656	2,154	Mardals	Norway
Tyssestrengane (highest fall 289 m, 948 ft)	646	2,120	Tysso	Norway
Sutherland (highest fall 248 m, 815 ft)	580	1,904	Arthur	S. Island, New Zealand

THE WORLD'S GREATEST WATERFALLS BY VOLUME

NAME	TOTAL HEIGHT Metres	Feet	WIDTH Metres	Feet	RIVER	LOCATION
Boyoma (7 cascades)	60	200	730	2,400	Upper Zaire	Zaire
Guaira	114	374	4,846	15,900	Parana	Brazil-Paraguay border
Khône	21	70	10,670	35,000	Mekong	Laos
Niagara (in two sections)						
American	50	167	300	1,000	Niagara	USA-Canada border
Canadian	48	160	760	2,500	Niagara	USA-Canada border

THE WORLD'S LARGEST ISLANDS —

ISLAND	AREA		LOCATION
	Sq km	Sq miles	
Greenland	2,175,600	840,000	Arctic Ocean
New Guinea	831,390	321,000	W. Pacific
Borneo	738,150	285,000	Indian Ocean
Madagascar	590,002	227,800	Indian Ocean
Baffin Island	476,065	183,810	Arctic Ocean
Sumatra	473,607	182,860	Indian Ocean
Honshu	230,300	88,920	N.W. Pacific
Great Britain	218,041	84,186	N. Atlantic
Victoria Island	212,197	81,930	Arctic Ocean
Ellesmere Island	196,236	75,770	Arctic Ocean
Sulawesi (Celebes)	189,484	73,160	Indian Ocean
South Island, New Zealand	150,460	58,093	S.W. Pacific
Java	130,510	50,390	Indian Ocean
North Island, New Zealand	114,687	44,281	S.W. Pacific
Cuba	114,494	44,206	Caribbean Sea
Newfoundland	112,300	43,359	N. Atlantic
Luzon	104,688	40,420	W. Pacific
Iceland	102,846	39,709	N. Atlantic
Mindanao	94,628	36,536	W. Pacific
Hokkaido	88,775	34,276	N.W. Pacific
Ireland	82,460	31,839	N. Atlantic
Hispaniola	76,498	29,536	Caribbean Sea
Tasmania	67,897	26,215	S.W. Pacific
Sri Lanka	65,610	25,332	Indian Ocean

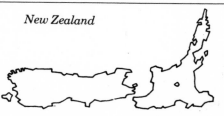

New Zealand

AVERAGE COMPOSITION OF THE EARTH'S CRUST

Element	Symbol	%
Oxygen	O	46·71
Silicon	Si	27·69
Aluminium	Al	8·07
Iron	Fe	5·05
Calcium	Ca	3·65
Sodium	Na	2·75
Potassium	K	2·58
Magnesium	Mg	2·08
Titanium	Ti	0·62
Hydrogen	H	0·14
Phosphorus	P	0·12
Carbon	C	0·09
Manganese	Mn	0·09
Sulphur	S	0·05
Chlorine	Cl	0·05
Barium	Ba	0·04
Fluorine	F	0·03
Strontium	Sr	0·02
Others	–	0·17
		100·00

CONTINENTS OF THE WORLD

CONTINENT	AREA Sq km	Sq miles
Africa	30,259,000	11,683,000
Antarctica	16,000,000	6,178,000
Asia	43,250,000	16,699,000
Europe	10,360,000	4,000,000
America: North America	21,500,000	8,301,000
South America	17,793,000	6,870,000
Central America	2,750,000	1,062,000
Oceania (Australia and the Pacific islands – Polynesia, Melanesia and Micronesia)	8,935,000	3,450,000

THE AGES OF THE EARTH

STEPS IN THE EVOLUTION OF LIFE

Pre-Cambrian Period Earlier than 600 million years ago	Algae, worms, jellyfish and other simple soft-bodied life forms

LOWER PALAEOZOIC ERA ('ANCIENT LIFE')

Cambrian Period 500–600 million years ago	Abundant marine invertebrates
Ordovician Period 425–500 million years ago	Earliest fish and molluscs

UPPER PALAEOZOIC ERA

Silurian Period 400–425 million years ago	Earliest land plants

The Ages of the Earth

Devonian Period **345–400 million years ago**	Earliest insects; the first bony fishes
Lower Carboniferous (Mississippian) **Period** **320–345 million years ago**	Earliest conifers (the great coal forests), tree ferns and club mosses
Upper Carboniferous (Pennsylvanian) **Period** **280–320 million years ago**	Earliest quadruped (*Ichthyostega*); earliest spiders; giant trees abundant
Permian Period **230–280 million years ago**	Earliest land reptiles (*Seymouria*)

MESOZOIC ERA ('MIDDLE ERA OF LIFE')

Triassic Period **180–230 million years ago**	Earliest dinosaurs
Jurassic Period **130–180 million years ago**	Earliest flying reptiles; first bird (*Archaeopteryx*); earliest mammals
Cretaceous Period (period of chalk **formation)** **64–130 million years ago**	Dinosaurs were abundant during the early part of this period but declined at its close; first flowering plants appeared, and hardwood trees were abundant, including many now familiar to us (beech, holly, ivy, oak, maple, poplar, magnolia, laurel)

CENOZOIC ERA ('RECENT LIFE')
Tertiary Period

Palaeocene Epoch (earliest recent **forms)** **54–64 million years ago**	Tremendous increase in mammals; forerunners of carnivores and hoofed mammals
Eocene Epoch **38–54 million years ago**	First true rodents; types of rhinoceros; *Hyracotherium*, a tiny, four-toed ancester of the horse, 30 cm (12 in) in height; appearance of deer, camels, pigs, cattle; ancestors of tapirs and elephants; sabre-toothed tiger
Oligocene Epoch **26–38 million years ago**	*Mesohippus*, a three-toed ancestor of the horse, 60 cm (24 in) in height
Miocene Epoch **7–26 million years ago**	Continued rise of modern mammals; *Merychippus*, a three-toed ancestor of the horse, 100 cm (40 in) in height
Pliocene Epoch **2–7 million years ago**	Ancestors of elephants, camels, rhinoceroses, and dogs abounded; *Pliohippus*, an ancestor of the horse, 150 cm (60 in) high, with one toe

Some common reptiles of Cretaceous times

QUATERNARY PERIOD

Pleistocene Epoch
1,750,000–50,000 BC

Man first appeared; the period of the Ice Ages; animal species included the woolly mammoth, 39·5 m (12 ft) high, and a woolly type of rhinoceros, *Coelodonta*, 19·7 m (6 ft) high, as well as most of the modern animals.

Holocene Epoch
50,000 BC–Present

All recent forms

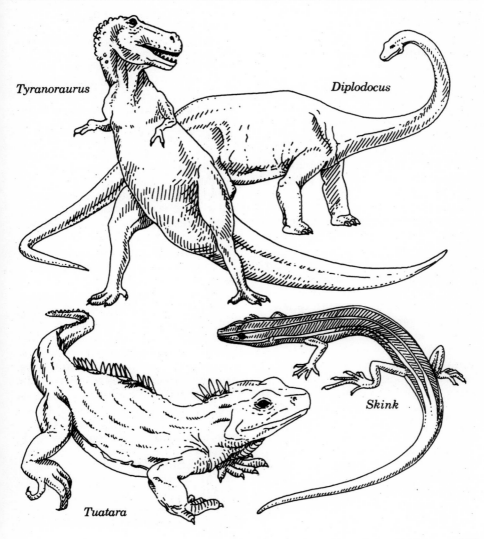

Tyranoraurus

Diplodocus

Skink

Tuatara

Wildlife in Danger

Largely as a result of man's activities, it has been estimated that as many as 100,000 species of animals and plants may be in danger of extinction. Some species are declining because they are not as well adapted as others in the fight for survival. The majority of animals and plants which have become rare in the last few hundred years are disappearing, however, because of man's greed or thoughtlessness.

Man has always hunted wild animals for food and skins but, in the past, traditional hunting methods probably did not cause many species to die out. Modern technology, however, has produced such things as guns with telescopic sights, the repeating rifle and the snowmobile which make it much easier for the hunter to kill. At the same time the human population has greatly increased. Demand for skins has also considerably increased and the prices that they can fetch has consequently gone up. These factors weigh very heavily against the chances of survival of many species of animals. Some have already become extinct, such as the Quagga, a kind of zebra which was once numerous in southern Africa. Excessive hunting led to its extermination by 1883.

Several species of whale, for example the blue whale (the largest animal ever to have lived on the Earth), have been almost exterminated. The blue whale didn't stand much of a chance against the great Russian and Japanese factory ships which slaughtered them with explosive harpoons for their oil and meat. Since 1963 the blue whale has had complete protection in all oceans and is slowly increasing in numbers.

The greatest danger to wildlife is the destruction of their natural habitats. Vast areas of tropical forest are being felled and burned, and the animals that once lived in them have vanished. The drainage of wetlands for industry, agriculture or housing has led to the disappearance of many animals and birds that were once quite common.

In the United States, the great prairies that once existed have been largely ploughed and turned over to grain and cattle. Once these prairies were roamed by vast herds of bison (sometimes incorrectly called 'buffalo'). The bison were hunted by the Indians for food and clothing, but that did not seriously affect their numbers. When the white man came, however, the bison were slaughtered in large numbers. Now only a few remain in reservations.

The introduction by man of alien species is a common cause of the extinction of many animals. The egg-laying mammals (monotremes) of Australia have suffered from the introduction of the dingo, which the Aborigines brought with them 10,000 years ago. Domestic livestock such as the goat, a voracious eater, may also threaten

Reserves have been established in India to save the tiger from extinction.

One of the world's rarest birds, the King of Saxony bird of paradise, is from New Guinea. Although trading in its plumes was banned in 1924, illegal trading continues. Destruction of its forest habitat further threatens its survival.

The leopard and other spotted cats are threatened by the fashion for fur coats.

The Quagga of southern Africa was hunted to extinction.

The blue whale was nearly exterminated for its meat and oil.

THE NUMBER OF ANIMAL SPECIES IN THE WORLD

Arthropods	900,000
Chordates	45,000
Molluscs	45,000
Protozoans	30,000
Worms	38,000
Other invertebrates	21,000
Total:	approximately 1,000,000

Species of mammals in danger of extinction: approx. 120
Species and subspecies of birds in danger of extinction: approx. 350

THE NUMBER OF PLANT SPECIES IN THE WORLD

Algae, fungi, etc.	60,000
Ferns, conifers, etc.	10,000
Flowering plants	250,000
Mosses and liverworts	23,000
Total:	approximately 350,000

Species of plants which may be threatened: approx 20,000

The American bison was once numbered in millions, now there are just a few.

Hunted for its eggs, meat and shell, the green turtle has been greatly reduced in numbers.

the food supplies of native animals. Many plants, too, are threatened with extinction where once-lush areas have been eaten bare by grazing livestock.

What can be done to help endangered species? The International Union for Conservation of Nature and Natural Resources (IUCN), a scientific organization with headquarters in Switzerland, studies threatened animals and birds, and some reptiles, amphibians, fish and plants, too. Its experts decide what must be done to save each species and also consult with the authorities in the countries concerned. The World Wildlife Fund (WWF), another international organization based in Switzerland, raises funds and works hard at persuading national governments to take the necessary action to save wildlife.

Reserves have been set up for a few endangered animals and plants. In India, the tiger would soon be extinct were it not for the special sanctuaries established by the Indian government. Zoos, too, can play an important part by breeding rare animals in captivity and so giving them a chance of survival.

TIME

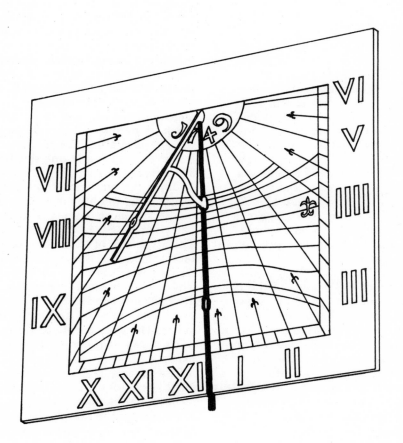

Time, Clocks and Calendars

The measurement of time owes its origin to early man's observation of the heavens – chiefly the movements of the Sun and the Moon, together with regular seasonal changes noted over long periods.

Clocks
Gradually, with the advance of knowledge over many centuries, man developed the means of calculating and measuring time on a more accurate basis, and early forms of clocks were invented. The earliest of these was the shadow clock introduced by the ancient Egyptians some 3,500 years ago. This eventually gave rise to the sundial but these devices were useless at night or when clouds obscured the Sun. The clepsydra (water clock) was used at these times, and sand clocks were helpful for the calculation of short intervals.

On one of the islands of the Nile, in those ancient times, 360 vessels were tended by 360 priests at a temple to the Egyptian god Osiris. Each of these vessels had a hole in the bottom, just the right size to allow milk, poured in to fill the container, to empty out in precisely 24 hours. The priests did this to each vessel in turn, day after day, throughout the year!

Before the invention of mechanical clocks, people frequently used candles and simple oil lamps, often marked in divisions to show how much time had elapsed, particularly during the night. Although the date of the invention of the first mechanical clock is not known, a device driven by water was certainly constructed in Peking in 1090.

The pendulum clock was invented in the 17th century by Christiaan Huygens, and the first watches appeared as early as 1500 in Nuremberg, Germany.

Modern quartz-crystal clocks have achieved an accuracy of one-thousandth of a second a day. The latest development in the measurement of time, an atomic clock using natural vibrations of the caesium atom, is considered to achieve accuracy to one second in 300 years.

Of all the many different kinds of interesting and elaborate clocks, one of the most famous is in the cathedral at Strasbourg, in France. The structure of this clock is, in fact, a model of the cathedral and on its tower there are three dials. The lowest, a revolving circle, is divided into the 365 days of the year. The figure of Apollo, on one side of the dial, points to the correct day of the year with an arrow.

The ingenious maker of the clock, Schwilgué, so built this mechanical calendar that, at midnight on the last day of each year, all the days of the week adopt new positions. An extra day is added each leap year, and the movable holiday of Easter is shown appropriately year by year. The middle dial on Schwilguè's clock is a normal one for telling the hours, but the top one indicates the position of each of the seven planets then known, as seen in the heavens from Earth (Neptune and Pluto had not been discovered when the clock was made).

There are two galleries on the upper part of the tower. Each quarter of an hour, a tiny human figure moves along the lower gallery and rings out the quarter: first quarter, a child; second quarter, a young man; third quarter, a middle-aged man; and, at the hour, an old man carrying Death and his scythe. At noon, the figures of 12 little monks proceed along the upper gallery, and a tiny cock cries out 'cock-a-doodle-doo!'

Another clock of world fame is London's Big Ben, although that is actually the name of the bell, not the clock itself. One of the sights of the city, if only because of its great size, Big Ben became well-known all over the world as a result of its chimes being broadcast regularly by the BBC during the days of World War II. Each of the clock's four dials is 7 metres (23 feet) in diameter and the bell weighs more than 13 tonnes.

Calendars

The Sun was responsible, in the first place, for man's measurement of the days and hours, but the Moon played its part in the calculation of weeks and months – and also of tides and their effects – in conjunction with the Sun. A period of 29 days, 12 hours, 44 minutes, 2·87 seconds represents the mean time taken from full Moon to full Moon, and this is known as the lunar month. Since

1926, however, a month is *legally* considered to be a calendar month.

Calendars of a sort were in use before the birth of Christ in many different parts of the world. There is, for instance, a 50-tonne Aztec monolith, found in Mexico in 1790, which is thought to be an early form of calendar inscribed on stone.

Julius Caesar introduced the Julian Calendar just over 2,000 years ago. This, being based on a year of $365\frac{1}{4}$ days, included the principle of the leap year. Despite its accuracy over a comparatively short period, the Julian Calendar was approximately 11 minutes out of true in the course of each year, because the Earth orbits the Sun in 365 days, 5 hours, 48 minutes, 46 seconds (mean solar time).

Over the centuries, the error accumulated until, in 1582, Italy introduced the Gregorian Calendar to rectify the miscalculation and adjust the passing of months and years precisely. This was done by counting century years as leap years only when they are divisible by 400, as will happen when we reach the year 2000. The Gregorian or New Style Calendar, named after Pope Gregory III who introduced it, is still in use today.

TIMES AROUND THE WORLD

When it is 1200 hrs (noon), Greenwich Mean Time,* clocks and watches around the world will normally show times as listed.

CITY	TIME	CITY	TIME
Adelaide	21.30	Melbourne	22.00
Amsterdam	13.00	Montreal	07.00
Ankara	14.00	Moscow	15.00
Athens	14.00	Nairobi	15.00
Auckland	24.00	New York	07.00
Belgrade	13.00	Oslo	13.00
Berlin	13.00	Ottawa	07.00
Bombay	17.30	Panama	07.00
Brisbane	22.00	Paris	13.00
Brussels	13.00	Peking	20.00
Budapest	13.00	Perth	20.00
Buenos Aires	09.00	Prague	13.00
Cairo	14.00	Quebec	07.00
Calcutta	17.30	Rangoon	18.30
Cape Town	14.00	Rio de Janeiro	09.00
Chicago	06.00	Rome	13.00
Copenhagen	13.00	San Francisco	04.00
Gibraltar	13.00	St John's (N.F.)	08.30
Helsinki	14.00	Singapore	19.30
Hobart	22.00	Stockholm	13.00
Hong Kong	20.00	Sydney	22.00
Istanbul	14.00	Teheran	15.30
Jerusalem	14.00	Tokyo	21.00
London	12.00	Toronto	07.00
Madeira	12.00	Vancouver	04.00
Madrid	13.00	Vienna	13.00
Malta	13.00	Winnipeg	06.00
Mauritius	16.00	Yokohama	21.00

*Greenwich Mean Time is based on the meridian at Greenwich, London. It dates, in practice, from the building of a clock, in 1852 and still in existence, at the Greenwich Observatory. GMT was adopted all over the world in 1884 and became Universal Time.

WEDDING ANNIVERSARIES

1st	Cotton	25th	Silver
5th	Wood	40th	Ruby
10th	Tin	50th	Gold
15th	Crystal	60th	Diamond
20th	China	70th	Platinum

DAYS OF THE WEEK

ENGLISH	LATIN	ANGLO-SAXON
Monday	Dies Lunae	Moon's Day
Tuesday	Dies Martis	Tiu's Day
Wednesday	Dies Mercurii	Woden's Day
Thursday	Dies Jovis	Thor's Day
Friday	Dies Veneris	Frigg's (or Freyja's) Day
Saturday	Dies Saturni	Saturn's Day
Sunday	Dies Solis	Sun's Day

DAYS OF THE MONTH

'Thirty days hath September,
April, June, and November.
All the rest have thirty-one,
Excepting February alone,
That has 28 days clear,
And 29 each leap year.'

THE WORLD
AND ITS PEOPLE

Languages of the World

PRINCIPAL LANGUAGES OF THE WORLD

LANGUAGE	NUMBER OF SPEAKERS	LANGUAGE FAMILY
Northern Chinese (Mandarin, Guoyu, or Beifanghira)	600,000,000	Sino-Tibetan
English	375,000,000	Indo-European
Russian	210,000,000	Indo-European
Hindustani (a combination of Hindi and Urdu)	200,000,000	Indo-European
Spanish	200,000,000	Indo-European
German	125,000,000	Indo-European
Arabic	120,000,000	Hamito-Semitic
Bengali	120,000,000	Indo-European
Portuguese	120,000,000	Indo-European
Japanese	110,000,000	Inrelated to any known language
Malay-Indonesian	95,000,000	Malayo-Polynesian
French	90,000,000	Indo-European
Italian	60,000,000	Indo-European
Cantonese (a dialect of Chinese spoken in the Kwang-tung area)	50,000,000	Sino-Tibetan
Korean	50,000,000	Unrelated to any known language
Marathi (spoken in west and central India)	50,000,000	Indo-European
Punjabi (spoken in Punjab region and Pakistan)	50,000,000	Indo-European
Tamil (spoken in Sri Lanka, south India and Malaysia)	50,000,000	Dravidian
Telugu (spoken in south India)	50,000,000	Dravidian
Javanese (spoken in Indonesia)	45,000,000	Malayo-Polynesian

Over 4,000 languages – living or dead – have been identified and more than 2,000 are spoken today. They are classified into families. One of the largest families is known as the Indo-European group of languages, all of which are derived from a common tongue spoken by nomadic tribes in northern Europe in about 3000 BC. Today, nearly half the people in the world speak an Indo-European language.

Over the centuries, languages have changed. Pronunciation of words has tended to alter and new words have often been added, especially when invaders speaking a different tongue settled among a conquered people. Even basic grammar can change over a long period of time. As a result, completely new languages have evolved from older ones. Modern English is very dissimilar to the Anglo-Saxon language that preceded it.

Sometimes, in a region, a local form of the main language of a country develops. It is then called a *dialect*. For instance, Catalan is a dialect of Spanish which originated in the province of Catalonia. The majority of the people of Spain speak Castilian Spanish, the classic form of the language originating in Castile. There is a small number of languages, called isolates, which have no known relation to any other. Examples of these are Basque and Korean.

Of the 2,000 different languages in use today, the most widely spoken are listed below. The six main international languages of the major historic colonial powers are English, Spanish, Russian, Arabic, Portuguese and French. Many people throughout the world speak one of these languages as well as their native tongue. In some former colonies the language of the old colonial authority remains as an official language.

Countries of the World

Population figures in the following list cannot be absolutely accurate as there are many areas of the world where no census is taken. Furthermore, some countries have not been fully surveyed, so the areas given here may in some cases be only approximate.

An asterisk (*) denotes that the country is a member of the British Commonwealth, and was part of the old British Empire.

AFGHANISTAN, Democratic Republic of   population: 19,800,000
Capital Kabul
Land area 636,270 sq km (245,664 sq miles)
Principal languages Pushtu, Dari (Persian), Turki
Currency 100 puls = 1 afghani

ALBANIA   population: 2,430,000
Capital Tirana
Land area 28,748 sq km (11,099 sq miles)
Principal languages Gheg, Tosk
Currency 100 qintars = 1 lek

ALGERIA　　　　　　　　　　　　　　population: 17,000,000
Capital Algiers
Land area 2,381,000 sq km (919,592 sq miles)
Principal languages Arabic, French
Currency 100 centimes = 1 dinar

ANDORRA　　　　　　　　　　　　　population: 30,700
Capital Andorra la Vella
Land area 466 sq km (180 sq miles)
Principal languages Catalan, French, Spanish
Currency French and Spanish currency both in use

ANGOLA　　　　　　　　　　　　　population: 5,400,000
Capital Luanda
Land area 1,246,700 sq km (481,351 sq miles)
Principal languages Portuguese, tribal languages
Currency 100 lwei = 1 kwanza

ARGENTINA　　　　　　　　　　　population: 25,400,000
Capital Buenos Aires
Land area 2,777,815 sq km (1,072,514 sq miles)
Principal language Spanish
Currency 100 centavos = 1 peso

*AUSTRALIA, Commonwealth of　　　population: 14,070,000
Capital Canberra
Land area 7,686,884 sq km (2,967,906 sq miles)
Principal language English
Currency 100 cents = 1 Australian dollar

AUSTRIA　　　　　　　　　　　　　population: 7,460,000
Capital Vienna
Land area 83,853 sq km (32,376 sq miles)
Principal language German
Currency 100 groschen = 1 schilling

*BAHAMAS, Commonwealth of the　　population: 218,000
Capital Nassau
Land area 13,864 sq km (5,353 sq miles)
Principal language English
Currency 100 cents = 1 Bahamas dollar

BAHRAIN　　　　　　　　　　　　population: 275,600
Capital Manama
Land area 570 sq km (220 sq miles)
Principal languages Arabic, Urdu
Currency 1,000 fils = 1 dinar

*BANGLADESH　　　　　　　　　population: 80,500,000
Capital Dacca
Land area 144,020 sq km (55,606 sq miles)
Principal language Bengali
Currency 100 paise = 1 taka

*BARBADOS
population: 258,000
Capital Bridgetown
Land area 430 sq km (166 sq miles)
Principal language English
Currency 100 cents = 1 Barbados dollar

BELGIUM
population: 9,800,000
Capital Brussels
Land area 30,513 sq km (11,781 sq miles)
Principal languages Dutch (Flemish), French, German
Currency 100 centimes = 1 franc

BENIN, People's Republic of (formerly Dahomey)
population: 3,200,000
Capital Porto Novo
Land area 112,622 sq km (43,483 sq miles)
Principal languages French, tribal languages
Currency 100 centimes = 1 franc CFA

*BERMUDA
population: 55,000
Capital Hamilton
Land area 53 sq km (20 sq miles)
Principal language English
Currency 100 cents = 1 Bermuda dollar

BHUTAN
population: 1,200,000
Capital Thimphu
Land area 46,600 sq km (18,000 sq miles)
Principal language Dzongkha
Currency 100 paisa = 1 rupee

BOLIVIA
population: 4,700,000
Capital La Paz
Land area 1,098,580 sq km (424,160 sq miles)
Principal languages Spanish, Quechua, Aymara
Currency 100 centavos = 1 Bolivian peso

*BOTSWANA (formerly Bechuanaland Protectorate)
population: 800,000
Capital Gaborone
Land area 575,000 sq km (222,000 sq miles)
Principal languages English, Setswana
Currency 100 thebe = 1 pula

BRAZIL, Federative Republic of
population: 116,400,000
Capital Brasilia
Land area 8,511,965 sq km (3,286,470 sq miles)
Principal language Portuguese
Currency 100 centavos = 1 cruzeiro

*BRUNEI
population: 201,260
Capital Bindar Seri Begawan
Land area 5,800 sq km (2,226 sq miles)
Principal languages Malay, English
Currency 100 cents = 1 Brunei dollar

BULGARIA, People's Republic of   population: 8,760,000
Capital Sofia
Land area 110,912 sq km (42,823 sq miles)
Principal languages Bulgarian, Turkish
Currency 100 stotinki = 1 lev

BURMA, Socialist Republic of the Union of   population: 30,830,000
Capital Rangoon
Land area 678,000 sq km (262,000 sq miles)
Principal language Burmese
Currency 100 pyas = 1 kyat

BURUNDI (formerly part of Ruanda-Urundi)   population: 3,900,000
Capital Bujumbura
Land area 27,834 sq km (10,747 sq miles)
Principal languages Kirundi, French
Currency 100 centimes = 1 Burundi franc

CAMBODIA
see Kampuchea

CAMEROON, United Republic of   population: 7,700,000
Capital Yaoundé
Land area 474,000 sq km (183,000 sq miles)
Principal languages French, English
Currency franc CFA

*CANADA, Dominion of   population: 23,500,000
Capital Ottowa
Land area 9,220,975 sq km (3,560,218 sq miles)
Principal languages English, French
Currency 100 cents = 1 Canadian dollar

CAPE VERDE   population: 360,000
Capital Praia
Land area 4,033 sq km (1,557 sq miles)
Principal languages Portuguese, tribal languages
Currency 100 centavos = 1 escudo

CENTRAL AFRICAN EMPIRE (formerly Central   population: 241,000
African Republic)
Capital Bangui
Land area 625,000 sq km (241,000 sq miles)
Principal languages French, Sangho
Currency franc CFA

CEYLON
see Sri Lanka

CHAD   population: 3,870,000
Capital N'djamena
Land area 1,284,000 sq km (496,000 sq miles)
Principal languages French, Arabic, tribal languages
Currency franc CFA

CHILE
population: 10,400,000

Capital Santiago
Land area 741,767 sq km (286,396 sq miles)
Principal language Spanish
Currency 1,000 escudos = 1 Chilean peso

CHINA, People's Republic of
population: 900,000,000

Capital Peking
Land area 9,597,000 sq km (3,705,000 sq miles)
Principal language Chinese
Currency 100 fens = 1 yuan (renminbi)

COLOMBIA
population: 26,500,000

Capital Bagotá
Land area 1,138,914 sq km (439,735 sq miles)
Principal language Spanish
Currency 100 centavos = 1 peso

COMOROS (Comoro Republic)
population: 290,000

Capital Moroni
Land area 1,862 sq km (719 sq miles)
Principal languages Comoran, French
Currency franc CFA

CONGO, People's Republic of the
population: 1,420,000

Capital Brazzaville
Land area 342,000 sq km (132,000 sq miles)
Principal languages French, tribal languages
Currency franc CFA

COSTA RICA
population: 2,000,000

Capital San José
Land area 51,100 sq km (19,730 sq miles)
Principal language Spanish
Currency 100 centimos = 1 colon

CUBA
population: 9,470,000

Capital Havana
Land area 114,524 sq km (44,218 sq miles)
Principal language Spanish
Currency 100 centavos = 1 Cuban peso

*CYPRUS
population: 639,000

Capital Nicosia
Land area 9,251 sq km (3,572 sq miles)
Principal languages Greek, Turkish
Currency 1,000 mils = 1 Cyprus pound

CZECHOSLOVAKIA
population: 14,970,000

Capital Prague
Land area 127,877 sq km (49,373 sq miles)
Principal languages Czech, Slovak
Currency 100 halers = 1 koruna

DENMARK population: 5,100,000
Capital Copenhagen
Land area 43,075 sq km (16,631 sq miles)
Principal language Danish
Currency 100 öre = 1 krone

DJIBOUTI (formerly French Somaliland; Afars and population: 125,000
Issas)
Capital Djibouti
Land area 23,000 sq km (9,000 sq miles)
Principal languages French, Somali, Dankali, Arabic
Currency 100 centimes = 1 Djibouti franc

*DOMINICA population: 78,000
Capital Roseau
Land area 751 sq km (290 sq miles)
Principal language English
Currency The French franc, pound sterling and East
Caribbean dollar are all legal tender

DOMINICAN REPUBLIC population: 4,700,000
Capital Santo Domingo
Land area 48,442 sq km (18,700 sq miles)
Principal language Spanish
Currency 100 centavos = 1 peso

ECUADOR population: 6,500,000
Capital Quito
Land area 276,000 sq km (106,508 sq miles)
Principal languages Spanish, Quechua and other
Amerindian languages
Currency 100 centavos = 1 sucre

EGYPT, Arab Republic of (formerly United Arab population: 40,000,000
Republic)
Capital Cairo
Land area 1,000,000 sq km (386,000 sq miles)
Principal language Arabic
Currency 100 piastres = 1 Egyptian pound

EQUATORIAL GUINEA population: 325,000
Capital Malabo
Land area 28,050 sq km (10,830 sq miles)
Principal languages Spanish, Arabic
Currency ekpwele

ETHIOPIA population: 30,180,000
Capital Addis Ababa
Land area 1,023,000 sq km (395,000 sq miles)
Principal language Amharic
Currency 100 cents = 1 birr

*FIJI　　　　　　　　　　　　　　　　　　population: 601,485
Capital Suva
Land area 18,272 sq km (7,055 sq miles)
Principal languages English, tribal languages
Currency 100 cents = 1 Fiji dollar

FINLAND　　　　　　　　　　　　　　　population: 4,740,000
Capital Helsinki
Land area 305,475 sq km (118,000 sq miles)
Principal languages Finnish, Swedish
Currency 100 pennia = 1 markka

FRANCE　　　　　　　　　　　　　　　population: 53,200,000
Capital Paris
Land area 550,634 sq km (212,600 sq miles)
Principal language French
Currency 100 centimes = 1 franc

GABON　　　　　　　　　　　　　　　　population: 950,000
Capital Libreville
Land area 267,667 sq km (103,346 sq miles)
Principal languages French, Bantu dialects
Currency franc CFA

*GAMBIA, The　　　　　　　　　　　　　population: 568,000
Capital Banjul
Land area 10,368 sq km (4,003 sq miles)
Principal languages English, tribal languages
Currency 100 bututs = 1 dalasi

GERMAN DEMOCRATIC REPUBLIC (DDR)　　population: 16,800,000
Capital Berlin (East)
Land area 108,179 sq km (41,768 sq miles)
Principal language German
Currency 100 pfennig = 1 ostmark

GERMANY, Federal Republic of　　　　population: 61,350,000
Capital Bonn
Land area 248,630 sq km (95,996 sq miles)
Principal language German
Currency 100 pfennig = 1 Deutsche mark

*GHANA　　　　　　　　　　　　　　　population: 9,600,000
Capital Accra
Land area 238,305 sq km (92,010 sq miles)
Principal languages English, tribal languages
Currency 100 pesewa = 1 cedi

GREECE　　　　　　　　　　　　　　　population: 9,200,000
Capital Athens
Land area 131,986 sq km (50,960 sq miles)
Principal language Greek
Currency 100 lepta = 1 drachma

*GRENADA population: 108,000
Capital St George's
Land area 344 sq km (133 sq miles)
Principal language English
Currency 100 cents = 1 East Caribbean dollar

GUATEMALA population: 6,800,000
Capital Guatemala City
Land area 108,889 sq km (42,042 sq miles)
Principal languages Spanish, Amerindian languages
Currency 100 centavos = 1 quetzal

GUINEA population: 5,140,000
Capital Conakry
Land area 245,857 sq km (95,000 sq miles)
Principal languages French, tribal languages
Currency 100 cauris = 1 syli

GUINEA-BISSAU (formerly Portuguese Guinea) population: 800,000
Capital Bissau
Land area 36,125 sq km (13,948 sq miles)
Principal languages Portuguese, tribal languages
Currency 100 centavos = 1 escudo

*GUYANA (formerly British Guiana) population: 800,000
Capital Georgetown
Land area 210,000 sq km (81,000 sq miles)
Principal languages English, Amerindian languages
Currency 100 cents = 1 Guyana dollar

HAITI population: 4,580,000
Capital Port-au-Prince
Land area 27,750 sq km (10,700 sq miles)
Principal languages French, Creole
Currency 100 centimes = 1 gourde

HONDURAS population: 2,831,000
Capital Tegucigalpa
Land area 112,088 sq km (43,227 sq miles)
Principal languages Spanish, tribal languages
Currency 100 centavos = 1 lempira

HUNGARY population: 10,670,000
Capital Budapest
Land area 93,032 sq km (35,920 sq miles)
Principal language Hungarian (Magyar)
Currency 100 filler = 1 forint

ICELAND population: 221,000
Capital Reykjavik
Land area 103,000 sq km (39,768 sq miles)
Principal language Icelandic
Currency 100 aurar = 1 krona

*INDIA
Capital New Delhi
Land area 3,166,828 sq km (1,222,712 sq miles)
Principal languages Putshu, Hindi, Baluchi, Bengali,·
Pali, Urdu, Hindustani, Assamese, Oriya, Bihari,
Rajasthani, Gujarati, Punjabi, Kashmiri, Tamil, Telegu,
Gondi and many others
Currency 100 paise = 1 rupee

INDONESIA
population: 141,600,000
Capital Jakarta
Land area 1,903,650 sq km (735,000 sq miles)
Principal languages Bahasa Indonesian, English and
many local languages and dialects spoken
Currency 100 sen = 1 rupiah

IRAN (formerly Persia)
population: 34,000,000
Capital Teheran
Land area 1,648,000 sq km (636,000 sq miles)
Principal languages Persian (Farsi), Kurdish
Currency 100 dinars = 1 rial

IRAQ
population: 12,200,000
Capital Bagdad
Land area 438,446 sq km (169,284 sq miles)
Principal languages Arabic, Kurdish
Currency 1,000 fils = 1 dinar

IRELAND, Republic of
population: 3,220,000
Capital Dublin
Land area 68,893 sq km (26,600 sq miles)
Principal languages English, Irish (Gaelic)
Currency 100 pence = 1 Irish pound

ISRAEL
population: 3,600,000
Capital Jerusalem
Land area 20,700 sq km (8,000 sq miles)
Principal languages Hebrew, Yiddish, Arabic and
several European languages
Currency 100 new agorot = 1 shekel

ITALY
population: 56,500,000
Capital Rome
Land area 301,245 sq km (116,300 sq miles)
Principal language Italian
Currency 100 centesimi = 1 lira

IVORY COAST
population: 7,300,000
Capital Abidjan
Land area 322,500 sq km (124,500 sq miles)
Principal languages French and many tribal
languages
Currency franc CFA

*JAMAICA   population: 2,110,000
Capital Kingston
Land area 10,991 sq km (4,244 sq miles)
Principal language English
Currency 100 cents = 1 Jamaican dollar

JAPAN   population: 114,200,000
Capital Tokyo
Land area 370,370 sq km (143,000 sq miles)
Principal language Japanese
Currency 100 sen = 1 yen

JORDAN   population: 3,000,000
Capital Amman
Land area 101,140 sq km (39,050 sq miles)
Principal language Arabic
Currency 1,000 fils = 1 dinar

KAMPUCHEA, Democratic (formerly Cambodia and   population: 7,700,000(?)
Khmer Republic)
Capital Phnom Penh
Land area 181,000 sq km (70,000 sq miles)
Principal language Khmer
Currency money officially abolished since 1978

*KENYA   population: 14,340,000
Capital Nairobi
Land area 582,600 sq km (224,960 sq miles)
Principal languages Arabic, Swahili and Bantu
Currency 100 cents = 1 Kenya shilling

*KIRIBATI (formerly Gilbert Islands)   population: 52,000
Capital Tarawa
Land area 956 sq km (369 sq miles)
Principal languages English, Gilbertese
Currency 100 cents = 1 Australian dollar

KOREA, Democratic People's Republic of (North Korea)   population: 16,000,000
Capital Pyongyang
Land area 122,370 sq km (47,250 sq miles)
Principal language Korean
Currency 100 jun = 1 won

KOREA, Republic of (South Korea)   population: 36,400,000
Capital Seoul
Land area 98,447 sq km (38,002 sq miles)
Principal language Korean
Currency 100 chon = 1 won

KUWAIT   population: 1,130,000
Capital Kuwait
Land area 24,280 sq km (9,375 sq miles)
Principal language Arabic
Currency 1,000 fils = 1 dinar

LAOS (Lao People's Democratic Republic)
Capital Vientiane
Land area 235,700 sq km (91,000 sq miles)
Principal languages Lao, French
Currency 100 ats = 1 kip

population: 2,900,000

LEBANON
Capital Beirut
Land area 10,400 sq km (4,000 sq miles)
Principal language Arabic
Currency 100 piastres = 1 Lebanese pound

population: 3,060,000

*LESOTHO (formerly Basutoland)
Capital Maseru
Land area 30,340 sq km (11,715 sq miles)
Principal languages English, Sesotho
Currency 100 cents = 1 South African rand

population: 1,250,000

LIBERIA
Capital Monrovia
Land area 112,600 sq km (43,500 sq miles)
Principal languages English, tribal languages
Currency 100 cents = 1 Liberian dollar

population: 1,500,000

LIBYA (Popular Socialist Libyan Arab Jamahiriyah)
Capital Tripoli
Land area 1,759,540 sq km (679,358 sq miles)
Principal language Arabic
Currency 1,000 dirhams = 1 dinar

population: 2,630,000

LIECHTENSTEIN
Capital Vaduz
Land area 160 sq km (62 sq miles)
Principal language German
Currency 100 centimes = 1 Swiss franc

population: 24,715

LUXEMBOURG
Capital Luxembourg
Land area 2,586 sq km (998 sq miles)
Principal languages Lutzeburgesch, French and German
Currency 100 centimes = 1 Luxembourg franc

population: 360,200

MADAGASCAR, Democratic Republic of
Capital Antananarivo
Land area 594,180 sq km (229,400 sq miles)
Principal languages Malagasy, French, English
Currency 100 centimes = 1 Malagasy franc

population: 8,000,000

*MALAWI, Republic of (formerly Nyasaland)
Capital Lilongwe
Land area 117,614 sq km (45,411 sq miles)
Principal languages English, Chinyanya,
Chitumbukaere
Currency 100 tambala = 1 kwacha

population: 5,310,000

*MALAYSIA population: 12,530,000
Capital Kuala Lumpur
Land area 334,110 sq km (129,000 sq miles)
Principal languages Malay, English, Chinese, Tamil
Currency 100 cents = 1 Malaysian dollar (ringgit)

MALDIVES, The population: 143,500
Capital Malé
Land area 298 sq km (115 sq miles)
Principal language Divehi
Currency 100 laris = 1 rupee

MALI population: 6,030,000
Capital Bamako
Land area 1,204,021 sq km (464,873 sq miles)
Principal languages French, Bambara
Currency 100 centimes = 1 Mali franc

*MALTA population: 309,000
Capital Valletta
Land area 246 sq km (95 sq miles)
Principal languages Maltese, English
Currency 100 cents = 1 Maltese pound

MAURITANIA (Mauritanian Islamic Republic) population: 1,480,000
Capital Nouakchott
Land area 1,030,700 sq km (398,000 sq miles)
Principal languages Arabic, French
Currency 5 khoums = 1 ougiya

*MAURITIUS population: 880,800
Capital Port Louis
Land area 1,865 sq km (720 sq miles)
Principal languages English, French, Creole, Hindi
Currency 100 cents = 1 rupee

MEXICO (United Mexican States) population: 62,330,000
Capital Mexico City
Land area 1,967,183 sq km (759,530 sq miles)
Principal languages Spanish, Amerindian languages
Currency 100 centavos = 1 peso

MONACO population: 25,050
Capital Monaco
Land area 190 hectares (467 acres)
Principal languages French, Monegasque
Currency 100 centimes = 1 French franc

MONGOLIA (Mongolian People's Republic) population: 1,500,000
Capital Ulan Bator
Land area 1,565,000 sq km (604,247 sq miles)
Principal language Mongol
Currency 100 möngö = 1 tugrik

MOROCCO
population: 18,340,000
Capital Rabat
Land area 659,970 sq km (254,814 sq miles)
Principal languages Arabic, Berber, French, Spanish
Currency 100 francs = 1 dirham

MOZAMBIQUE, People's Republic of
population: 11,000,000
Capital Maputo
Land area 784,961 sq km (303,073 sq miles)
Principal language Portuguese
Currency 100 centavos = 1 escudo

*NAURU
population: 7,254
Capital Makwa
Land area 2,130 hectares (5,263 acres)
Principal language English
Currency 100 cents = 1 Australian dollar

NEPAL
population: 11,700,000
Capital Kathmandu
Land area 141,400 sq km (54,600 sq miles)
Principal languages Nepali, Maithir, Bhojpuri
Currency 100 pice (paisa) = 1 Nepalese rupee

NETHERLANDS, The
population: 13,880,000
Seat of government The Hague
Capital Amsterdam
Land area 41,160 sq km (15,892 sq miles)
Principal language Dutch
Currency 100 cents = 1 guilder (florin)

*NEW ZEALAND
population: 3,130,000
Capital Wellington
Land area 268,704 sq km (103,747 sq miles)
Principal language English
Currency 100 cents = 1 NZ dollar

NICARAGUA
population: 2,240,000
Capital Managua
Land area 148,000 sq km (57,000 sq miles)
Principal language Spanish
Currency 100 centavos = 1 cordoba

NIGER
population: 4,990,000
Capital Niamey
Land area 1,187,000 sq km (458,300 sq miles)
Principal languages French, Arabic, tribal languages
Currency franc CFA

*NIGERIA, Federal Republic of
population: 73,000,000
Capital Lagos
Land area 923,770 sq km (356,670 sq miles)
Principal languages English, Hausa, Igbo, Yoruba
Currency 100 kobo = 1 naira

NORWAY population: 4,050,000
Capital Oslo
Land area 323,895 sq km (125,056 sq miles)
Principal language Norwegian
Currency 100 öre = 1 krone

OMAN (formerly Muscat and Oman) population: 750,000
Capital Muscat
Land area 212,380 sq km (82,000 sq miles)
Principal language Arabic
Currency 100 baiza = 1 riyal

PAKISTAN population: 75,600,000
Capital Islamabad
Land area 803,943 sq km (310,403 sq miles)
Principal languages Urdu, Punjabi, Sindhi, Pushtu,
Baluchi, Brahvi
Currency 100 paisa = 1 rupee

PANAMA population: 1,780,000
Capital Panama City
Land area 75,650 sq km (29,210 sq miles)
Principal language Spanish
Currency 100 centesimos = 1 balboa

*PAPUA NEW GUINEA population: 2,960,000
Capital Port Moresby
Land area 462,840 sq km (178,700 sq miles)
Principal language English
Currency 100 toea = 1 kina

PARAGUAY population: 2,750,000
Capital Asuncion
Land area 406,752 sq km (157,047 sq miles)
Principal languages Spanish, Guarani
Currency 100 centimos = 1 guarani

PERU population: 15,500,000
Capital Lima
Land area 1,285,215 sq km (496,223 sq miles)
Principal languages Spanish, Quechua, Aymara
Currency 100 centavos = 1 sol

PHILIPPINES, The population: 45,030,000
Capital Quezon City (a suburb of Manila)
Land area 300,000 sq km (115,830 sq miles)
Principal languages Filipino, English and Spanish
Currency 100 centavos = 1 peso

POLAND population: 34,900,000
Capital Warsaw
Land area 312,683 sq km (120,727 sq miles)
Principal language Polish
Currency 100 groszy = 1 zloty

PORTUGAL   population: 8,750,000
Capital Lisbon
Land area 91,631 sq km (35,379 sq miles)
Principal language Portuguese
Currency 100 centavos = 1 escudo

QATAR   population: 200,000
Capital Doha
Land area 11,000 sq km (4,247 sq miles)
Principal language Arabic
Currency 100 dirham = 1 riyal

ROMANIA   population: 21,650,000
Capital Bucharest
Land area 237,500 sq km (91,700 sq miles)
Principal language Romanian
Currency 100 bani = 1 leu

RWANDA   population: 4,400,000
Capital Kigali
Land area 26,330 sq km (10,170 sq miles)
Principal languages Kinyarwanda, French
Currency 100 centimes = 1 Rwanda franc

*ST LUCIA   population: 113,000
Capital Castries
Land area 616 sq km (238 sq miles)
Principal language English
Currency 100 cents = 1 East Caribbean dollar

SALVADOR, El   population: 4,000,000
Capital San Salvador
Land area 21,393 sq km (8,260 sq miles)
Principal language Spanish
Currency 100 centavos = 1 colon

SAN MARINO   population: 19,200
Capital San Marino
Land area 61 sq km (24 sq miles)
Principal language Italian
Currency Italian and Vatican City currencies are in
general use

SAO TOME E PRINCIPE   population: 82,750
Capital São Tomé
Land area 964 sq km (372 sq miles)
Principal language Portuguese
Currency 100 centavos = 1 escudo

SAUDI ARABIA   population: 9,160,000
Capital Riyadh
Land area 2,400,000 sq km (927,000 sq miles)
Principal language Arabic
Currency 100 halalas = 1 riyal

SENEGAL
population: 5,090,000
Capital Dakar
Land area 197,720 sq km (76,340 sq miles)
Principal language French
Currency franc CFA

*SEYCHELLES
population: 62,000
Capital Victoria (on island of Mahé)
Land area 404 sq km (156 sq miles)
Principal languages English, French, Créole
Currency 100 cents = 1 rupee

*SIERRA LEONE
population: 3,470,000
Capital Freetown
Land area 73,326 sq km (28,311 sq miles)
Principal languages English, tribal languages
Currency 100 cents = 1 leone

*SINGAPORE
population: 2,310,000
Capital Singapore
Land area 616 sq km (238 sq miles)
Principal languages Malay, Chinese, Tamil, English
Currency 100 cents = 1 Singapore dollar

*SOLOMON ISLANDS
population: 196,850
Capital Honiara (on Guadalcanal Island)
Land area 29,785 sq km (11,500 sq miles)
Principal languages English, Melanesian languages
Currency Australian dollar, Solomon Islands dollar

SOMALIA (Somali Democratic Republic)
population: 3,200,000
Capital Mogadiscio
Land area 630,000 sq km (243,000 sq miles)
Principal languages Somali, Arabic, Italian, English
Currency 100 cents = 1 Somali shilling

SOUTH AFRICA, Republic of
population: 26,000,000
Administrative capital Pretoria
Legislative capital Cape Town
Judicial capital Bloemfontein
Land area 1,140,519 sq km (440,354 sq miles)
Principal languages Afrikaans, English, Xhosa, Zulu,
Sesotho
Currency 100 cents = 1 rand

SPAIN
population: 35,700,000
Capital Madrid
Land area 504,879 sq km (194,934 sq miles)
Principal languages Spanish (Castilian), Catalan,
Galician, Basque
Currency 100 centimes = 1 peseta

*SRI LANKA (formerly Ceylon)
Capital Colombo
Land area 65,610 sq km (25,332 sq miles)
Principal languages Sinhala, Tamil
Currency 100 cents = 1 rupee

population: 13,940,000

SUDAN
Capital Khartoum
Land area 2,500,000 sq km (967,500 sq miles)
Principal language Arabic
Currency 100 piastres = 1 Sudan pound

population: 17,000,000

SURINAM
Capital Paramaribo
Land area 163,000 sq km (63,000 sq miles)
Principal languages Sranan (Taki Taki), Dutch,
English, Spanish, Hindi, Javanese, Chinese
Currency 100 cents = 1 Surinam guilder

population: 450,000

*SWAZILAND
Capital Mbabane
Land area 17,400 sq km (6,700 sq miles)
Principal languages English, Siswati
Currency 100 cents = 1 lilangeni (plural emalangeni);
South African rand also in use

population: 528,000

SWEDEN
Capital Stockholm
Land area 411,479 sq km (158,872 sq miles)
Principal language Swedish
Currency 100 öre = 1 krona

population: 8,200,000

SWITZERLAND
Capital Bern
Land area 41,288 sq km (15,941 sq miles)
Principal languages German, French, Italian,
Romansch
Currency 100 centimes = 1 franc

population: 6,300,000

SYRIA (Syrian Arab Republic)
Capital Damascus
Land area 185,680 sq km (71,690 sq miles)
Principal language Arabic
Currency 100 piastres = 1 Syrian pound

population: 8,300,000

TAIWAN (formerly Formosa)
Capital Taipei
Land area 35,989 sq km (13,895 sq miles)
Principal language Chinese (Mandarin and Amoy
dialects)
Currency 100 cents = 1 new Taiwan dollar

population: 15,000,000

*TANZANIA (a union formed in 1964 between   population: 17,500,000
Tanganyika, Zanzibar and Pemba)
Capital Dar es Salaam; moving to Dodoma
Land area 939,706 sq km (363,708 sq miles)
Principal languages Swahili, English
Currency 100 cents = 1 Tanzanian shilling

THAILAND   population: 45,000,000
Capital Bangkok
Land area 514,000 sq km (198,500 sq miles)
Principal language Thai
Currency 100 satang = 1 baht (tical)

TOGO   population: 2,200,000
Capital Lomé
Land area 56,000 sq km (22,000 sq miles)
Principal languages Ewe, Mina, Dajomba, Tim, Cabrais
and other tribal languages
Currency franc CFA

*TONGA (Friendly Islands)   population: 90,150
Capital Nuku'alofa (on the island of Tongatapu)
Land area 700 sq km (270 sq miles)
Principal languages Polynesian, English
Currency 100 seniti = 1 pa'anga

*TRINIDAD AND TOBAGO   population: 1,070,000
Capital Port-of-Spain
Land area 4,828 sq km (1,864 sq miles)
Principal language English
Currency 100 cents = 1 Trinidad and Tobago dollar

TUNISIA   population: 6,030,000
Capital Tunis
Land area 164,150 sq km (63,380 sq miles)
Principal languages Arabic, French
Currency 1,000 millimes = 1 dinar

TURKEY   population: 40,200,000
Capital Ankara
Land area 779,452 sq km (300,946 sq miles)
Principal language Turkish
Currency 100 kurus = 1 Turkish pound (lira)

*TUVALU (formerly Ellice Islands)   population: 5,900
Capital Funafuti
Land area 24 sq km (9 sq miles)
Principal languages English, Ellice
Currency 100 cents = 1 Australian dollar

*UGANDA
population: 11,170,000
Capital Kampala
Land area 236,860 sq km (91,430 sq miles)
Principal languages English, Bantu languages, Kiswahili
Currency 100 cents = 1 Uganda shilling

USSR (Union of Soviet Socialist Republics)
population: 260,000,000
Capital Moscow
Land area 22,400,000 sq km (8,650,000 sq miles)
Principal languages Russian, Ukrainian, Uzbek and several others
Currency 100 kopeks = 1 rouble

UNITED ARAB EMIRATES (a federation consisting of the former Trucial States; Abu Dhabi, Dubai, Sharjah, Ajman, Umm al Qawain and Fujairah joined in 1971, Ras al Khaimah joined in 1972)
population: 652,900
Capital Abu Dhabi
Land area 92,100 sq km (35,560 sq miles)
Principal language Arabic
Currency 100 fils = 1 dirham

UNITED KINGDOM OF GREAT BRITAIN AND NORTHERN IRELAND (comprises England, Scotland, Wales and Northern Ireland. It does not include the Channel Islands or the Isle of Man, which are dependencies of the Crown, but have their own legislative and taxation systems.)
population: 56,000,000
Capital London
Land area
England: 130,362 sq km (50,333 sq miles)
Wales: 20,761 sq km (8,016 sq miles)
Scotland: 78,772 sq km (30,414 sq miles)
Northern Ireland: 14,121 sq km (5,452 sq miles)
Total land area 244,016 sq km (94,215 sq miles)
Principal languages English, Welsh, Gaelic
Currency 100 pence = 1 pound sterling

USA (United States of America)
population: 218,060,000
Capital Washington DC
Land area 9,363,169 sq km (3,615,120 sq miles)
Principal language English
Currency 100 cents = 1 dollar

UPPER VOLTA
population: 6,100,000
Capital Ouagadougou
Land area 274,200 sq km (105,900 sq miles)
Principal languages French, tribal languages
Currency franc CFA

URUGUAY   population: 2,760,000
Capital Montevideo
Land area 177,508 sq km (68,536 sq miles)
Principal language Spanish
Currency 100 centesimos = 1 peso

VATICAN CITY STATE   population: 1,000
Land area 44 hectares (108·7 acres)
Principal language Italian
Currency 100 centesimi = 1 lira (Italian and Vatican
City currencies in use)

VENEZUELA   population: 12,700,000
Capital Caracas
Land area 912,050 sq km (352,143 sq miles)
Principal language Spanish
Currency 100 centimos = 1 bolivar

VIETNAM, Socialist Republic of   population: 47,150,000
Capital Hanoi
Land area 329,566 sq km (127,245 sq miles)
Principal language Vietnamese
Currency 100 xu = 1 dong

*WESTERN SAMOA   population: 151,275
Capital Apia (on island of Upolu)
Land area 2,842 sq km (1,097 sq miles)
Principal languages English, Samoan
Currency 100 sene = 1 tala (dollar)

YEMEN ARAB REPUBLIC (North Yemen)   population: 5,240,000
Capital San'a
Land area 195,000 sq km (75,000 sq miles)
Principal language Arabic
Currency 100 fils = 1 riyal

YEMEN, The People's Democratic Republic of (South   population: 1.600,000
Yemen)
Capital Aden
Land area 336,700 sq km (130,000 sq miles)
Principal language Arabic
Currency 1,000 fils = 1 dinar

YUGOSLAVIA   population: 21,560,000
Capital Belgrade
Land area 255,804 sq km (98,766 sq miles)
Principal languages Serbo-Croat, Slovene, Macedonian
Currency 100 paras = 1 dinar

ZAIRE (formerly Congo Democratic Republic)   population: 25,600,000
Capital Kinshasa
Land area 2,345,500 sq km (905,600 sq miles)
Principal languages French, Lingala, Kiswahili,
Tshiluba, Kikongo
Currency 100 makuta = 1 Zaire

*ZAMBIA   population: 5,140,000
Capital Lusaka
Land area 752,620 sq km (290,590 sq miles)
Principal languages English, tribal languages
Currency 100 ngwee = 1 kwacha

*ZIMBABWE (formerly Rhodesia)   population: 6,800,000
Capital Salisbury
Land area 390,622 sq km (150,820 sq miles)
Principal languages English, Shona, Ndebele
Currency 100 cents = 1 Zimbabwe dollar

The United Nations

As World War II drew to a close in 1945, a conference was held in Washington between statesmen of the four great powers on the Allied side – Britain, China, the USSR and the USA. They planned a worldwide organization of countries pledged to prevent war and to replace the defunct League of Nations.

On 26 June 1945 the UN came into being with the signing of the UN Charter by 51 nations at a meeting in San Francisco. The present headquarters is in New York.

The Charter read:

'We the peoples of the United Nations, determined to save succeeding generations from the scourge of war, which twice in our lifetime has brought untold sorrow to mankind, and

'To reaffirm faith in fundamental human rights, in the dignity and worth of the human person, in the equal rights of men and women and of nations large and small, and

'To establish conditions under which justice and respect for the obligations arising from treaties and other sources of international law can be maintained, and

'To promote social progress and better standards of life in larger freedom, and for these ends

'To practise tolerance and live together in peace with one another as good neighbours, and

'To unite our strength to maintain international peace and security, and

'To insure, by the acceptance of principles, and the institution of methods, that armed force shall not be used, save in the common interest, and

'To employ international machinery for the promotion of the economic and social advancement of all peoples, have resolved to combine our efforts to accomplish these aims.

'Accordingly our respective Governments, through representatives assembled in the city of San Francisco, who have exhibited their full powers found to be in good and due form, have agreed to the present Charter of the United Nations and do hereby establish an international organization to be known as the United Nations.'

The Charter became effective on 24 October 1945, when the UN formally came into existence.

There are six major organs contained within the UN:
1 **The General Assembly** This consists of all UN members, and meets once a year. Each member may have up to five representatives but is entitled to only one vote. The members discuss matters concerned with world peace and security and make recommendations to the Security Council.
2 **The Security Council** Consisting of 15 members, the Security Council sits continuously. Its function is to arrange the settlement of disputes and stop aggression. Five of the Council's seats are held permanently by Britain, China, France, USSR and the USA. The other ten are occupied temporarily by countries elected periodically in the General Assembly. The Council can take no action in an emergency if any one of its permanent members uses the veto (forbids action).
3 **The Economic and Social Council** This consists of 54 members elected by the General Assembly for periods of three years. The purpose of this body is to help raise the standards of life all over the world. It is concerned with economic and social problems such as health, education, full employment and human rights, more particularly in the underdeveloped areas of the world.
4 **The Trusteeship Council** This consists of the permanent members of the Security Council.
5 **The International Court of Justice** The principal judicial organ of the United Nations. The judges are elected for nine-year terms.
6 **The Secretariat** This is composed of the Secretary-General who is appointed, as a rule, for a period of five years and his staff.

The United Nations also runs special agencies. These are: International Atomic Energy Agency (IAEA); International Labour Organization (ILO); Food and Agriculture Organization of the United Nations (FAO); United Nations Educational Scientific and Cultural Organization (UNESCO); World Health Organization (WHO);

International Monetary Fund (IMF); International Bank for Reconstruction and Development (The World Bank); International Finance Corporation (IFC); International Civil Aviation Organization (ICAO); International Telecommunications Union (ITU); World Meteorological Organization (WMO); Intergovernmental Maritime Consultative Organization (IMCO); General Agreement on Tariffs and Trade (GATT); International Development Association (IDA); Universal Postal Union (UPU); Office of the United Nations High Commissioner for Refugees (UNHCR); United Nations Children's Fund (UNICEF).

MEMBERS OF THE UNITED NATIONS

There are to date 152 member countries

MEMBER	YEAR OF ADMISSION	MEMBER	YEAR OF ADMISSION	MEMBER	YEAR OF ADMISSION
Afghanistan	1946	Republic		Greece	1945
Albania	1955	of	1971	Grenada	1974
Algeria	1962	Colombia	1945	Guatemala	1945
Angola	1976	Comoros	1975	Guinea	1958
Argentina	1945	Congo	1960	Guinea-	
Australia	1945	Costa Rica	1945	Bissau	1974
Austria	1955	Cuba	1945	Guyana	1966
Bahamas,		Cyprus	1960	Haiti	1945
The	1973	Cz'lovakia	1945	Honduras	1945
Bahrain	1971	Denmark	1945	Hungary	1955
Bangladesh	1974	Djibouti	1977	Iceland	1946
Barbados	1966	Dominica	1978	India	1945
Belgium	1945	Dominican		Indonesia	1950
Benin	1960	Republic	1945	Iran	1945
Bhutan	1971	Ecuador	1945	Iraq	1945
Bolivia	1945	Egypt	1945	Irish	
Botswana	1966	El Salvador	1945	Republic	1955
Brazil	1945	Equatorial		Israel	1949
Bulgaria	1955	Guinea	1968	Italy	1955
Burma	1948	Ethiopia	1945	Ivory Coast	1960
Burundi	1962	Fiji	1970	Jamaica	1962
Byelorussian		Finland	1955	Japan	1956
SSR	1945	France	1945	Jordan	1955
Cameroon	1960	Gabon	1960	Kampuchea,	
Canada	1945	Gambia	1965	Dem.	1955
Cape Verde	1975	German		Kenya	1963
Central		Democratic		Kuwait	1963
African		Republic	1973	Laos	1955
Empire	1960	Germany,		Lebanon	1945
Chad	1960	Federal		Lesotho	1966
Chile	1945	Republic		Liberia	1945
China,		of	1973	Libya	1955
People's		Ghana	1957	Luxembourg	1945

MEMBER	YEAR OF ADMISSION	MEMBER	YEAR OF ADMISSION	MEMBER	YEAR OF ADMISSION
Madagascar	1960	Portugal	1955	Tobago	1962
Malawi	1964	Qatar	1971	Tunisia	1956
Malaysia	1957	Romania	1955	Turkey	1945
Maldive Islands	1965	Rwanda	1962	Uganda	1962
Mali	1960	St Lucia	1979	Ukrainian SSR	1945
Malta	1964	São Tomé and Principe	1975	USSR	1945
Mauritania	1961	Saudi Arabia	1945	United Arab Emirates	1971
Mauritius	1968	Senegal	1960	United Kingdom	1945
Mexico	1945	Seychelles	1976		
Mongolia	1961	Sierra Leone	1961	United States of America	1945
Morocco	1956	Singapore	1965		
Mozambique	1975	Solomon Islands	1978	Upper Volta	1960
Nepal	1955	Somalia	1960	Uruguay	1945
Netherlands	1945	South Africa	1945	Venezuela	1945
New Zealand	1945	Spain	1955	Vietnam	1977
Nicaragua	1945	Sri Lanka	1955	Western Samoa	1976
Niger	1960	Sudan	1956	Yemen Arab Republic	1947
Nigeria	1960	Surinam	1975		
Norway	1945	Swaziland	1968	Yemen, People's Dem. Repub. of	1967
Oman	1971	Sweden	1946		
Pakistan	1947	Syria	1945		
Panama	1945	Tanzania	1961	Yugoslavia	1945
Papua New Guinea	1975	Thailand	1946	Zaire	1960
Paraguay	1945	Togo	1960	Zambia	1964
Peru	1945	Trinidad and			
Philippines	1945				
Poland	1945				

Largest Cities of the World

The following cities are ranked according to the size of population in their metropolitan areas. The figures are the most recent.

CITY	POPULATION	CITY	POPULATION
New York	11,572,000	Bombay	5,970,575
Tokyo	11,403,744	Seoul	5,536,000
Shanghai	10,820,000	Cairo	5,384,000
Mexico City	8,589,630	São Paulo	5,186,752
Buenos Aires	8,352,900	Philadelphia	4,777,414
Peking	7,570,000	Djakarta	4,576,009
London	7,379,014	Tientsin	4,280,000
Moscow	7,061,000	Rio de Janeiro	4,252,009
Los Angeles	6,974,103	Detroit	4,163,517
Chicago	6,892,509	Delhi	3,647,023

Monarchies

COUNTRY	RULER	DATE OF ACCESSION
Belgium	King Baudouin (married Dõna Fabiola de Mora y Aragòn in 1960)	1951
Bhutan	King Jigme Singye Wangchuck	1972
Denmark	Queen Margrethe II (married Count Henri de Monpezat [Prince Henrik of Denmark] in 1967)	1972
Japan	Emperor Hirohito (married Princess Nagako in 1924)	1926
Jordan	King Hussein	1952
Liechtenstein	Prince Franz Josef II (married Countess Gina von Wilczek in 1943)	1938
Luxembourg	Grand Duke Jean (married Princess Joséphine Charlotte of Belgium in 1953)	1964
Monaco	Prince Rainier III (married Miss Grace Kelly in 1956)	1949
Morocco	King Hassan II	1961
Nepal	King Birendra Bir Bikam Shah Deva	1972
Netherlands	Queen Beatrix (married Prince Claus George Willem Otto Frederik Geert of the Netherlands, Jonkheer van Amsberg, in 1966)	1980
Norway	King Olav V (married Princess Märthe of Sweden in 1929)	1957
Saudi Arabia	King Khalid bin Abdul Aziz Al Saud	1975
Spain	King Juan Carlos I de Borbón y Borbón (married Princess Sophia of Greece, 1962)	1975
Sweden	King Carl XVI Gustav (married Fraulein Silvia Renate Sommerlath in 1976)	1973
Thailand	King Bhumibol Adulyadej (married Princess Sirikit Kityakara in 1950)	1946
Tonga	King Taufa' ahau Tupou IV	1965
UK	Queen Elizabeth II (married Prince Philip, Duke of Edinburgh, in 1947)	1952

SPORTS
AND GAMES

Equestrian Events

Show jumping

The earliest record of competition jumping is of a steeplechase held in Ireland in 1752. Show jumping or as it was then called 'leaping', began to appear in horse shows in England in the late 1870s although contests for high and wide leaps were included in the Royal Dublin Society's show in 1865. By the beginning of the 20th century show jumping had become a popular sport and three jumping events were included in the Paris Olympic Games of 1900. In 1907, at the first International Horse Show to be held at Olympia in London, competitors had the chance to enter 11 jumping events.

It was not until after 1948 that civilians began to take a major part in show jumping competitions as up until then they had been dominated by the army.

Despite the set-back of two world wars, show jumping has grown into a major world sport enjoyed by riders, horses and spectators alike.

Show jumping is an event where a horse and rider jump a course of fences designed and built specially for each competition. The rider with the least number of faults at the end is the winner.

The same rules apply to all show jumping competitions and a rider will be given:

Four faults for knocking down a fence;
Three faults for a refusal (this includes circling or swerving round the side of a jump);
Three faults for a second refusal of the same fence;
Eight faults if the rider or his horse falls (a horse is judged to have fallen if its shoulder touches the ground);
Four faults for a foot or feet in the water or on the landing tape;
A quarter of a fault for every second over the time set for jumping the course.

A rider will be eliminated if:

The horse refuses the same fence three times;
Does not pass the start or finish on his horse;
Takes the wrong course;
Receives unofficial help;
Starts before the bell.

If at the end of the first round two or more riders have an equal number of faults or no faults (a clear round), they will be asked to jump the course again. This is called a 'jump off'. If there is still a tie at the end of the first jump off there will either be a second jump off or the rider with the fastest time will be the winner.

The four basic fences are.

The upright is made from poles or planks in a vertical plane.

The parallel is usually made from two poles both at the same height and set apart from one another.

The pyramid has a central pole with a lower pole on either side.

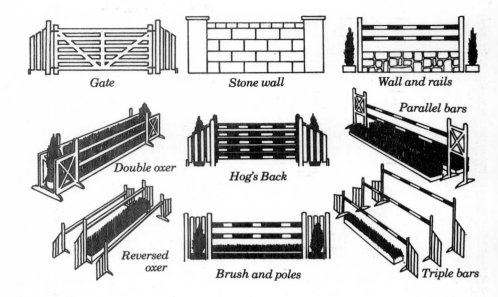

Gate

Stone wall

Wall and rails

Double oxer

Hog's Back

Parallel bars

Reversed oxer

Brush and poles

Triple bars

This can be jumped from either side.

Staircase or triple bar consists of three poles, each higher than the one in front.

Children under the age of 18 are not allowed to enter the major international competitions but a lot of small shows and gymkhanas will include classes for children. Many famous show jumpers start at these shows, working their way up through the various shows. At the small shows there will usually be three rings, with a different range of jumps in each. The classes will be divided into pony sizes; experience and previous winnings will also be taken into account.

The puissance is a competition to test a horse's jumping power. It starts with several fences and continues until the final

competitors are asked to jump only two fences, one spread and one upright, which are raised after each jump. Britain only allows three jump offs, because of the vast heights of the fences the horse is pushed to its limit. In 1949 Captain Alberto Larra-guibel Morales of Chile jumped the amazing height of 2·47 metres (8 ft $1\frac{1}{4}$ in). This is still the world record.

Shows and competitions
In Europe each country is allowed to hold one official international horse show each year; the USA is allowed to hold two. This will include a Nations Cup World Team Championship. Teams of four riders compete against teams from other countries. Each team jumps two rounds. The lowest score in the team is not counted. The six best scores from the various competitions held around the

world are added together to find the winning team of the prized President's Cup.

A special saddle is used for show jumping which has a special place for the rider's knee when he is in the forward jumping position.

SOME OF THE SHOWS HELD IN BRITAIN.

April
The Badminton Horse Trials
The Hickstead Spring Meeting

May
The Royal Windsor Horse Show

June
The Cardiff International Show Jumping Championships, Wales
The Royal Bath and West Show
The South of England show, Sussex
The Royal Show, Stoneleigh, Warwickshire

July
The Royal International Horse show, Wembley: since 1975 this meeting has incorporated the July meeting at Hickstead enabling Nations Cup competitions to be held at Wembley.

September
Burghley Horse Trials

October
Horse of the Year Show, Wembley: this includes the competition for 'Leading Show Jumper of the Year' and 'Junior Show Jumper of the Year'.

December
The International Show Jumping Championships, Olympia, London

SOME OF THE OVERSEAS SHOWS

The Aachen International Show, Germany: this is one of the largest shows and has one of the toughest courses a horse and rider will have to face in the year's competitions.

The Rome Show in May: This has been described as one of the most beautiful shows of the year.

The Dublin Horse Show: held at Balls Bridge in early August.

Dressage

Dressage originated from the time when men trained their horses to survive against their enemies in battle. A horse would be trained to kick backwards with both legs to kill an enemy creeping up on him from behind. He was also taught to rear up on his back legs to ward off any attack on him or his rider from the front with a knife or a sword. He would even be trained to leap into the air to avoid or jump over an enemy concealed on the ground.

These movements can still be seen performed in the dressage exhibitions given by the famous Lippizzaner horses of the Spanish School of Riding in Vienna.

Most of the dressage seen today in competitions has been modified. Dressage was first included in the Olympic Games in 1912. Britain and America were late in taking dressage seriously, giving the experienced European riders a great advantage in earlier competitions. The dressage competitions were first held at Goodwood and have helped to promote dressage in Britain.

Dressage competitions are divided into standards of difficulty. These are Elementary, Medium, and Advanced (Prix St Georges). Dressage is a form of training to make a horse supple, calm, collected and keen to obey perfectly the commands the rider gives. These are given with the hands, legs and seat.

A special saddle is used for

dressage which is cut very straight and has a deep seat allowing the rider to sit well into the saddle. This gives the rider maximum use of his legs. A special girth is also used called a Lonsdale girth which buckles low down so that it is not felt through the sides of the saddle.

The official size for a dressage arena is 60 metres (198 ft) by 20 metres (66 ft). This may be smaller for Elementary dressage and small shows. Each competitor performs individually and has to memorize the programme before the show. The rectangular arena is marked with letters along the sides, in the corners and down the centre. The programme will have told the rider what pace he is to perform between the different letters. Each move is marked individually and marks are also given for general impression. Each movement is marked out of six. At large shows there are three judges (there may be only one at a small show). The three judges' total marks for a rider are added together and divided by three to give an average. This is then subtracted from the possible total score. If there are 15 movements the possible total would be 90. The competitors' final score is given as penalties so the rider with the lowest score is the winner or leader if it forms part of a competition. The movements are based on three movements. The trot, the walk and the canter.

The walk
The three paces used in the walk are the medium, collected and extended. A medium walk should contain four steps to one step of a relaxed walk. A collected walk is more springy than the medium walk with the horse collected up. The extended walk is when the horse is striding out as far as possible with even steps. This is the most difficult walk.

The trot
Collected, working, medium and extended are the four types of trot. The working trot is an ordinary trot, while in the medium trot the power comes from the horse's back legs. A collected trot is where the horse is gathered in and the extended trot is with a lengthened stride.

The canter
There are four types of canter, the same as for the trot. The stride is short in the collected canter and lengthened for the extended. All the movements should be carried out smoothly and with precise balance.

The three-day event
The three-day event started in Europe where it was used for cavalry endurance tests and training. This consisted of rides over long distances and varied in length. The winner needed to have speed as well as stamina. They took place on roads and tracks and were very dangerous. During one competition in 1902 in which the riders had to ride from Brussels to Ostend, 16 of the 29 horses which started, died.

France at this time used long distance cross-country riding for military training and not as a competition. As jumping was not

The walk

The trot

The canter

The gallop

popular until the late 18th century all these were ridden on the flat. Perhaps the first competition to include all aspects of riding was held in France in 1902 which was called the Championnat du Cheval d'Armes and included dressage, steeplechase, a 31-mile ride on roads and tracks, and show jumping. This became popular with other regiments in other parts of the world and was included in the Olympic Games of 1912 which were held in Stockholm.

The three-day event as we know it now is held, as the name implies, over three days. Dressage on the first day, speed and endurance tests on the second (this includes riding on roads and tracks, steeplechase, and cross-country) and show jumping on the final day.

By the second day the rider will have gained penalty points from the dressage tests. He now has to ride over roads and tracks for anything from 6 to 12 miles. This is to test the horse's endurance and is not ridden at a great speed but at a fast trot or a slow canter. The steeplechase which follows is ridden at a fast gallop. After this there is more road work and the rider may dismount and run with his horse to give it a rest. When this section is finished the rider has a compulsory ten minute break while the horse is checked by a veterinary surgeon to see that it is fit to take part in the cross-country event which follows. The cross-country event is held over a distance of three to five miles and the horse and rider will have to negotiate 30 to 40 fences. The rider will have walked the course beforehand.

This section is perhaps the most exciting requiring skill, speed and stamina.

The fences are varied and will

have been built to form a natural part of the countryside. They can include log piles, stiles, water troughs, stone walls, tree trunks and ditches. Some of them will require the horse to jump into water, down steep slopes or onto ground which is much lower than the take-off. At some of the jumps the rider will have the choice of taking the longer, but easier, route or the quicker, but more difficult, approach. A rider will be given penalty points for:

A first refusal, 20 faults;
A second refusal (at the same fence), 40 faults;
A fall of rider or horse in the zone around the jump, 60 faults.

The rider will be eliminated for:
A third refusal;
Taking the wrong course;
A second fall in the steeplechase;
A third fall of horse or rider in the cross-country section.

The horses which are still in the competition on the third day will again be checked by a veterinary surgeon. If they are passed fit they will enter the final stage which is show jumping. This will decide the winner of the gruelling three-day event.

Cross-country events are held in smaller forms than the big three-day events, in these smaller forms children are allowed to take part.

Outstanding Sportswomen

Adams, Sharon Sites Born USA, sailor. The first woman to cross the Pacific Ocean solo in a boat. She left Yokohama, Japan and took 75 days to reach San Diego, USA, 9,513 km (5,911 miles) away.

Blankers-Koen, Francina E. Born Netherlands 1918, athlete. Winner of four gold medals in the 1948 Olympics for 100 m and 200 m sprints, 80 m hurdles and 4 × 100 m relay.

Board, Lillian Born UK, athlete. Winner of 4 × 100 m relay in world record time of 3 min 30·8 sec at the European Games in Athens in 1969.

Comaneci, Nadia Born Romania 1961, gymnast. The only woman to gain seven perfect scores at the 1976 Olympics. She became the overall winner of the European section.

Connolly, Maureen ('Little Mo') Born USA 1934, tennis player. Won three successive US championships at Forest

Hills before she was 17. She won the Wimbledon championship at her first attempt in 1952 and held it for three years. In 1953 she won the Australian, French, Wimbledon and US titles and so became the first woman to hold the four major championships simultaneously.

Cook, Sylvia Born UK, sailor. She partnered John Fairfax in *Brittania II*, a 35 ft rowing boat, on their voyage across the Pacific in 1971–2. The journey took them nearly a year to complete.

Court, Margaret (née Smith) Born Australia 1942, tennis player. Won the 'grand slam' in 1970 by holding the US, French and Australian championships, and the Wimbledon title. In 1971 she retained the Australian title but lost Wimbledon and France to Yvonne Goolagong, and the US title to Billie Jean King, possibly the greatest woman tennis player, ever.

Davies, Sharron Born UK, swimmer. Won the 200 m freestyle in 2 min 4·11 sec in 1978 and the 400 m in 4 min 18·59 sec in 1979 at Coventry. These are British national long course records. She also won the 200 m individual medley in 2 min 17·55 sec at Amersfoot, Netherlands and the 400 m individual medley in 4 min 47·67 sec. Both these British records still stand.

De la Huntey, Shirley, MBE (née Strickland) Born Australia 1925, athlete. The only woman ever to have won 7 medals (3 gold, 1 silver and 3 bronze) in the 1948, 1952 and 1956 Olympic Games. Unofficially she is thought to have deserved a further bronze.

Dod, Charlotte Born UK 1871, died 1960, a versatile all-round sportswoman. In 1887, at 15 years of age, she won Wimbledon. She won it another four times between 1887 and 1893. She also won the British Ladies Golf championship in 1904 and gained a silver medal for archery at the 1908 Olympics. She played hockey for England in 1899. She was also an excellent skater.

Earhart, Amelia Born USA 1898, died 1937(?), aviator. In 1917 Amelia decided that she wanted to fly, this was an extraordinary choice for a woman at that time. Her first airplane was a Kinner Canary. In 1928, with Bill Stultz, she crossed the Atlantic, the first woman to do so in an airplane. In 1932 she flew solo from America to Ireland – another first for a woman. Tragically, in an attempt to fly round the world she disappeared in 1937 and was never found.

Ederle, Gertrude Caroline Born USA 1906, swimmer. Swam the English Channel from Cap Gris-Nez to Deal on 6th August 1926. She took 14 hr 39 min and was the first woman to swim the Channel.

Ender, Cornelia Born East Germany 1958, swimmer. Winner in the 1976 Olympics of four gold medals (100 m and 200 m freestyle, 100 m butterfly and 4 × 100 m medley).

Frazer, Dawn, OBE (now Mrs Ware) Born Australia 1937, swimmer. Australia's finest swimmer, she won four gold medals in the 100 m freestyle in 1956, 1960 and 1964, and in the 4 × 100 m freestyle in 1956. She also won four silvers.

Hambleton, Kitty Born USA. Holder of the world land speed record driving the SMI *Motivator* (a 4,800 hp rocket-powered 3-wheeler) in the Alvard Desert, Oregon. She clocked up a recorded time of 524·016 mph.

Henie, Sonja Born Norway 1912, died 1969, ice skater. The only woman to win three gold medals in succession at the 1928, 1932 and 1936 Olympics for figure skating. She also held 10 world and 8 European titles. She later became a very popular Hollywood film star.

Heyhoe-Flint, Rachel, MBE Born UK, cricketer. Captain of the English cricket team, she scored 1,789 runs between December 1960 and July 1979 in test matches.

James, Naomi Born New Zealand, sailor. Circumnavigated the world via Cape Horn in the Bermuda sloop *Express Crusader*. She left Dartmouth, England on the 9th September 1977 and rounded Cape Horn on 19th March 1978, arriving back in Dartmouth on 8th June 1978.

Kanetaka, Kaoru Born Japan, traveller, author, lecturer. She set the world commercial propellor-driven flight record for circumnavigation, Tokyo to Tokyo in 81 hours. The first Japanese woman to visit the South Pole, the first Japanese woman to parachute jump and the first Japanese woman to take a balloon over the Alps and to hang-glide.

King, Billie Jean (née Moffitt) Born USA 1943, tennis player. Six times singles champion at Wimbledon with a total of 20 Wimbledon titles between 1961 and 1979. A player of incredible stamina and consistency, she has probably done more for young tennis players than any other champion.

Kim, Nelli Born USSR 1957, gymnast. The most gifted competitor in the Russian gymnastic team at the 1976 Olympics. Gained a perfect score twice and was second in both the European and World championships in 1975. Her grace and skill are considered perfection.

Korbut, Olga Born USSR 1958, gymnast. Miss Korbut has probably done more to popularize gymnastics than any other gymnast. She was the first woman to perform a backward somersault on the beam. She won three gold medals and one silver at the 1972 Olympics.

Kulakova, Galina Born USSR 1942, skier. Won gold medals for the 5 km, 10 km and 3·5 km relay at the 1972 Olympics and the 4 × 5 km relay in the 1976 Olympics. She also won one silver and two bronze medals in 1968 and 1976.

Lacoste, Catherine Born France, golfer. The only woman to win the US Open, US Amateur and British and French Open championships (1965–9).

Latynina, Larissa Semyonovna Born USSR 1934, gymnast. She holds ten individual world titles and five team titles, she has also won six individual gold medals and was a member of three winning teams. She also gained five silver and four bronze medals and therefore holds 18 medals in all. This is an Olympic record for any sport.

Lopez, Nancy Born USA, golfer. When Nancy Lopez turned professional she won nine tournaments in her first year, her winnings reached an all-time record.

Moser, Annemarie (née Proell) Born Austria 1953, skier. Probably the finest woman skier in the world. She won the Women's Alpine World Cup six times, in 1971–5 and 1979. She won 11 consecutive downhill races and between 1970 and 1979 won 62 individual events.

Mould, Marion (née Coakes) Born UK, showjumper. Winner of the Queen Elizabeth Cup three times on *Stroller* in 1965, 1971, and on *Elizabeth Ann* in 1976.

Phillips, Fran Born Canada. On the 5th April 1971 she was the first woman to set foot on the North Pole.

Prior-Palmer, Lucinda Born UK 1953, horse rider. Thought to be the most consistent rider in Britain, winner of the Badminton Three-day Event four times, on *Be Fair* in 1973, *Wide Awake* in 1976, *George* in 1977 and *Killane* in 1979.

Rand, Mary Denise MBE Born UK, athlete. Jumped an incredible 6·7 m (22 ft 2¼ in) at the 1964 Olympics.

Rodnina, Irina Born USSR 1949, ice skater. Winner of ten world pairs titles, gained the highest number of maximum marks in the 1974 European pairs title, considered to be the most graceful of all women skaters.

Smythe, Patricia, OBE Born UK 1928, horse rider. Winner of the British Women's Show Jumping Association championships eight times, 1952, 1953, 1955, 1957, 1958, 1959, 1961 and 1962. Riding *Flanagan* she won three of these, the only horse to have won three times.

Tabei, Junko Born Japan 1939, mountaineer. She started climbing when she was nine. On 16th May 1975 accompanied by Ang Tsering, her Sherpa guide, she conquered Mount Everest. She had already climbed Annapurna in 1970.

Wickham, Tracy, MBE Born Australia, swimmer. Holder of the 200 m, 400 m and 800 m freestyle world records.

Gymnastics

This sport has gained unbelievably in popularity over the last few years. The inspiration to hundreds of young girl gymnasts came from a young girl gymnast from Russia called Olga Korbut and a young girl from Romania called Nadia Comaneci. It was at the 1972 Munich Olympic Games, that the tiny Olga Korbut thrilled the thousands of spectators with her energetic and daring performance. But perhaps the main reason for the crowd taking this tiny girl to their hearts was the sight of her crying with disappointment after she had made two mistakes on the beam. Despite her two mistakes she won three gold medals and one silver at Munich.

Olga became the star of gymnastics with a huge following. It came as a surprise when in 1975 at the Montreal Olympics a new girl emerged as the overall Olympic champion. This was Nadia Comaneci. Nadia gained full marks for seven of her exercises. The first time this has ever happened in the history of the Olympic Games. It is without doubt that these two young girls are responsible for the popularity of gymnastics today.

Since 1948 all gymnastics have been judged and marked in the same way throughout the world. The way of marking is laid down in a Code of Points.

In major competitions each gymnast has to perform on four pieces of apparatus. These are the broad horse, the asymmetric bars, the beam and the floor. Each girl has to perform a compulsory and a voluntary programme.

In the compulsory section the mark is out of ten and is given for rhythm, precision, correctness, and co-ordination. Marks will be lost for lack of control, requiring help, falling or faulty movements. The voluntary exercises are marked out of ten but these ten marks are divided between the different things the judges are looking for. The difficulty of the movement is marked out of three. There are two grades of difficulty in women's gymnastics, medium and superior, Seven medium and three superior exercises must be included in the gymnastics, medium and superior. will lose marks for leaving out a movement. Composition is marked out of 0·5 and is where a gymnast is judged for the way in which she puts her performance together. Execution and extent are marked out of four and the general impression made by the gymnast on the judges is marked out of one. Originality is marked out of 1·5 and it is here that a daring and exciting performance will gain marks.

A young girl interested in becoming a gymnast will probably start by joining a club. There may be one at school, if so it will probably be connected to the regional school's gymnastic association. The competitions organised through this association will enable a good gymnast to become a national champion.

If there is no club at school, the

gymnast will have to join a local gymnastics club. The club will probably have a fully qualified coach who will instruct the new member in the basics of gymnastics. A good gymnast may be asked to join a special group which will offer the opportunity for extra coaching. The training will be hard and require many hours of dedicated work. A gymnast who is a member of a leading club and who trains hard will be able to enter major competitions at national and international levels. But most gymnasts climb to the top through local championships. A gymnast entering any competition will need mental concentration as well as physical perfection.

In Britain probably the most sought after prize is the Champions Cup; a competition held at London at the Royal Albert Hall and which is held in January. This is where the six top girl gymnasts (men also) in the country compete against each other.

Training

The training to become a top gymnast is very hard, requiring hours of regular training. Ballet lessons will also be included in a young gymnast's training as this strengthens the legs as well as giving grace of movement.

Before performing on the apparatus or the floor a gymnast will warm up for at least half an hour to get the body ready for the physical extremes needed in gymnastics.

Vaulting

Women vault across the horse by placing their hands in the centre of the horse. In competitions women are allowed two vaults. A vault is divided into two parts when it is being judged. The first from when the gymnast starts her run up to the horse to when she touches the horse. This is judged on how the body is placed on the horse and for the flight through the air. The second part is from leaving the horse to the landing. This is marked on the distance the gymnast travels before landing and on the landing itself. This must be smooth and balanced. Marks will be lost for a fall or staggering.

In all vaults the gymnast's hands must touch the horse.

Some of the vaults a gymnast uses

The Horizontal Vault is the simplest vault and the body and the legs must be kept straight. The body should be in a horizontal position when it passes over the horse. The back is to the horse on landing.

In a Handspring Vault, the body, the arms and the legs are all kept straight when landing on the horse. The legs should be straight above the head as the gymnast moves through a handstand to land with the back to the horse.

A Yamashita Vault named after a Japanese male gymnast, Haruhiro Yamashita, is a variation on a basic handspring. On leaving the horse the body goes into a pike position, straightening out and landing with the back to the horse.

Turns can be added to handsprings. A half turn before landing on the horse, a handspring over the horse and then a full turn before landing facing the horse, is just one of the combinations which can be put together.

Somersaults can be incorporated with handsprings and cartwheels in a variety of different ways. It depends upon how daring the gymnast is and how advanced.

The beam
This consists of a beam of wood 1·2 metres (4 ft) from the ground, 4·9 metres (16 ft) in length and only 10 centimetres (4 in) wide. Balance and perfect line combined with deep concentration are needed for any work on the beam. In competitions, the gymnast will be expected to use the whole length of the beam and include in her programme walking, running, jumps, leaps, cartwheels, and if she is a top gymnast, acrobatic exercises. Her performance must be smooth and flowing, any hesitation will lose marks. She must also include three pauses of not more than three seconds each. This will show the judges that she has perfect balance. Before the gymnast can begin her exercises she has to get onto the beam. This is important as she must land on the beam with her body perfectly balanced in order to be able to move smoothly into her next movement. The gymnast does not think of the mount as merely a way of getting onto the beam but as the start of the exercise with which she has chosen to open her performance. This may be a handstand, a cartwheel or any of the other movements used in work on the beam. She can use a spring board to help her or she may walk or run up to the beam. Whatever she does she will be marked and timed from the moment her feet leave the ground. She will also lose marks if she falls from the beam and she must regain the beam within ten seconds.

Movements on the beam
A cat leap with a turn is where the gymnast raises one foot from the beam, followed by the other and turns through 360 degrees back to her original position.

There are various hold positions (pauses). A gymnast may choose to stand sideways on the beam with one leg straight on the beam and the other held to the side as high as it will go.

An arabesque hold is where the legs are in a full splits position with one foot on the beam and the other high in the air. The arms are held horizontally to the legs and the head is down.

The way the gymnast leaves the beam is important. She may choose any way of getting off the beam but as well as being perfectly executed it must be of a superior standard of difficulty. She must also land on her feet without falling or staggering.

Back support: Body in front of bar with upper thighs resting on bar. Supported by straight arms.

Cartwheel: Complete turn through 360 degrees sideways from feet to hands to feet.

Dismount: Final movement of an exercise descending from the apparatus being used.

217

Beam exercises demand perfect balance

Front handstand: Body vertical, supported on hands.

Front support: Body behind bar, hips resting on bar.

Hip circle: Rotation round bar with hips in contact throughout.

Hold position: Any position held for three seconds or more.

Kip: Usually performed on the bars. A swing over the bar, head and feet coming together. Continuing to front support.

Mount: Movement bringing gymnast onto apparatus.

Movement: One particular part of an exercise.

Overgrasp: Palms' downwards grasp of bars.

Pike: Body bent at waist with straight legs.

Rear lying hang: Uses high bar and low bar. Hands hold high bar, body straight supported by buttocks on low bar.

R.O.V.: Bonus factors taken into account when judging. Risk, originality and virtuosity.

Straddle: Legs straight and held apart.

Tuck: Body bent at waist with bent legs held up to the chest.

Undergrasp: Palms under bars, holding bar upwards.

Uprise: Arms straight, body straight, swinging to front support.

Walkover: 360 degree turn, forwards or backwards, rotating round shoulder.

Floor exercises
It is in this section of gymnastics that a gymnast's skills of self-

Floor exercises are a combination of
gymnastic skill and musical interpretation

expression, suppleness and agility are all put together. The one to one and a half minute performance is carried out on a 12 metre (39 ft) square mat. This is made of plywood with a layer of sponge in the centre. The exercise is performed to music which must be chosen with great care as the rhythm of the music and the gymnasts movements must complement each other. The arms, the hands and the head must be used with expression to fit with the powerful and quick movements across the mat. It is here that the gymnast's basic ballet training becomes apparent.

The gymnast must use the whole area of the mat, moving diagonally across it as well as from side to side. She will lose marks if she steps over the edge of the mat. She will also be judged on general posture, lightness, suppleness, turns, balances and relaxation; as well as for the way she interprets the music.

The routine will include springs, body waves, leaps, jumps, rolls, cartwheels, flic-flacs, somersaults, splits, pauses and variations on all these movements. It is perhaps the most exciting secton out of the competition.

Some of the movements used in floor exercises

A flic-flac is where the gymnast leaps forward from one foot with arms stretched forwards and upwards, while at the same time turning through 180 degrees. She then circles backwards onto her hands and pushes off again to do more flic-flacs across the mat.

Exercises on the parallel bars require strong arm and stomach muscles

Tinsicas are used to cross the mat using the arms as well as the legs. Using her first leg to push off with she bends so that one hand after the other touches the mat. This brings her legs into a straddle position above her head with her body straight. Her first foot touches the floor as her first hand leaves it. She then pushes off with her second hand which brings her back to the position she started in.

NAMES AND THEIR MEANINGS

NAME	MEANING
Abigail	Father rejoiced (Hebrew)
Adela	Noble (German)
Adelaide	Noble sort (German)
Agatha	Good (Greek)
Agnes	Pure, chaste (French)
Alice	Noble sort (French)
Alison	a pet name for Alice
Alma	Loving, kind (Latin)
Amabel	Lovable (Latin)
Amanda	Fit to be loved (Latin)
Amelia	Labour (German)
Amy	Loved (French)
Angela	Messenger (Greek)
Angelica	Angelic (Greek)
Anita – *see* **Ann**	
Ann, Anna, Anne,	He has favoured me (Western form of the Hebrew
Annette, Nancy, Nanette	Hannah)
Annabel	derived from Amabel
Annis – *see* **Agnes**	
Anthea	Flowery (Greek)
April	the name of the month
Arabella	Easy to be entreated (Scottish)
Audrey	Noble strength (Anglo-Saxon)
Averil	Boar battle (Anglo-Saxon)

NAME	MEANING
Barbara	Strange, foreign (Greek)
Beatrice, Beatrix	Bringer of joy (Latin)
Belinda	Snake
Bella	Beautiful (Italian) (pet form of names such as Isobel or Arabella)
Berenice	Bringer of Victory (Greek)
Bertha	Bright (Teutonic)
Beverley	Beaver stream (from an English surname derived from a place name
Brenda	Sword (Irish)
Bridget	The high one (Old Irish)
Bronwen	White breast (Welsh)
Candida	White (Latin)
Carol, Caroline	feminine forms of Charles, 'Man'
Catherine – *see* **Katharine**	
Cecilia, Cecily, Cicely	Blind (from the Roman family name, *Caecilius*, from the root *caecum*)
Celia	Heavenly (Latin)
Charlotte	feminine form of Charles, 'Man'
Charmian	A little joy (Greek)
Chloe	A green shoot (Greek)
Christina, Christine	Of Christ
Clara, Clare, Clarice, Clarinda, Clarissa	Bright, clear (Latin)
Colette – *see* **Nicole**	
Constance	Constancy
Cynthia	Of Cynthus (Mount Cynthus in Greece)
Daphne	Bay or laurel (Greek)
Deborah	Bee (Hebrew)
Deirdre	The raging one or the broken-hearted one (Irish)
Denise	from the Greek Dionysos, god of wine (French)
Diana	Roman Moon goddess
Dilys	Certain, perfect, genuine (Welsh)
Dinah	Dedicated (Hebrew)
Dolores	Sorrows (Spanish)
Dora – *see* **Dorothy**	
Dorcas	Roe or gazelle (Greek)
Doreen	probably an Irish version of Dorothy
Doris	A Dorian girl (from a region in Greece)
Dorothy, Dorothea	Gift of God (Greek)
Dulcie	Sweet (Latin)
Edith	Rich, happy (Anglo-Saxon)
Edna	possibly from a Hebrew word meaning rejuvenation
Eileen, Aileen	Irish equivalent of Helen or possibly Evelyn
Eithne, Aine	Fire (Celtic)
Elaine	Old French form of Helen
Eleanor, Leonora, Ellen, Ella	forms of Helen

NAME	MEANING
Elfreda	Elf, and strength (Anglo-Saxon)
Elizabeth, Elisabeth, Elsa	My God is satisfaction (Hebrew)
Elspeth	Scottish form of Elizabeth
Emily	from *Aemilus*, a Roman family name
Emma	Whole (Teutonic)
Ena	Fire (Irish)
Enid	Life, soul (Welsh)
Erica	female form of Eric, 'Kingly'
Esmé	Loved (a Scottish name derived from the French *Aimé*)
Esmeralda	Emerald (Spanish)
Estelle	Star (French)
Esther	Star (Persian) from the goddess Astarte
Ethel	Noble (Anglo-Saxon)
Eunice	Well and victory (Greek)
Eva, Eve	Life (Hebrew)
Evelyn, Evelina	from the surnames Aveline, Eveling and Evelyn
Fay	an abbreviation of Faith
Felicity	Happiness (Latin)
Fenella	White shoulder (Gaelic)
Fiona	Fair (Gaelic)
Flora	Roman goddess of Flowers
Florence	from the city, also Blooming (Latin)
Frances	feminine form of Francis, 'Frenchman'
Freda – *see* Winifred	
Gail	diminitive of Abigail
Gemma	Gem (Latin)
Gertrude	Spear, and strength (Teutonic)
Gillian	English form of Julian (a)
Gladys	Welsh form of Claudia, 'Lame'
Gloria	Glory (Latin)
Glennis, Glynis	Valley
Greta	Swedish abbreviation of Margaret
Gwendolen, Gwendolyn, Gwenda	White (Welsh)
Gwyneth	Blessed, happy (Welsh)
Hannah	God has favoured me (Hebrew)
Harriet	English form of the French Henrietta
Helen, Helena	The bright one (Greek)
Henrietta	female form of Henry, 'Ruler'
Hester – *see* Esther	
Hilary	Cheerful (Latin)
Hilda	War, battle (Teutonic)
Honor	Reputation (Anglo-Norman)
Ida	Labour (Teutonic)
Imogen	Daughter, girl (Old English)
Irene	from Eirene, the Greek goddess of peace
Isabel, Isabella Isobel	French and Spanish forms of Elizabeth
Ita	Irish form of Ida

NAME	MEANING
Jacqueline	the feminine form of Jacques (James), 'Follower' (French)
Jane	feminine form of John, 'Jehovah has favoured'
Janet, Jean	derived from Jane
Jemima	Dove (Hebrew)
Jennifer	from Guenevere King Arthur's wife (Welsh)
Jessica	He beholds (Hebrew)
Jessie	Scottish diminutive of Janet
Jill	pet form of Gillian
Joan, Joanna, Johanna	derived from Jane
Jocelyn, Joscelin	derived from surnames based on the folk name Goth
Josephine	feminine form of Joseph, 'Jehovah added'
Joyce	derived from the Breton saint, Jodoc
Judith	Jewess (Hebrew)
Julia	feminine form of Julius
June	the name of the month
Karen	Danish form of Katharine
Katharine, Katherine	Pure (Greek)
Kathleen – *see* **Katharine**	
Kay, Kitty	pet forms of Katharine
Laura	Laurel tree (Latin)
Leah	Cow (Hebrew)
Lena – *see* **Helen**	
Lesley	from a Scottish surname
Lettice	Gladness (Latin)
Linda	Serpent (Teutonic)
Lindsay	from a Scottish surname
Lois	the name of the grandmother of Timothy, meaning unknown (Greek)
Lola	diminutive of Dolores
Lorna	name invented by R. D. Blackmore in his novel *Lorna Doon*
Louisa, Louise	feminine form of Louis
Lucia, Lucy	Light (Latin)
Lydia	Woman of Lydia (Greek)
Lynn	Lake (Celtic)
Mabel	form of Amabel
Madeline, Madeleine	Woman of Magdala (Hebrew)
Madge – *see* **Margaret**	
Maire	Irish form of Mary
Marcia	feminine form of Mark, Marcus
Margaret	Pearl (Greek)
Margery, Marjorie	forms of Margaret
Marie	French form of Mary
Marilyn	American form of Mary
Marina	Of the sea (Latin)
Marion, Marian	diminutive of Mary or Mary + Ann
Martha	Lady (Aramaic)

NAME	MEANING
Mary	Wished-for child (Hebrew)
Matilda, Maud, Maude	Might, strength and battle (Teutonic)
Maureen	Irish diminutive of Maire (Mary)
Mavis	Song-thrush (Anglo-Saxon)
Maxine	feminine form of Maximilian (French)
May	pet form of Margaret or Mary, or the name of the month
Meg – *see* **Margaret**	
Melanie	Black or dark complexioned (Greek)
Melissa	Bee (Greek)
Merle	Blackbird (French)
Michelle	feminine form of the French Michel (Michael)
Mildred	Mild and strength (Anglo-Saxon)
Millicent	Work and strong (Anglo-Saxon)
Minnie	diminutive of Wilhelmina
Mirabel	Wonderful, glorious (Latin)
Miranda	Worthy of admiration (Latin)
Miriam	Longed-for, desired (Hebrew)
Moira, Moyra	forms of Maire, Irish for Mary
Molly – *see* **Mary**	
Mona	Noble (Irish)
Monica	from mother of St Augustine
Morag	Great (Gaelic)
Muriel, Meriel	Sea and bright (Celtic)
Naomi	Pleasant (Hebrew)
Natalie	Birth (French, German, Russian and other European countries form is Natasha)
Nelly	pet form of Ellen, Eleanor and Helen
Nessie, Nesta	Welsh diminutive of Agnes
Nicola, Nicolette, Nicole	feminine forms of Nicholas, 'Victory of the people'
Nona	Ninth (Latin)
Nora, Norah	abbreviated form of Honora (Irish)
Noreen	Irish diminutive of Nora
Norma	Precept, pattern (Latin)
Olga	Holy (a Russian name of Norse origin)
Olivia, Olive	from the tree
Olwen	White track (Welsh)
Oonagh – *see* **Una**	
Pamela	a name invented in a classic novel by Sir Philip Sidney
Patricia	feminine form of Patrick, 'Noble'
Pauline	feminine form of Paul, 'Small'
Peggy – *see* **Margaret**	
Penelope	Bobbin or weaver, faithful wife of Odysseus (Greek)
Philippa	feminine form of Philip, 'Lover of horses'
Phoebe	The shining one (Greek)
Phyllis	Leafy (Greek)
Polly – *see* **Mary**	

NAME	MEANING
Priscilla	feminine form of the Roman family name *Priscus* (*priscus*, meaning former or old)
Rachel	Ewe (Hebrew)
Rebecca	Heifer (Hebrew)
Rhoda	Rose (Greek)
Rita – *see* **Margaret**	
Roma	the name of the city
Rosalind	Horse and serpent (Teutonic)
Rosamund, Rosamond	Horse and protection (Teutonic)
Ruth	Vision of beauty or friend (Hebrew)
Sadie – *see* **Sarah**	
Sally – *see* **Sarah**	
Sandra	diminutive of Alessandra (Alexandra)
Sarah, Sara	Princess (Hebrew)
Selina	The Moon (Greek) or Heaven (Latin)
Sharon	biblical place name
Sheena	Gaelic form of Jane
Sheila	Irish form of Celia, from Cecilia
Shirley	surname derived from a place name
Sibyl, Sybil	a prophetess in ancient Greece
Sonia, Sonya	Russian diminutive of Sophia
Sophia, Sophie	Wisdom (Greek)
Stella	Star (Latin)
Susan, Susanna,	Lily (Hebrew)
Tabitha	Roe or Gazelle, Aramaic equivalent of Dorcas
Teresa, Theresa	Reaper (Greek) or from the name of an island near Crete (Greek)
Tess, Tessa	pet forms of Theresa
Thelma	an invented name in a novel by Marie Corelli
Tina	pet form of names such as Christina
Tracy	diminutive of Theresa
Trixie – *see* **Beatrice**	
Una, Oona	probably based on the Irish word for lamb
Ursula	She-bear (Latin)
Valerie	from Roman family name *Valerius*, probably derived from the word for strong
Vanessa	a name invented by Jonathan Swift
Vera	Faith (Russian)
Veronica	Of a true image (Latin)
Victoria	Victory (Latin)
Viola	Violet (Latin)
Virginia	from the Roman family name *Virginius*
Vivien	Alive (Latin) or derived from Ninian, an Irish saint
Wanda	Stem or stock (Teutonic)
Wendy	first used by J. M. Barrie in his play *Peter Pan*
Winifred	White wave or stream (Celtic)
Yvonne	feminine form of Yvon, 'Yew'
Zoë	Life (Greek)

BOYS' NAMES

NAME	MEANING
Abraham	Father of a multitude (Hebrew)
Adam	Red (from colour of skin) or Man of earth (Hebrew)
Adrian	Of the Adriatic (Latin)
Allan, Allen, Alan	Harmony, cheerful (Celtic)
Alastair – *see* |Alexander	
Albert	Noble and bright (German)
Alec – *see* Alexander	
Alexander	Protector of men (Greek)
Alexis	Helper, defender (Greek)
Alfred	Elf counsel (Anglo-Saxon)
Algernon	With whiskers (Norman-French)
Alick – *see* Alexander	
Ambrose	Pertaining to the Immortals (Latin)
Andrew	Manly (Latin)
Angel	Messenger (Latin)
Angus	One choice (Scottish)
Anthony, Antony	Worthy, strong (Latin)
Archibald	Genuine, simple and bold (Teutonic)
Arnold	Eagle power (Teutonic)
Arthur	Bear (Celtic) or from Roman family name, *Artorius*
Aubrey	Elf ruler (from French form of the Old German Alberich)
Augustus	Venerable, consecrated (Latin)
Barnabas	Son of exhortation or consolation (Hebrew)
Barry	Spear (Irish)
Bartholomew	Son of Talmi (Hebrew)
Basil	Kingly (Greek)
Benedict	Blessed (Latin)
Benjamin	Son of good fortune (Hebrew)
Bernard	Bear and hard (Teutonic)
Bertram	Bright raven (Teutonic)
Beverley	Beaver stream (from an English place name)
Brendan	Stinking hair (Irish)
Brian	Hill or strong, powerful (Celtic)
Bruce	surname of Robert the Bruce, King of Scotland
Bruno	Brown (Teutonic)
Caleb	Bold, impetuous (Hebrew)
Cecil	from the Roman family name *Caecilius* (the root *caecus* means blind)
Cedric	name first used by Sir Walter Scott in his novel *Ivanhoe*
Charles	Man (Teutonic)
Christian	Belonging to Christ
Christopher	Christ-bearer (Greek)

NAME	MEANING
Claud, Claude	from a Roman family name, probably derived from *claudus*, lame
Clement	Mild, merciful (Latin)
Clifford	derived from a place name
Clive	surname of Robert Clive of India
Colin	derived from Nicholas (French)
Conrad	Bold counsel (Teutonic)
Cornelius	from a Roman family name, probably derived from *cornu*, horn
Craig	Crag, stony hill (Celtic)
Cyril	Lord, master (Greek)
Daniel	God has judged (Hebrew)
David	Beloved (Hebrew)
Denis, Dennis	Of Dionysos, god of wine (Greek)
Derek	The people's ruler (Teutonic)
Desmond	Worldly, sophisticated (Celtic)
Dick – *see* **Richard**	
Dominic	Belonging to God (Latin)
Donald	World mighty or proud chief (Celtic)
Dougal	Black stranger (Celtic)
Douglas	Dark blue (Celtic river name)
Duncan	Brown warrior (Old Irish)
Ebenezer	Stone of help (Hebrew)
Edgar	Happy, rich and spear (Anglo-Saxon)
Edmund, Edmond	Happy, rich and protection (Anglo-Saxon)
Edward	Happy, rich and guardian (Anglo-Saxon)
Edwin	Happy, rich and friend (Anglo-Saxon)
Egbert	Sword bright (Anglo-Saxon)
Emanuel	God is with us (Hebrew)
Enoch	Skilled (Hebrew)
Erasmus	Beloved, desired (Greek)
Eric	Kingly (Teutonic)
Ernest	Sincere, earnest (Teutonic)
Esmond	Grace, beauty and protection (Anglo-Saxon)
Eugene	Noble, well-born (Greek)
Eustace	Tranquil or fruitful (Greek)
Everard	Boar and hard (Teutonic)
Ewen	Well born (Celtic)
Ezra	Help (Hebrew)
Felix	Happy (Latin)
Ferdinand	Journey and venture, risk (Teutonic)
Fergus	Man and choice (Old Irish)
Francis	Frenchman or free
Frank	diminutive of Francis
Frederick	Peace and ruler (Teutonic)
Gabriel	Strong man of God (Hebrew)
Gareth	first used by Tennyson in his *Gareth and Lynnet*
Gary	Mighty spear (Anglo-Saxon)
Gavin	White hawk (Welsh or Teutonic)

NAME	MEANING
Gene – *see* **Eugene**	
Geoffrey	Land and peace (Teutonic)
George	Farmer, tiller of the soil (Greek)
Gerald	Spear and rule (Teutonic)
Gerard	Spear and hard (Teutonic)
Gilbert	Pledge and bright (Teutonic)
Giles	Kid (Latin)
Glyn	Valley (Welsh)
Godfrey	God's peace (Teutonic)
Godwin	God's friend (Anglo-Saxon)
Gordon	From the cornered hill (Scottish family name)
Graham	From the grey home (Scottish family name)
Gregory	Watchful (Greek)
Guy	Guide, leader (French)
Hamish	Scottish form of James
Harold	Host, army and power (Anglo-Saxon)
Hector	Holding fast (Greek)
Henry	House, home and ruler (Teutonic)
Herbert	Host, army and bright (Teutonic)
Hew – *see* **Hugh**	
Horace	Roman family name
Howard	probably from the surname, meaning heart, soul and protection
Hubert	Heart, soul and bright (Teutonic)
Hugh, Hugo	Heart, mind
Humphrey, Humphry	Giant and peace (Teutonic)
Ian	Gaelic form of John
Isaac	God may laugh (Hebrew)
Ivor, Ifor	meaning uncertain (Old Norse)
Jack	pet name for John
Jacob	God supplanted (Hebrew)
James	form of Jacob
Jeremiah, Jeremy	May Jehovah raise up, exhalt (Hebrew)
Jerome	Sacred name (Greek)
Jesse	Jehovah exists (Hebrew)
Job	Pious and persecuted (Hebrew)
Jocelyn, Joscelin	derived from surnames based on the folk name Goth
Joel	Jehovah is God (Hebrew)
John	Jehovah has favoured (Hebrew)
Jolyon – *see* **Julian**	
Jonah, Jonas	Dove (Hebrew)
Jonathan	Jehovah has given (Hebrew)
Joseph	Jehovah added (Hebrew)
Joshua	Jehovah is generous (Hebrew)
Julian	a derivative of Julius
Julius	a Roman family name, the most famous member being Julius Caesar
Justin	Just (Latin)

NAME	MEANING
Keith	Place (a Scottish surname derived from a place name)
Kenneth	Handsome (Celtic)
Kevin	Comely birth (Celtic)
Laurence, Lawrence	Laurel or bay tree (Latin)
Lee	Meadow (derived from the surname)
Leo	Lion (Latin)
Leonard	Lion and hardy, bold (Teutonic)
Leopold	People and bold (Teutonic)
Leslie	from a Scottish surname
Lionel	Young lion (French)
Luke, Lucas	Of Lucania (Latin)
Magnus	Great (Latin)
Malcolm	Servant or disciple of Columba (Celtic)
Mark, Marcus	derived from the Roman god Mars
Martin	Of Mars (Latin)
Matthew	Gift from God (Hebrew)
Maurice	Dark, a Moor (Latin)
Maximilian	a combination of two Roman names, *Maximus* and *Aemilianus* (German)
Mervyn	probably derived from the surname
Michael	Who is like God (Hebrew)
Miles	Merciful (Slavonic, Norman-French)
Montague	from the Norman surname
Morris – *see* Maurice	
Mortimer	from the Norman surname
Nathan	Gift (Hebrew)
Nathaniel	God has given (Hebrew)
Ned – *see* Edward	
Neil – *see* Nigel	
Neville	from the Norman surname
Nicholas	Victory of the people (Greek)
Nigel	Black (Latin) or Champion (Irish)
Noel	Birthday (Old French)
Norman	Northman
Oliver	Elf host (Anglo-Saxon) and from olive tree
Oscar	A god and spear (Teutonic)
Oswald	A god and power (Teutonic)
Patrick	Nobleman (Latin)
Paul	Small (Latin)
Percival	Pierce the valley (French)
Percy	Norman family surname, taken from the village of Perci
Peregrine	Stranger, a traveller, a pilgrim (Latin)
Peter	Rock (Greek)
Philip	Lover of horses (Greek)
Quentin, Quintin	a derivative of Latin word *quintus*, meaning fifth
Ralph	Counsel and wolf (Anglo-Saxon)
Randolph	Shield and wolf (Anglo-Saxon)

NAME	MEANING
Ray	derivative of Raymond
Raymond	Wise protection (Teutonic)
Reginald	Counsel, might and hard (Teutonic)
Rex	King (Latin)
Richard	Ruler and hard (Teutonic)
Robert	Fame and bright (Teutonic)
Robin – *see* **Robert**	
Roderick	Fame and rule (Teutonic)
Rodney	Renowned (Teutonic)
Roger	Fame and spear (Teutonic)
Roland	Fame of the land (Teutonic)
Rolf	Fame and wolf (Teutonic)
Rollo – *see* **Rolf**	
Rory	Red (Irish)
Roy	Red (Gaelic)
Rufus	Red-haired (Latin)
Rupert	a form of Robert
Samuel	Name of God (Hebrew)
Sean	Irish form of John
Sebastian	Man of Sebastia (a city, meaning venerable, in Greece)
Selwyn	House and friend (an old English surname)
Sidney	from the surname of an English family
Simon	Hearkening or little hyena (Hebrew)
Solomon	Little man of peace (Hebrew)
Stanley	surname derived from a place name
Stewart, Stuart	name of the royal house of Scotland and an extensive clan originating in the office of steward, the manager of a large household
Teddy – *see* **Edward**	
Terence	from the Roman family name
Theodore	God's gift (Greek)
Theophilus	beloved of God
Thomas	Twin (Aramaic)
Timothy	Honour, respect and god (Greek)
Tobias, Toby	God is good (Hebrew)
Tony – *see* **Anthony**	
Trevor	from the surname
Tristram	Tumult, din (Celtic)
Valentine	Strong, healthy (Latin)
Vernon	a surname and a place name in France
Victor	Conqueror (Latin)
Vincent	Conquering (Latin)
Vivian	Alive (Latin)
Wallace	a Scottish surname equivalent to the English and Welsh, Walsh
Walter	Rule and folk (Teutonic)
Wilfred	Will and peace (Anglo-Saxon)
William	Will and helmet (Teutonic)

FORTUNE-
TELLING

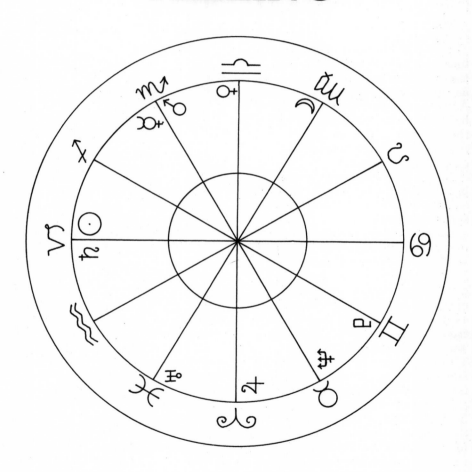

Most people at some time in their lives are interested in fortune-telling. The time-honoured art of foretelling the future is, broadly speaking, called divination. Its methods include all magical and supernatural means – anything outside the bounds of strict 'reason'. Despite the advance of science, some means of fortune-telling are still seriously regarded.

Astrology

This is probably one of the oldest forms of fortune-telling. In ancient times it included what is now known as the science of astronomy. Astrology was probably originated by the ancient Babylonians and then spread to Greece, Egypt and Arabia. India also has been claimed as an original source.

Astrologers believe that a person's characteristics and life are affected by the alignment of the stars and planets at the exact time and place of her birth. Here, however, fortune-tellers and serious astrologers disagree. Astrologers regard it more as a genuine science rather than as a means of foretelling exact future events. It studies the probable trend of the conditions a person will experience in her life.

In astrology the celestial sphere is divided into 12 parts called houses, six above the horizon and six below. The seven heavenly bodies known to the ancients, the Sun, Saturn, Jupiter, Mars, Venus, Mercury and the Moon, and the three recently discovered planets, Uranus, Neptune and Pluto are used. The zodiac is the belt of the celestial sphere, representing the path taken by the Sun as it appears to circle the Earth. It is divided into 12 sections, each with its own sign and name and each ruling one part of the human body. For this reason, in the past, astronomy was also linked with medicine, and even today astrology is used to indicate health trends. The word zodiac is linked with zoology, and several of the names are those of animals. The houses of astrology are quite distinct from the 12 divisions of the zodiac, though these too are sometimes termed 'houses'. The astrological reading of the heavenly bodies in relation to the divisions of the zodiac at the time of someone's birth is known as that person's horoscope.

Cartomancy

This is fortune-telling by means of cards. Ordinary playing cards are very commonly used. Hearts traditionally represent the emotions and affairs of the heart; Clubs friendship; Diamonds financial and home affairs; Spades matters of duty and will-power. The cards are laid out in a pattern and then a reading is taken. Several variations of pattern exist including the 'cross', 'wheel of fortune' and the 'mystic star'.

A more famous pack of cards used for cartomancy is the traditional tarot pack. These cards were introduced into Europe in the 14th century by gypsies, to whom the 78 cards have a particular significance. Fifty-six of the cards are the same as those found in a normal pack, except that the suits have different names; Cups instead of Hearts, Wands instead of Clubs,

Pentacles instead of Diamonds and Swords instead of Spades. The remaining 22 cards are trumps. Each trump has a picture such as the Devil, the Tower, the Hanged Man, and so on. The origin of these symbols and their meaning is unknown. The readings generally follow a set convention though variations exist.

Crystal-gazing (Scrying)

Scrying is seeing into the future by means of the traditional crystal ball but a mirror, pool of ink or water, or any shiny or reflecting surface can be used as well. These help the fortune-teller to concentrate. Imagination plays a great part as pictures are conjured up much in the same way as one might see images in the flames of a fire. Self-hypnotism also cannot be ruled out. In rural districts, particularly in the recent past, girls would gaze into a mirror in order to 'see' the face of her future husband-to-be, the wish probably being father to the thought. There are few records of great accuracy and in general crystal-gazing is more a part of fairground fun than a serious pursuit.

Dreams

These have been used throughout the ages to divine the future and in olden days dream 'interpreters' were highly paid. It could be a rather precarious occupation if one happened to be 'interpreter' to an emperor or king, for anyone who made a wrong interpretation would fall from favour. Classical literature gives many examples of dreams foretelling the future, though there have also been some historically recorded instances of surprisingly accurate forecasts. It is said, for example, that by a dream Abraham Lincoln foresaw his own assassination. Many books have been written about the interpretation of dreams, certain symbols being taken as a warning or sign of coming events. Unfortunately, these symbols are not always given single meanings; for instance, at least three possible interpretations arise from a dream about snakes. Different countries tend to have different conventions and the meaning of a symbol may differ from one area to another. In psychoanalysis dreams are regarded more seriously but on a very different basis. In this case dreams are used to explore a person's subconscious. The two approaches should not be confused.

Palmistry

Again a very ancient art, palmistry was used centuries ago by Indians, Greeks, Egyptians and Chinese. Gypsies in particular are famed for it. Some people regard it as a serious science, making claims which their opponents equally hotly deny.

A palmist reads a person's character and the main events of her life from the lines and general contour of the hand. Different parts of the hand are linked with the planets: the thumb with Venus, the first finger with Jupiter, the second with Saturn, the third with Apollo (Sun) and the fourth with Mercury. The 'mounts' are the slight swellings on the palm and are named after the Moon and Mars. The chief lines are those of Life,

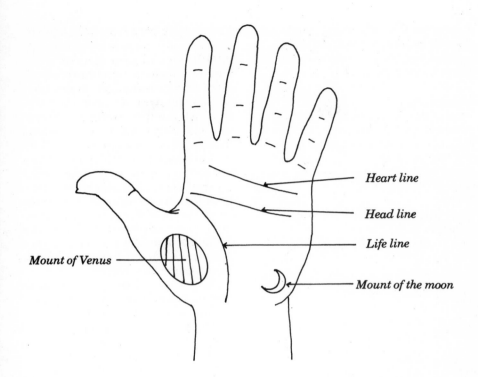

Heart line

Head line

Life line

Mount of the moon

Mount of Venus

Heart and Head, but other minor marks are taken into consideration. A full reading is very complicated. The left hand is usually read but the right is also studied, in some cases.

Palmistry was once regarded very seriously but it later fell into disrepute because of the way unscrupulous and often inept palmists used it to exploit believers, preying on fear and superstition. A law was brought in to prevent this and a palmist could be charged as a vagrant. Various interesting legal cases are on record.

Necromancy

This, often regarded as a 'black art', was a way of divining the future by calling up the spirits of the dead. The Bible gives one well-quoted example, that of Saul and the Witch of Endor. In England, particularly, this art was employed to reveal the whereabouts of hidden treasure and the diviner would sometimes end up in the pillory, accused of fraud. If it was thought that the Devil had assisted the diviner, the matter was regarded more seriously and cases are mentioned in old witch-hunt trials, though strangely enough the witches were never punished too severely. It seems to have been a slightly more acceptable form of black magic, probably because the hunt for buried treasure was a motive very easily understood and even approved of. In a different context the 'witch' would have had a much rougher time.

Numerology

This is the 'science' of lucky numbers and lucky days. Numerical values are attached to the letters of the alphabet and the name of the fortune-seeker is then translated into figures. The method is shown below. The lucky number is obtained by adding all the numbers together until only a single digit remains. The numbers of a birth date can also be added. Today numerology is more a form of amusement than serious fortune-telling.

Omens

They were regarded as signs of coming events. Signs such as the flight of birds, movement of insects, certain trees, plants and the behaviour of certain animals were thought to be warnings of future happenings. Traditionally a family would adopt one standard omen which was always associated with a coming event or disaster. You may even know of some yourself, though not regard them too seriously. They are generally passed down and many have become quite famous. Norse mythology contains numerous references to omens.

Some people still tell fortunes by means of tea-leaves left in cups. The shapes formed by the leaves in the bottom of the cup are interpreted as symbols or omens. Again, it is chiefly a form of amusement today, though not all omens have been regarded lightly.

Oracle

The most famous oracle was at Delphi in Greece. The oracle was in a chasm near the temple of the Sun god, Apollo, where a priestess sat on a three-legged stool called a tripod. After going into an ecstatic trance, she answered questions asked by those seeking guidance for the future. The answers were deliberately ambiguous (allowing for several interpretations), which rather let the priestess off the hook if she made a mistake. This kind of 'insurance policy' has been used by many diviners.

The powers of the priestess were said to come from fumes and the strange atmospheric conditions arising from a river running at the foot of the chasm. Before the priestess was installed there, several people had committed suicide by casting themselves down the chasm, having been affected in some way by these fumes. Other diviners have similarly used a trancelike state to relate messages and visions relating to the future.

NUMEROLOGY

1	2	3	4	5	6	7	8	9
A	B	C	D	E	F	G	H	I
J	K	L	M	N	O	P	Q	R
S	T	U	V	W	X	Y	Z	

Working from the above, Tom Smith would have the numbers
$2+6+4+1+4+9+2+8=36$.
$36 = 3+6 = 9$ (the final total and thus the lucky number)

The final result must always be a single digit, numerals always being added together until this is arrived at. The Christian name used is the one by which the person is generally known, being Tom rather than Thomas in the above example. The answer would have been different for Thomas.

ASTROLOGICAL MEANING OF THE PLANETS

Jupiter	♃	Wisdom
Saturn	♄	Responsibility
Sun	☉	Vitality
Mercury	☿	Intelligence
Venus	♀	Love
Mars	♂	Energy
Moon	☽	Feeling
Uranus	♅	Change
Neptune	♆	Imagination
Pluto	♇	Power

DISTANCES BETWEEN PLANETS ALSO SHOWN BY SYMBOLS

0°	☌	Conjunction
30°	⚺	Semi-sextile
60°	⚹	Sextile
90°	□	Square
120°	△	Trine
150°	⚻	Quincunx
180°	☍	Opposition

SIGNS OF THE ZODIAC AND RELATION WITH HUMAN BODY

Aries	♈	Head	March 20
Taurus	♉	Throat	April 20
Gemini	♊	Lungs	May 21
Cancer	♋	Stomach	June 21
Leo	♌	Heart	July 22
Virgo	♍	Bowels	August 23
Libra	♎	Kidneys	September 23
Scorpio	♏	Bladder	October 23
Sagittarius	♐	Thighs	November 22
Capricorn	♑	Knees	December 21
Aquarius	♒	Ankles	January 21
Pisces	♓	Feet	February 19

The Sun enters the signs of the zodiac on approximately the above dates throughout the year.

GENERAL
INFORMATION

Knots

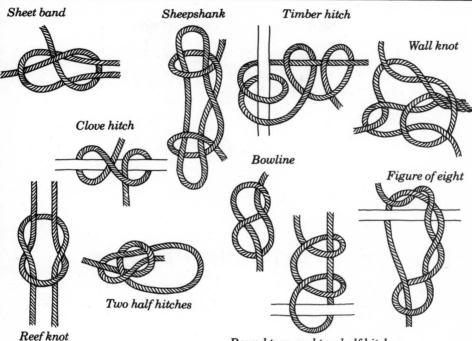

Sheet band

Sheepshank

Timber hitch

Wall knot

Clove hitch

Bowline

Figure of eight

Two half hitches

Reef knot

Round turn and two half hitches

The Reef Knot is used for tying together two ropes of equal size. It tends to slip if the ropes are of unequal diameter. These should be tied with a sheet bend.

The Sheet Bend is for tying together two ropes of different diameters. If the end is passed round again the result is a Double Sheet Bend.

The Clove Hitch is a knot by which a rope is secured around another rope or a rod that it crosses. When fastened it will neither slip up nor down.

A Bowline makes a fixed loop at the end of a rope that will never slip. It can be used for making fast to a ring, post, bollard or cleat.

The Sheepshank is used for shortening a rope.

The Figure of Eight is a knot used for stopping a rope running through a block.

The Half-hitch is used to tie a rope to a ring or post.

The Round Turn and Two Half-hitches holds a rope to a ring or post even more securely than a simple Half-hitch.

The Timber Hitch is used for dragging things along, such as a piece of wood.

The Wall Knot is used to finish off a rope that is unravelling.

Foreign Words and Phrases

Fr = French L = Latin Ger = German It = Italian

à bas (Fr) down with
ab incunabilis (L) from the cradle
ab initio (L) from the beginning
à bon marché (Fr) cheap; a good bargain
ad astra (L) to the stars
ad hoc (L) arranged for this purpose; special
ad infinitum (L) to infinity
ad interim (L) in the meantime
ad nauseam (L) to disgust, satiety
affaire d'amour (Fr) a love affair
affaire de coeur (Fr) an affair of the heart
affaire d'honneur (Fr) an affair of honour; a duel
a fortiori (L) with stronger reason
à la belle étoile (Fr) under the stars
à la mode (Fr) according to the fashion, custom
al fresco (It) in the open air
alter ego (L) one's other self
amour-propre (Fr) vanity; self-love
anno mundi (L) in the year of the world
à pied (Fr) on foot
a priori (L) from the cause to the effect (in reasoning)
à propos (Fr) to the point
au contraire (Fr) on the contrary

au courant (Fr) fully acquainted with
au fait (Fr) well acquainted with
au fond (Fr) at bottom
auf wiedersehen (Ger) goodbye till we meet again
au revoir (Fr) goodbye till we meet again
à votre santé (Fr) to your health
bel esprit (Fr) a wit
ben trovato (It) cleverly invented
bête noire (Fr) a black beast; one's abomination
billet doux (Fr) a love letter
bona fide (L) genuine
bonhomie (Fr) good nature
bon mot (Fr) witty saying
bonne bouche (Fr) a tasty titbit
bon vivant (Fr) a good liver; gourmand
carte blanche (Fr) a blank paper; full discretionary powers
casus belli (L) that which causes or justifies a war
causa sine qua non (L) an indispensible cause or condition
cause célèbre (Fr) a law-suit that excites much attention
ceteris paribus (L) other things being equal
chacun son goût (Fr) everyone to his taste
comme il faut (Fr) as it should be; well-bred
compos mentis (L) in right mind
contretemps (Fr) an unlucky accident or hitch
corrigenda (L) things to be corrected
coup de grâce (Fr) a finishing stroke
coup d'état (Fr) a violent or illegal change in the government of a country
de facto (L) in point of fact, actual
dei gratia (L) by God's grace
de jure (L) rightful by law
de profundis (L) out of the depths
de rigueur (Fr) required by etiquette
deus ex machina (L) providential intervention at a critical moment
en bloc (Fr) in a lump; wholesale
en famille (Fr) at home, among one's family
enfant terrible (Fr) a terrible child, who asks awkward questions for example
en masse (Fr) all together
en passant (Fr) in passing; by the way
en rapport (Fr) in harmony, sympathy
entre nous (Fr) between ourselves
erratum, errata (L) error, errors (especially those noted in list attached to book)
esprit de corps (Fr) the animating spirit of a group or collective body of people
ex cathedra (L) from the chair (of high authority)
ex officio (L) in virtue of one's office
fait accompli (Fr) a thing already done
faux pas (Fr) a false step; mistake in behaviour
genius loci (L) the guardian spirit of a place
honi soit qui mal y pense (Old Fr) evil to him who evil thinks
hors de combat (Fr) out of the fight; disabled
hors-d'oeuvre (Fr) an extra dish served at the beginning of a meal
ich dien (Ger) I serve

idée fixe (Fr) a fixed idea
in absentia (L) in (his or her) absence
in extremis (L) at the point of death
in memoriam (L) in memory of
in perpetuum (L) for ever
in situ (L) in its original place
inter alia (L) among other things
in toto (L) completely
ipse dixit (L) he himself said it
ipso facto (L) in the fact itself
je ne sais quoi (Fr) I know not what
laissez-faire (Fr) leave matters alone; policy of non-interference
magnum opus (L) great work
modus operandi (L) manner of working
mutatis mutandis (L) with necessary alterations made
nil desperandum (L) there is no reason to despair
noblesse oblige (Fr) much is expected from those in high position
nolens volens (L) willing or unwilling
nom de plume (Fr) a pen-name
non sequitur (L) it does not follow; an illogical inference
obiter dictum (L) a thing said by the way
omnia vincit amor (L) love conquers all
outré (Fr) eccentric
par excellence (Fr) by virtue of special excellence; above all others
pari passu (L) at an equal pace
passim (L) everywhere
pax vobiscum (L) peace be with you
per annum (L) by the year
per capita (L) by the head; each
per se (L) by itself; considered apart
persona non grata (L) an unacceptable person
pièce de résistance (Fr) the chief dish of a meal; main item
pied-à-terre (Fr) a lodging for occasional visits
poco a poco (It) little by little
post mortem (L) after death
prima facie (L) at first view or consideration
pro forma (L) for the sake of form
pro patria (L) for our country
pro rata (L) proportionally
quid pro quo (L) one thing for another; tit-for-tat
raison d'être (Fr) the reason for a thing's existence
reductio ad absurdum (L) reduction to a logical absurdity
re vera (L) in truth
sans souci (Fr) without care
sauve qui peut (Fr) let him save himself who can
savoir-faire (Fr) tact, quickness to see and do the right thing
sic (L) so (written)
sine die (L) indefinitely
sine qua non (L) without which, not; indispensable
sobriquet (Fr) nickname
sotto voce (It) in an undertone

stet (L) let it stand; do not delete
sub judice (L) under judicial consideration
summum bonum (L) the principal good
tant mieux (Fr) so much the better
tant pis (Fr) so much the worse
vice versa (L) the other way round; the reverse
viva voce (L) orally
voilà (Fr) behold; there is
vox populi (L) the voice of the people; public opinion
zeitgeist (Ger) spirit of the times

Weights and Measures

AVOIRDUPOIS WEIGHT

16 drams (dr)	= 1 ounce (oz)
16 ounces	= 1 pound (lb)
14 pounds	= 1 stone (st)
28 pounds (US 25 lb)	= 1 quarter (qr)
4 quarters	= 1 hundredweight (cwt)
20 hundredweight	= 1 ton

METRIC WEIGHT

1,000 milligram (mg)	= 1 gram (g)
1,000 gram	= 1 kilogram (kg)
1,000 kilogram	= 1 tonne

IMPERIAL LENGTH

12 inches (in)	= 1 foot (ft)
3 feet	= 1 yard (yd)
5½ yards	= 1 rod, pole or perch
40 poles	= 1 furlong (fur)
8 furlongs	= 1 mile
1,760 yards	= 1 mile

METRIC LENGTH

10 millimetres (mm)	= 1 centimetre (cm)
100 centimetres	= 1 metre (m)
1,000 metres	= 1 kilometre (km)

NAUTICAL MEASURE

6 feet	= 1 fathom
100 fathoms	= 1 cable
10 cables	= 1 nautical mile
6,080 feet	= 1 nautical mile
3 nautical miles	= 1 league

LIQUID MEASURE

4 gills	= 1 pint (pt)
2 pints	= 1 quart (qt)
4 quarts	= 1 gallon (gal)

METRIC LIQUID MEASURE

1,000 millilitres (ml)	= 1 litre (l)
1,000 cubic centimetres (cc)	= 1 litre

IMPERIAL MEASURES OF SURFACE

144 square inches	=1 square foot
9 square feet	=1 square yard
$30\frac{1}{4}$ square yards	=1 square rod, pole or perch
40 square poles	=1 rood
4 roods	=1 acre
640 acres	=1 square mile

METRIC MEASURES OF SURFACE

100 square metres	=1 are
100 ares	=1 hectare
100 hectares	=1 square kilometre

IMPERIAL MEASURES OF VOLUME

1,728 cubic inches	=1 cubic foot
27 cubic feet	=1 cubic yard

MEASUREMENTS

TRIANGLE
area $=\frac{1}{2}$ ah

SQUARE
area $= a^2$

CIRCLE
diameter (d) $= 2r$
circumference $= 2\pi r$
area $= \pi r^2$
NB the constant $\pi = 3\cdot1415$

TRAPEZOID
area $=\frac{1}{2}$ (m + n)h

CUBE
surface area $= 6a^2$
volume $= a^3$

SPHERE
surface area $= 4\pi r^2$
volume $= \frac{4}{3}\pi r^3$

CONE
curved surface area $= \pi rl$
total surface
area $= \pi rl + 2\pi r = \pi r(l + r)$
volume $= \frac{1}{3}\pi r^2 h$

CYLINDER
curved surface area $= 2\pi rh$
total surface
area $= 2\pi rh + 2\pi r^2 = 2\pi r(h + r)$

PYRAMID
surface area $= a^2 + 2la$
volume $= \frac{3}{4}a^2 h$

ELLIPSE
area $= \pi ab$

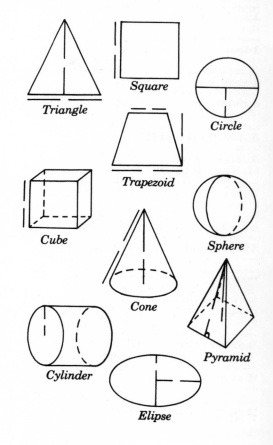

Triangle

Square

Circle

Trapezoid

Cube

Sphere

Cone

Pyramid

Cylinder

Elipse

244

METRIC MEASURES OF VOLUME

1,000 cubic centimetres	= 1 cubic decimetre	**1,000 cubic decimetres**	= 1 cubic metre

CONVERSION TABLE

WEIGHT

1 ounce	= 28·350 gram	**1 kilogramme**	= 2·205 pounds
1 pound	= 0·454 kilograms	**1,000 kilograms**	= 0·984 tons
1 ton	= 1·016 tonnes		

LENGTH

1 inch	= 2·540 centimetres	**1 centimetre**	= 0·394 inch
1 foot	= 30·480 centimetres	**1 metre**	= 3·281 feet
1 yard	= 0·914 metres	**1 metre**	= 1·094 yards
1 mile	= 1·609 kilometres	**1 kilometre**	= 0·621 mile

LIQUID MEASURE

1 Imperial pint	= 0·568 litres	**1 litre**	= 0·220 Imperial gallons
1 American pint	= 0·473 litres	**1 litre**	= 0·264 American gallons
1 Imperial gallon	= 4·546 litres		
1 American gallon	= 3·785 litres		

SURFACE MEASURE

1 square foot	= 0·093 square metre	**1 square metre**	= 1·196 square yards
1 square yard	= 0·836 square metres	**1 are**	= 119·599 square yards
1 acre	= 4,046·850 square metres	**1 hectare**	= 2·471 acres
1 square mile	= 258·998 hectares	**1 square kilometre**	= 0·386 square mile

MEASURE OF VOLUME

1 cubic inch	= 16·387 cubic centimetres	1 cubic centimetre	= 0·061 cubic inch
1 cubic yard	= 0·765 cubic metre	1 cubic metre	= 1·308 cubic yards

TEMPERATURE

To convert degrees Fahrenheit (°F) to degrees Centigrade (°C), use the following formula: $C = \frac{5}{9} (F - 32)$.

To convert degrees Centigrade (°C) to degrees Fahrenheit (°F), the formula is: $F = \frac{9}{5} C + 32$.

To convert degrees Centigrade (°C) to degrees Kelvin (°K) or absolute, the formula is: $K = C + 273$.

The Greek Alphabet

NAME	CAPITAL	LOWER CASE	ENGLISH EQUIVALENT
Alpha	A	α	a
Beta	B	β	b
Gamma	Γ	γ	g
Delta	Δ	δ	d
Epsilon	E	ε	è
Zeta	Z	ζ	z
Eta	H	η	ẽ
Theta	Θ	θ	th
Iota	I	i	i
Kappa	K	κ	k
Lambda	Λ	λ	l
Mu	M	μ	m
Nu	N	ν	n
Xi	Ξ	ξ	x
Omicron	O	o	ŏ
Pi	π	π	p
Rho	P	ρ	r
Sigma	Σ	σ	s
Tau	T	τ	t
Upsilon	Y	υ	u or y
Phi	Φ	ϕ	ph
Chi	X	χ	ch
Psi	Ψ	ψ	ps
Omega	Ω	ω	o

Roman Numerals

I	1	**XVI**	16	**CD**	400	**MMM**	3,000
II	2	**XVII**	17	**D**	500	$\overline{\text{MV}}$	4,000
III	3	**XVIII**	18	**DC**	600	$\overline{\text{V}}$	5,000
IV	4	**XIX**	19	**DCC**	700	$\overline{\text{X}}$	10,000
V	5	**XX**	20	**DCCC**	800	$\overline{\text{L}}$	50,000
VI	6	**XXX**	30	**CM**	900	$\overline{\text{C}}$	100,000
VII	7	**XL**	40	**M**	1,000	$\overline{\text{D}}$	500,000
VIII	8	**L**	50	**MM**	2,000	$\overline{\text{M}}$	1,000,000
IX	9	**LX**	60				
X	10	**LXX**	70				
XI	11	**LXXX**	80	**EXAMPLES**			
XII	12	**XC**	90	**1980**	MCMLXXX		
XIII	13	**C**	100	**1981**	MCMLXXXI		
XIV	14	**CC**	200	**1979**	MCMLXXIX		
XV	15	**CCC**	300				

Latin Abbreviations

AD *anno Domini* (in the year of the Lord)
ad lib. *ad libitum* (at pleasure)
a.m. *ante meridiem* (before noon)
c. *circa* (about)
do. *ditto* (the same)
et al. *et alii* (and others)
etc. *et cetera* (and the rest, and so on)
et seq. *et sequens* (and the following)
ex lib. *ex libris* (from the books of)
fl. *floruit* (flourished)
ibid. *ibidem* (in the same place)
id. *idem* (the same)
i.e. *id est* (that is)
ign. *ignotus* (unknown)
incog. *incognito* (unknown, unrecognized)
in loc. *in loco* (in its place)
loc. cit. *loco citato* (in the place cited)
N.B. *nota bene* (note well)
nem. con. *nemine contradicente* (nobody contradicting, unanimously)
no. *numero* (number)

non seq. *non sequitur* (it does not follow)
ob. *obiit* (died)
op. *opus* (work)
op. cit. *opere citato* (in the work cited)
pinx. *pinxit* (he painted)
p.m. *post meridiem* (afternoon)
p.p. *per procurationem* (by proxy)
pro tem. *pro tempore* (for the time being)
prox. *proximo* (of the next month)
p.s. *post scriptum* (postscript)
Q.E.D. *quod erat demonstrandum* (which was to be demonstrated)
q.v. *quod vide* (which see)
R.I.P. *requiescat in pace* (rest in peace)
seq. *sequentes, sequentia* (the following)
ult. *ultimo* (in the last month)
v. *vide* (see); *versus* (against)
verb. sap. *verbum sapienti sat est* (a word to the wise is enough)
viz. *videlicet* (namely, that is to say)

INDEX

Your Own Notes